BUY, REHAB, RENT, REFINANCE, REPEAT
Date: 10/29/19

332.6324 GRE
Greene, David
Buy, rehab, rent, refinance,
repeat : the BRRRR rental

Buy,
Rehab,
Rent,
Refinance,
Repeat

The BRRRR Rental Property Investment Strategy Made Simple

David Greene

BiggerPockets®
PUBLISHING

Praise for
Buy, Rehab, Rent, Refinance, Repeat

"I am simply blown away by the way David takes something as intimidating and complex as scaling a real estate portfolio and simplifies it to the point anyone can do it. Buy, Rehab, Rent, Refinance, Repeat is a true gem and guaranteed to make you a better investor and a wealthier individual."
—Hal Elrod, international bestselling author of *The Miracle Morning*

"David has committed himself to mastering real estate and it shows! This book has everything you'll need to become a black belt real estate investor and build wealth like the pros. From A-Z (or B-R), David covers just what you'll need to execute like a master and build wealth."
—David Osborn, New York Times
bestselling author of *Wealth Can't Wait*

"This book is what we've all been waiting for! David clearly breaks down each step of the process, with clear details and a meat-and-potatoes approach to sharing exactly how to excel at each step of the process. Mastering BRRRR really WILL help you master real estate—and this book will show you how."
—Pat Hiban, New York Times bestselling author
and host of the Real Estate Rockstars podcast

"*The only thing wrong with this book is that it wasn't written sooner! This BiggerPockets classic covers every single step in the process. Best of all, the principles are universal and can be applied to all types of real estate, from a single-family house to a 100-unit apartment complex, and everything in between. The BRRRR strategy as detailed in David's book is an absolute must-have tool for any successful real estate investor!*"

—Andrew Cushman, real estate investor
and blogger on BiggerPockets.com

"*David follows up his success with Long-Distance Real Estate Investing with another heavy hitter! David's first book helps you choose your market, and this one shows you what to do once you've got it. The whole process is covered, with fantastic advice for how to master each step and become a true real estate black belt. If you want a guide for how to build a real estate investing business, you need this book.*"

—Rock Thomas, Founder and CEO of March to a Million

Buy , rehab , rent , refinance , repeat : the BRRRR rental property investment strategy made simple
David Greene

Published by BiggerPockets Publishing LLC, Denver, CO
Copyright © 2019 by David Greene.
All Rights Reserved.

Publisher's Cataloging-in-Publication data
Names: Greene, David M., author.
Title: Buy , rehab , rent , refinance , repeat : the BRRRR rental property investment strategy made simple / by David Greene.
Description: Includes bibliographical references. | Denver, CO: BiggerPockets Publishing, 2019.
Identifiers: LCCN 2018960519 | ISBN 9781947200081 (pbk.) | 9781947200098 (ebook)
Subjects: LCSH Real estate investment--United States. | Real estate management--United States. | Real estate business--United States. | Investments. | Finance, Personal. | BISAC BUSINESS & ECONOMICS / Real Estate / General | BUSINESS & ECONOMICS / Real Estate / Buying & Selling Homes
Classification: LCC HD255 .G74 2019 | DDC 332.63/24--dc23

Published in the United States of America
Printed on recycled paper

10 9 8 7 6 5 4 3

MIX
Paper from
responsible sources
FSC® C008955

Dedication

To Josh Dorkin and Brandon Turner,

To Brandon, host of the BiggerPockets Podcast and creator of the term "BRRRR." You have been the biggest influence on my life in the last year, a terrific friend, inspiring figure, and great role model for what it means to be successful, humble, trustworthy, and noble. Your mind is a catalyst for great ideas. Thank you for your friendship.

To Josh, creator of BiggerPockets and superdad. Thank you for the opportunity you've created for our community and for investors everywhere. Your example in following what's important in life over what's easy is inspiring and encouraging. Thank you for passing me the baton and setting us all up for success.

Table of Contents

CHAPTER SEVEN | Tenant Tips

PART FIVE | THE REFINANCE PROCESS

CHAPTER EIGHT | Choosing Your Lender

PART ONE

Introduction to BRRRR

Owning real estate has the ability to change lives. When my parents bought their first home around 1985 in Manteca, California, they paid around $60,000. That house is now worth about $375,000. Had they rented it out, the tenants would have paid off the entire mortgage for them during the time they'd owned it. At a 10 percent down payment, my parents would have turned $6,000 or so into $375,000—all while letting the tenants create the wealth for them.

Had they applied the cash flow from rent payments toward the loan principal, the loan mortgage would probably have been paid off twice. Had they reinvested that second mortgage amount into real estate, they could have started this same process over with about four new houses.

Imagine the financial power that comes from owning a large portfolio of cash-producing rental property that appreciates in value while the tenants pay your loan down for you. Imagine using someone else's money to fund this portfolio, then taking the wealth you've created and spending those same dollars over and over to buy new properties. With each new property you start a new wealth-building cycle, increase your efficiency and effectiveness, and create equity to fund your next purchase. Soon you end up with a powerful wave, carrying you to financial freedom.

This book is about how to create that wave, which can be easily leveraged, and builds wealth in several different ways. Owning real estate for a significant period of time is virtually guaranteed to build you wealth. Cash flowing assets have the ability to carry you to great heights that you couldn't have achieved through working a traditional job.

Real estate also has the ability to completely destroy you, your wealth, and your plans for a better future. Rarely do we see a source of power that is all good or all bad. In most cases, power helps or hurts depending on how it's used or the ability of the one who's using it. But those who want the big reward have to also take the big risk. Success isn't found in avoiding anything that could go wrong. It's found in harnessing your strengths to make them work for you and creating systems that mitigate risk and enhance efficiency.

So how do we learn to harness power? The process of developing or harnessing power that will propel you to achieve great things, including financial freedom, is called mastery. Mastery is the process that allows you to harness the same power that can destroy you, force it to help you, and unlock your own true potential. Whether it's riding a bike, surfing a wave, or learning a martial art, mastery is the process of harnessing and controlling a great power to make it work for you, not against you.

In my book *Long-Distance Real Estate Investing: How to Buy, Rehab, and Manage Out-of-State Rental Properties*, I tackled the controversial topic of buying rental property in "someone else's backyard." In the book, I took a contested subject (the ability to build wealth by buying in any market) and showed people how they could use it to build their wealth while avoiding losing money.

I challenged the conventional thinking that long-distance investing was risky "just because." I helped expose that the logic that led to the advice "only invest in your own backyard" was well-intentioned but outdated in today's technology-driven world. I showed people how it's unwise only to focus on what can go wrong. They also need to consider what can go right! I detailed the systems I use to grow my own wealth through real estate. These systems are the process I used to harness the power, to ride the wave that led me to the result I wanted.

This book is intended to serve a similar purpose, but on a different topic. I want everyone to see that while anyone can buy real estate and benefit from its power to grow wealth, there is a way to do it that is the *best*. The BRRRR method will teach you how to become a black belt real estate investor and get the most out of your capital, time, effort, energy, and resources. Mastering BRRRR *is* mastering real estate. BRRRR is an acronym that stands for Buy, Rehab, Rent, Refinance, Repeat. It is a way of describing the order of buying a rental property and then pulling your capital back out in the most efficient way possible. In this book, I'm going to cover how to master each of the five steps of the BRRRR process, and in the process, how to come closer to mastering the power of real estate.

For too long, people have focused on *not losing money*. This has led to inaction, excuses, lost time, and lost opportunity to build wealth. Now, I'll be the first to tell you the power of real estate can work against you, and you need to understand how to protect your capital. But *that is only half the game*. This book is going to teach you the other half of the game—how to master real estate investing and let the power of that wave carry you to massive financial prosperity through practical advice and practical philosophy.

My goal is not just to teach you to grow your wealth at a consistent rate. I want to show you how to do it at an exponential rate. I do this by showing you not only how to find success at each element of the BRRRR process, but also how you can use success in one area to help you in the others. This creates exponentially increasing returns, a wave that develops momentum and becomes more powerful the longer it propels.

I commend you for being committed to this process and showing that commitment by purchasing this book. I'm excited to share with you not only what BRRRR is, but also why the very best do it, and just how it will reward you for doing real estate the right way. Unlike flipping houses, the BRRRR model will enable you to take advantage of all the benefits of buying houses cheaply, without the headaches or expenses associated with a quick sale. When you use the BRRRR model correctly, you begin building a foundation that will later become a skyscraper-sized portfolio of properties.

Many people will tell you what not to do. That's easy. This book is going to tell you what to do, how to do it, and why! You'll find this book is broken into seven parts, with one part for each of the five phases of BRRRR and one part for digging deeper into the mastery of BRRRR. By the time you're done reading this, you should have a better understanding not only of the most efficient way to structure your investments, but also of how to master each phase of the investment cycle.

My Story

If I'm going to be sharing why I believe you should be utilizing the BRR-RR method, I feel I owe it to you to explain a little about myself and my background so you can understand how it worked for me.

I am a police officer. I've worked this blue-collar job for the last ten years. When I realized how real estate could build my wealth, I became obsessed with buying as much of it as I could. Because I did not come from a wealthy family or understand the process of raising money, my only option was to make as much money at my job as I could and save as much of that as possible.

How did that look for me? I worked about 90 hours a week for several years, slept in my car several times a week, gained a ton of weight, became very unhealthy, and sacrificed my social life, all at the altar of real estate investing.

While I paid a heavy price (pardon the weight gain joke) this allowed me to save enough money to put down payments and cover the rehab costs on two to three properties a year. These properties became the foundation of my real estate investing and eventually led to where I am now. As grateful as I am to have them, there is no way I could continue that process forever. I barely made it through the five years I did it!

The good news is, I went from buying two houses a year in the beginning of 2017 to two a month today. I didn't find a way to make more money. I didn't utilize shady or "creative strategies." I didn't inherit anything. All I did was find a way to use the money I was making more efficiently. I finally figured out it shouldn't only be me working so hard—my money should be, too.

Had I read a book like this back then, I have zero doubt I would now own at least 20 to 30 houses more than I do right now. Part of me kicks myself for being so stuck in my ways, but another part of me knows it's that frustration at doing things the wrong way that drove me to write this book—so I can help other people avoid my mistakes. *The good news for you is you don't have to take the hard road I did for so long.* I'm going to show you the shortcut.

Fast forward nine years from when I bought my first property, and I'm rolling along nicely now. Learning to BRRRR at a high level is what allowed me to master all the other aspects of real estate investing that are involved in the BRRRR process. By winning at all five levels, I get the very most out of my deals, my capital, and my opportunities. Each of these "wins" compounds themselves, increasing my likelihood to win even bigger on the next deal.

Now that I've figured out the BRRRR method, it's become the only way I buy property. What I learned mastering BRRRR opened the door for me to become a top-producing real estate agent. (Success often opens doors you never knew were there—one more reason we should pursue mastery.) In my first year of full-time sales, I won the rookie of the year award for my Keller Williams office, ended as the top selling agent, built a team of full-time staff, was featured on several podcasts, wrote my first book, and was featured on HGTV's *House Hunters*. Not a bad year!

What I'm trying to say is, pursuing the mastery of real estate investing created countless exciting opportunities for me, and I have no doubt it can do the same for you. The effort you put into learning real estate investing will pay you dividends in the end, and furthering education is one of the best investments you can ever make!

How BRRRR Supercharged My Success

Once I learned BRRRR and started buying more houses, agents started sending me the best deals first. My contractors gave me better pricing and more attention when I took on more rehabs. When my portfolio grew, property managers started giving me better pricing as well. As my volume increased, every aspect of real estate investing got easier. Real estate investing, while challenging at first, had become progressively easier with each deal and each new relationship I formed.

When someone starts buying houses (or doing anything, really) they aren't very efficient at it. Frankly, they usually suck. At least I do. That's why experienced investors often give advice to newbies that if they really want to learn, they need to find an easy property to get into the market with and buy something. Even if you don't make any money on your first deal, the education itself is priceless!

That's how life works. The first time we do anything, it sucks. The first time we ski, drive, try to read, lift weights, go running, start a new job, *whatever it is*, we aren't going to be very good at it. Success comes through repeating a process over and over until our brains figure it out—usually by spotting patterns of things that worked and things that did not, and remembering them.

One of the most devastating things I see in real estate is when someone pays the price up front to learn real estate investing, and right when they finally start to get good at it, and are ready to make money, they run out of capital and are stuck. It's like putting in all the time in the gym to build up a base, then quitting before the big race.

Can you imagine? It sucks! I want to teach you how to avoid that. There is a better way to invest in real estate than a big down payment and paying a contractor to make your property barely livable. Learning and mastering this process will make sure you never run out of capital, never stop getting better, and are not limited by the hours in the week you have to work as I was for so long.

Those who have mastered something can get superior results with much less effort. The less effort something takes, the more fun it is, and the more you can accomplish in other parts of your life. We don't want to spend our whole lives working to learn and succeed at real estate investing. By committing to mastery now, you give your future self an opportunity to actually enjoy the wealth you'll be building by taking action today.

CHAPTER ONE

Getting to Know the BRRRR Method

Many people take no care of their money till they come nearly to the end of it, and others do just the same with their time.

—JOHANN WOLFGANG VON GOETHE

Why BRRRR Is Better Than Traditional Financing

At its most basic understanding, BRRRR is the best way to buy a property if your goal is to own more than one or two. It allows you to recover the largest amount of your capital out of the project as possible. This will help you for myriad reasons we will cover in the book.

The BRRRR method is an alternative to the traditional method of buying a property. When I refer to the traditional method, I am defining it as putting down a large down payment, then spending the minimal amount of money necessary to get the place rent-ready. This is the formula most investors have been following for decades. It requires the least amount of thought, effort, and foresight, and is therefore the easiest. However, what is easiest isn't always what's best.

Before we go any further, I'll explain the process of buying a home in the traditional sense, then compare that to how the BRRRR model works. Once you have a firm grasp of the two, it will make more sense why the traditional model isn't the most effective way to buy real estate.

The Traditional Method Explained

The majority of real estate is bought using someone else's money. This is usually a bank, mortgage broker, or some other lending institution. While the majority of home buyers in America are purchasing for the purpose of living in the property themselves, most investors take advantage of the opportunity to use someone else's money, too.

In the traditional method, financing is the *first* step of the whole process. The home buyer gets approved for a loan, uses it to buy the property, then fixes it up and rents it out. The investor puts capital in when they buy (the down payment) and capital in when they rehab (what you pay the contractor to get it ready to rent out). Then they are done. The amount the bank allows the home buyer to borrow is based on the value of the property before any improvements are made.

If the investor did well, the home is now worth more than they paid for it, they are receiving a good return on investment (ROI), and they have a sizeable amount of equity in the property. In the traditional model, this would be considered a success, and for many years, the majority of investors stopped here.

Once the property is stabilized and rented, the investor would start saving money to buy their next property and repeat the process. This model is simple and usually requires less work. It is with this exact process I bought every one of my rentals from 2009 to 2016. It wasn't the best way to buy real estate, but it was all I knew.

The problem with this method is that while I'm adding value and creating equity through purchasing real estate, the majority of that value stays in the property. While that looks nice on a spreadsheet, there is one major problem with this—I can't use that money to buy more property. The single, most important act a real estate investor can do to grow their wealth is to add value to a property—be it through purchasing below market value or adding value through a rehab.

The problem with the traditional model is *you leave so much equity in the deal when you are done that you can't access this capital to buy the next property*, and the next property is where you always make the most money! It is through the acquisition of real estate at great prices that we create wealth, and holding that property for long periods of time that we build wealth. It is very difficult to do this when all your wealth is stuck in the last property you bought!

The BRRRR Method

So if we need money to make money, but our money gets left in the property we just bought, how do we solve this dilemma? Enter the BRRRR method. The BRRRR method works the same as the traditional method, but in a different order. That one small difference leads to a radically different result.

When an investor utilizes the BRRRR method, they start off by paying cash for the property, rather than financing it. I know for many people this can seem weird, but bear with me. There are many ways to get that cash, and many other advantages to paying cash that I will discuss later. For now, just make sure you note that money is put into the project in step one: buying the property.

Next, the investor manages the rehab portion. More money is put into the project. In real estate, investors can add value to their property in two ways.

1. They pay less than what it's worth, "buying" equity.
2. They increase the value by improving the property's condition, "forcing appreciation" or "building" equity through the rehab process.

It's important to note, in the BRRRR method, these are the *first* two things the investor does. With BRRRR you are adding value *before* you are financing anything.

After the rehab portion, the investor puts the property up for rent and immediately starts collecting cash flow. This cash flow is higher than in the traditional method in the beginning because there is not yet a mortgage on the property.

Once the property is bought, rehabbed, and rented out, *then* the investor refinances it. The amount financed is based on the value of the property after it has been fixed up (when it's higher). This differs from the traditional model where the amount financed is based on the value of the property before it is fixed up (when it's lower). This is the key fact that makes BRRRR so cost-effective. When the bank is evaluating the property to give you a loan, it's valuing a property that's fixed up and worth more with the BRRRR method. With the traditional method, the bank is evaluating the property before it's been fixed up, making it worth less.

Because so many houses are bought with financing, many people just assume you can only get a loan to buy a house, but that's not true. In *Part*

Five: The Refinance Process of this book, we will talk about how lenders give loans. For now, just understand a loan can be secured by an asset at any time, not just upon purchase.

What's important to understand at this point is that ultimately, the BRRRR method gets you more of your capital out of your project because of the order in which you conduct the various stages of buying a rental. In the traditional method, you finance it first. In the BRRRR method, you finance it last. This one seemingly insignificant difference in the order in which you finance your property is the difference between someone like me buying two houses a year or buying 24 houses a year. It's insanely impactful.

Small hinges swing big doors, and BRRRR is the ultimate small hinge.

How BRRRR Increases Your ROI

The best investors use the BRRRR method for several reasons. One of the biggest is the fact it increases your ROI significantly. Increasing your ROI makes your money work more efficiently for you, and working efficiently is what BRRRR is all about.

I'm going to explain to you just how BRRRR accomplishes this, but before I do, I'm going to explain what ROI is and how it's calculated.

ROI Defined

ROI is a metric used to describe how an investment performs. It is one of the simplest ways to compare investments, and it's used across all investment vehicles, not just real estate.

ROI is the percent of your total investment you can expect to receive in a year. If your ROI is 5 percent, you could expect to receive 5 percent of your investment back in a 12-month period. That means if you invested $10,000, you could expect to receive a $500 return.

ROI is one of the first metrics you need to understand in your journey of mastering finance. It is incredibly useful—and universal—because it's a language spoken by pretty much every businessperson. If you put money in a bank CD (certificate of deposit) at a 5 percent return, 5 percent would be your ROI. If you lend someone money at an 8 percent return, 8 percent would be your ROI.

When applying ROI to real estate investing, we typically are only referring to cash flow when discussing ROI. This is an important distinction because real estate is a unique investment that makes its owners money in several ways, such as appreciation, cash flow, paying down debt, etc. Note that when we talk about ROI, we are only talking about the cash flow portion of your profit, nothing else. Because it's specific to cash flow, ROI in real estate is also referred to as a "cash on cash" return.

The formula for calculating ROI is very simple. You take your yearly profit and divide it by the amount of money you've invested. We call this amount of money you've invested your "basis" because it is often made up of more than one source of capital. With investing, we spend money on the down payment, closing costs, rehab costs, holding costs, etc. The accumulation of all these expenses added up is your basis.

In order to calculate your ROI, you would take your monthly cash flow and multiply it by 12 (because there are 12 months in a year). Then divide that number by your basis and boom! You've got your ROI.

Example:

You have a property in which you've invested $50,000 of capital.
The property cash-flows $400 a month after expenses.

$$\$400 \times (12) = \$4,800$$

$$\$4,800 / \$50,000 = 9.6\%$$

Your ROI is 9.6 percent, meaning you would earn back 9.6 percent of your investment basis each year.

How to Increase Your ROI

Every good financial planner or businessperson is interested in increasing their ROI. Because there are two numbers included in the formula for ROI (yearly profit and investment basis), there are two methods to increase your ROI.

1. You can increase your profit
2. You can decrease your basis

Pretty simple right? Understanding these formulas makes real estate seem much more manageable.

There are several ways to increase your profit. The most basic way is to earn more (raise rent) or spend less (decreases expenses). Entire books have been written on these methods and it's important you understand them. Good investors know techniques to earn more money and spend less on their properties.

In *Part Three: The Rehab Process* of this book, I'm going to discuss some ways we can do this using the BRRRR method. However, trying to increase cash flow is a difficult proposition. Rents only go up so fast, and if you try to increase them beyond what the market can withstand you'll end up with vacancy and *less* rent. Expenses can only be dropped so much, and trying to decrease them beyond a reasonable level can leave you with less than ideal talent helping you accomplish your goals and run your property.

Once I realized this, I started looking for ways to decrease my basis as opposed to just increasing my profit. I found that to be *much* easier, and that's when I started using BRRRR the most.

The reason this worked so well is your cash flow tends to increase as rents increase. Rents only increase so fast, and sometimes not at all. This creates a restraint on your ability to pump up the profit portion of the formula and takes control away from your ability to impact your investment.

Decreasing your basis is much different. You have much, much more control over this portion of the process. BRRRR works so well because it allows you to reduce the basis by using a few simple techniques and restructuring the order in which you finance the property.

And in case you were wondering, decreasing the basis can have a BIG impact on your ROI.

Consider this: if you use the BRRRR method instead of the traditional method, and are able to decrease your basis from $50,000 to $20,000 (by borrowing the $30,000 difference), your cash flow would decrease by about $150 a month at today's interest rates.

However, your total ROI would significantly increase.

Example:

$250 (new cash flow) x 12 = $3,000

$3,000 / $20,000 (new basis) = 15%

Your new ROI is 15 percent, up from 9.6 percent. That is a 61 percent increase in ROI by simply doing nothing but borrowing more money against your investment because you switched up the order in which you financed it.

Now, this is actually a much less dramatic sample than some of the deals I do myself. I used it to prove a point that even on a deal that isn't a killer, BRRRR can increase your ROI massively just because lowering your basis is more impactful than increasing your cash flow.

Many new investors fail to grasp this and assume they can only increase their ROI slowly, year after year, as rents tick upward. Experienced investors look for ways in which they can take more control over their investments to make them perform better.

BRRRR Gets the Most Out of Your Capital

Increasing your ROI is good, but it's really only one of many ways BRR-RR makes you a better investor. In my opinion, an even better benefit of BRRRR is the fact it allows you to make your capital work harder for you, not just your ROI.

As an investor, the amount of capital you have available to you is extremely important. To me, it was worth working 90-hour weeks! Without capital, you can't buy deals. If you can't buy deals, you can't add equity to your net worth. You can't add cash flow to your passive income. You can't get repetitions in buying, rehabbing, and managing property—hurting your ability to improve. Without capital, you can't invest in other people's deals. You can't make loans. You can't flip houses. Really, you can't do much but read and talk.

Ensuring you have capital available to continue investing is of utmost importance. You can be the smartest investor in the world but if you don't have any capital to put into play, you aren't making any more money than the worst investor. While many believe in putting as much down on a property as possible (to increase cash flow by lowering the mortgage), this is a too-simple way to look at investing that doesn't consider enough of the facts.

By borrowing an extra $30,000, we lose $150 in cash flow (at least initially, although some of that $150 is going toward the principal and isn't really "lost"). But what we've gained is the ability to reinvest that money for *more* cash flow than we lost by borrowing it. If we make sure the ROI we make on our money is higher than the interest rate we are paying to borrow the money, we come out on top.

For example, let's say we invest that $30,000 at the same return we received in the last deal (15 percent). A 15 percent return on $30,000 would be $375 a month.

$$\$30,000 \times .15 = \$4,500$$

$$\$4,500 / 12 \ (\# \text{ of months in a year}) = \$375$$

Compare that to the $150 we lost to borrow it. That's a difference of $225 in our bank account every single month.

Would you rather have $375 (plus another property, plus the equity you've added to it, plus the opportunity to raise rents in the future, plus the mortgage pay down from your tenant, plus the future appreciation of the property) or $150?

In other words, why wouldn't you want to borrow money at a 4–5 percent interest rate (from the bank) when you can invest it at 15 percent, plus get all the other perks of owning investment property? Thinking from a perspective that only considers losing cash flow by borrowing more money against a property is incredibly shortsighted.

This example I'm providing is pretty modest. I often hit returns of over 70 percent on the houses I BRRRR, and that is on the *bad ones*. It's not a gimmick, it's all in the math. As you continue to read, you'll see exactly how you can do the same thing.

A 70 percent ROI isn't a bad consolation prize on a property you miss on. BRRRR allows you to make much better use of your capital than the traditional method. Once you see more examples of how this works in real life, and you realize how it allows you to capitalize on the power of the wave that real estate investing creates, I'm convinced you too will never invest any other way again.

BRRRR Increases the Velocity of Your Money

Velocity of money is a cool term used to describe how many times you can make the same source of capital work for you. The faster you send out money and recover it along with a profit, the faster you can build your wealth. I like to think of it as how many houses I can buy with the same dollar. There is a stark difference between saving up a dollar to invest, and investing a dollar, getting it back, and investing it again. That difference amounts to *massive* savings when compounded over time.

If I buy a property that earns me a 10 percent return each year, I have to wait ten years before I can get that money back and reinvest it again. If I buy a property and pull out 100 percent of the capital I put into it, I can then immediately buy another property. There is a LOT of wave power you can make up in a ten-year period when it comes to buying real estate.

This may not seem very significant to you right now, but consider a few facts:

If I can pull out 100 percent of my cash from each BRRRR deal (an easy, round number), and buy a new property every three months (time to buy, rehab, rent, and refinance), that is four new properties a year, with the exact same capital.

Currently I average $25,000 in equity and $400 in cash flow on each single-family home I BRRRR. If rents increase by 5 percent a year, over five years, my cash flow is likely to have increased from $400 to $650 a month.

At the end of five years, *even if every property I buy never appreciates a dollar*, I will have added $500,000 to my net worth (for example, 20 houses at $25,000 in equity each) and $13,000 in cash flow to my passive income (20 houses at $650 a month each).

Even if rents didn't continue to increase, I would still have $8,000 a month in cash flow. Compare that to one house, with $400 a month in cash flow, and $25,000 total added to my net worth. Can you see the huge difference between investing in rental properties using the BRRRR strategy and not?

When it comes to investing in real estate, you have two main options. Learn to BRRRR or use the traditional method. From all accounts I can see, BRRRR is better from many angles, but one of the biggest is the increase it can have on increasing the velocity of your money. Buying a good deal will grow your wealth; buying a whole bunch of them, much faster, will skyrocket your wealth!

BRRRR Increases the Efficiency of Your Investing

As you'll see in *Part Three: The Rehab Process*, using the BRRRR method can also increase the efficiency of your rehab, as well as the appraised value of your property when you're finished. In addition to that:

- Grow your properties' emergency fund faster and get better prices on the rehabs of your properties.
- Learn which types of properties will make good investments.
- Find the best agents, wholesalers, contractors, and others to work with.
- Make a small amount of capital stretch further than you can imagine.
- Buy properties under value in markets likely to appreciate in rent.
- Create a pipeline of more deals than you can buy at one time and build out processes that take the stress out of real estate investing.
- Rehab properties efficiently, under budget, and on time while recovering large amounts of the initial capital you invested.
- And so much more!

The BRRRR method is the most efficient way to buy property, period, and that is why it's a game changer when you learn how to harness its power. It's so powerful, in fact, that I often advise newbie investors *not* to buy their first property until they've saved, found, partnered with others, or otherwise secured enough capital to buy a fixer-upper property with cash. You'll often hear me say buying your first house is *so* critical to your success, and it is. Buying the first property helps remove a lot of the emotional hurdles involved with undertaking a new endeavor.

However, the second house matters, too! If you can BRRRR on your first purchase, your next deal will come that much faster. If you BRRRR that one, the third will come even faster. Your learning curve will be so radically steeper, so incredibly better, that it will be worth it to take longer to get started in order to move so much faster once you begin.

A Story from My Own Life

When I first decided I wanted to try the BRRRR model, I realized I didn't have enough capital available to buy a property without financing it. Because buying properties with cash opens up doors to make massive returns, I knew this was something I needed to figure out. I considered many options including using credit cards, borrowing the money, or selling an existing property.

My ultimate solution was to find the property that was performing poorest in my portfolio, sell it, and reinvest the money in a new market.

I mentioned this property in the book *Long-Distance Real Estate Investing*. It was a property in Arizona that had increased in value while rents had remained stagnant. When I sold it, it was making me about $250 a month in cash flow and I ended up with $65,000 after paying all the fees associated with the sale of a home.

That $65,000 became my "seed" money to start buying in Florida. With it, I bought my first house for cash, fixed it up, and then refinanced it. I actually ended up pulling more out of the property than I had put in it ($15,000 more). This left me with $80,000 to invest instead of my original $65,000. I bought another property two months later, and continued the process.

That one property I sold in Arizona ended up turning ten properties in Florida, and counting. My cash flow on that capital increased from $250 a month to about $4,000 a month, and that equity has increased from about $65,000 to $315,000.

This doesn't take into consideration the relationships I've developed that continue to bring me deals (and make me money) to this day! By building relationships with contractors, I'm given better pricing and a higher priority in their schedules. The relationships with property managers give me reduced rates, better service, and access to deals before they hit the MLS (Multiple Listing Service). Because of my relationships with lenders, I'm given lines of credit and access to loan products that other investors can't get because of their lack of network. These relationships may just be more valuable than the actual monetary value attached to my properties.

What You Will Learn from This Book

At its core, this book is about breaking down the five elements that make up the BRRRR strategy. To reiterate:

1. Buy
2. Rehab
3. Rent
4. Refinance
5. Repeat

In each of the book's corresponding parts, I am going to show you how I've learned to master each element. Sharing the secrets, systems, and methods practiced by myself and other high-performing investors, you'll learn how to succeed at real estate investing at a much deeper level than simply analyzing properties and choosing paint colors.

In all reality, entire books on each element of BRRRR could be written. In this book, I will highlight the most important aspect of each element of BRRRR, and show you how to master it to find greater success and ease when it comes to building your own portfolios.

If you want to be great at anything, you first must choose to focus on mastering it. Simply understanding concepts won't create mastery. Being able to recite definitions won't create mastery. Memorizing idioms like "buy low, sell high," won't do anything but trick yourself into believing you know more than you really do. Mastery is more than just being able to copy a movement over and over. It's understanding why that movement works, and finding new ways to use it in different areas of your life.

This is my goal. To help you master the art of Buying, Rehabbing, Renting, Refinancing, and ultimately Repeating the process of buying rental homes, increasing your passive income, and growing your net worth. If I do my job successfully, you too will be willing to do whatever it takes to get serious about investing and catching that wave that will carry you to financial freedom.

While I'm sure you have at minimum some interest in the power of real estate to build wealth, I want you to consider how, just like with every other investment vehicle, you can lose money in real estate, too. Real estate is a powerful vehicle, but if you want to use it to help you, not hurt you, you need to learn to master it.

There is a way to structure your investing so you won't lose money, or if you do, you can bounce back. The more you understand about what you're doing, the more likely you are to avoid mistakes and see threats to your wealth on the horizon. By learning how to master real estate investing, you will also learn how to avoid losing money.

Wildly successful real estate investor Grant Cardone raises money and buys ungodly amounts of multifamily property because he has mastered the art of finding people to believe in him and investing that money in real estate. He can captivate an audience and make them believe in themselves better than most walking this earth.

Those who do the best at their chosen vocation do so because they've mastered it. Those who swing and miss the least do so because they really understand what it is they are doing. Those who consistently win, time in and time out, do so because they have mastered their field. Don't believe when people tell you "it's a numbers game" when referring to being successful. Numbers play a role, but its skill that determines how well you'll perform.

How Learning to BRRRR Will Make You a Better Investor

Once you understand how real estate is valued, financed, and improved, you can learn to get the utmost out of each step of the process.

This will make you a better overall investor, because in the process of learning to BRRRR, you will learn how to excel at each individual stage that makes up the process. By breaking the investment cycle into five parts, we make each part a job of its own. If we win at all five stages of the investment cycle, we win big with our overall investment.

Breaking big problems down into smaller pieces is how experts approach obstacles. The best sports coaches break their game film down to watch with the players. The best business owners divide their companies into smaller parts and put a different person in charge of each department. Mastery of the whole begins with mastery of the parts.

Because every property you buy is its own small business, it makes sense to break down the process of buying, rehabbing, and managing a property into smaller pieces so we can better master each one. Small business owners look for ways to increase their investments' efficiency at every level. As investors, we should, too.

Once you've done this successfully, you'll find that there is a synergistic quality to real estate investing that takes place at each level. Learning to buy better deals will help you get better at finding areas with stronger rents. Learning to manage your rehabs more effectively will help you develop skills that will also help you find better lenders, or get higher appraisals on your refinances.

Developing skills in one area of real estate investing will lead to improving your skills in other areas as well. When you expand your skill set as a business person, your whole business wins. There is big wealth to be made in real estate, so the reward for learning more about it is a worthy one to pursue!

Let me give you an example of how this works in real life: Say you dedicate yourself to learning to find better deals. You study lead generation techniques, you dedicate yourself to a process, and you work that process to a successful result. As a result of this process, you find that you are routinely buying deals for 50 percent of their ARV (after repair value). Big win!

You're obviously thrilled with this new level of success you've reached. You quickly realize you want to figure out just what you did to achieve this. After all, if you can figure out what you did right, you can replicate it and amplify it, leading to even bigger successes. This is exactly what good, profitable businesses do.

As you reverse engineer your own success, you realize the secret to it is your ability to speak with motivated sellers. Most of your competition is looking for the same motivated sellers you are. You're not using any techniques that are different than anyone else. Your secret is that you are the best at proposing your value to these sellers. You explain how you'll be making an all-cash offer and exactly what that means to them, and you do this better than your competition. You lay out how you won't have any contingencies to back out of the deal, and you'll be buying the house "as is."

Now, every other person chasing these same motivated sellers is saying the same thing, but you're *explaining why this matters to them*. You may not be offering the most money, but you're providing them with an opportunity to move on with their life without waiting to see if the deal is going to close. You're saving them Realtor fees, you're paying all the closing costs, and you're allowing them to move without worrying if the deal will close.

Because you do such a good job of this, more sellers agree to sell to you. You build a great reputation for yourself as someone who closes and always keeps their word. When they talk about you to others, they say nothing but good things. You've become so great at sharing the value you bring others, they all want to work with you.

Once you've realized this is the key to your success, you look for ways to replicate this in other elements of the investment cycle. It's helping you a ton in the "buy" part, so why wouldn't it work during the "rehab" part as well? You start looking for ways to incorporate this new skill into more areas of your business, and you come up with a great idea.

Why not use this great skill to start communicating your value to the contractors working on your rehabs as well? If buying right is the most important thing you can do to make money in real estate, surely rehabbing right is the second most important. It only makes sense to apply your skills to this area next. You decide to call your contractor and give it a shot.

The next morning you call the contractor and explain that starting in six months, you plan on buying one new property every month—and you'd like to give all the business to them. You remind them you pay on time, every time, and the two of you have a great business relationship. You understand not every contractor is a great businessperson, so you take it upon yourself to explain to them just how much money they'll be making from you. You also assure them you will send them every referral you have.

After this talk, you explain that since you'll be offering so much value in the way of volume and referrals, and because you're an ideal client, you are going to expect a 15 percent decrease in the profit margin the contractor is making from you. You remind them that even with this decrease, their overall profit will be increasing dramatically and so will their ability to grow their business.

You see the light bulb flick on in their head. They are already thinking about how they can now hire more people, buy more equipment, and pay for more marketing—all because the business you bring in allows them to plan for more growth. You are going to be an instrumental part in the organization's next steps, and they are realizing just how important and valuable you really are.

With a proposition like this, of course they agree to reduce the profit they make off you. And, if you get lucky, they should be doing your projects at cost if you give them enough referrals. What an incentive for you to continue to grow your brand! You've now put yourself in a much stronger business position, improved your skill at explaining your value, and improved your bottom line.

This is how it works when you learn to master the skills that make a successful investor. As you grow in one area, it starts to expand into other areas, and your success compounds on itself. You are now theoretically twice as successful as before, and you're only getting started! There are so many more ways you can now apply this "super power" of yours that can only help your business. With each new success, it becomes even easier to achieve the next one.

Recovering More of Your Capital Allows You to Buy More Deals

This may sound like common sense, but I'd like to share a perspective you may not have previously considered when it comes to buying more deals. Obviously more properties (as long as they're good properties) will lead to more wealth, but there's more than that. Buying more properties doesn't just provide more real estate, it also provides more practice. And that practice is what will turn you into a black belt investor.

A black belt is a rank someone achieves in martial arts. It is the highest rank possible, and symbolizes mastery over the techniques taught in that particular discipline. Every serious martial artist wants to be a black belt in their discipline. So, how does a black belt get to that level of excellence?

They practice. A lot. Black belts train for years to master the techniques taught by their teachers. They develop muscle memory, they practice the technique correctly, every time, without fail. Black belts don't cut corners, they don't settle for mediocrity, and they pay a price to achieve that level of success.

As investors, we can do the same thing. We can practice analyzing properties until we can do it with our eyes closed. We can learn how to run a rehab of a property in a way that comes in at budget and on time. We can look into what made us successful, replicate, and amplify that, over and over, until we are successful at every level of real estate.

Learning the BRRRR process will give you opportunity to do this. It will give you the ability to break each part of the investment cycle into a "technique" that can be mastered, just like a martial artist. Once you've mastered these techniques, you will be a force to be reckoned with, capable of doing major damage in the wealth building space!

How Getting More Capital Back in a Deal Will Make You a Better Investor

While learning to BRRRR will do a lot for your business, the very best reason to learn is because you get so much more capital back at the end of the deal. More capital back at the end of the deal means more capital to buy your next deal. Doing more deals means your skill grows with each one. This won't just improve one area of your business, it will improve *many* areas of your business. To name a few:

- Your systems and processes.

- Your ability to communicate with and find more talented staff.
- The speed at which you analyze a deal.
- The "hacks" you recognize to add more value to a deal.
- Your relationship with your lender and track record.
- Your ability to articulate to others what you are doing, why it works, and why they should be involved, too.
- Your ability to recognize patterns of success (where good deals come from, who gives you the best advice, etc.).
- Your ability to estimate rehab costs.
- Your ability to raise money in the future.
- Your ability to find "lead sources" where more deals are likely to come from.

You see, it's not just that getting more money out of a deal allows you to buy more deals (although that's great); it's also that the more deals you buy, the more reps you get in, and the better of an investor you become. Repetition is the building block of mastery.

How Learning to BRRRR Will Supercharge Your Wealth

Let's take a look at two different stories of investors who chose different routes. In this story, both investors made investing in real estate a top priority. Both investors were able to raise the same amount of money, and both investors bought properties that performed the exact same way. The only difference is in the way they went about building their portfolio. One used the traditional method, the other used the BRRRR method.

Investor A: Traditional Tom

Traditional Tom was a quality assurance manager at a plant in Idaho. Tom had worked in this plant for many years, and so did his father and his grandfather before him. Tom's whole family had provided for themselves by going to high school, graduating, taking a job at the plant, and "putting in their time." Tom found comfort in following the footsteps of those who came before him and always preferred the beaten bath.

But then Tom realized the impact real estate investing could have on his family's future. He decided to jump in and start purchasing buy-and-hold rental properties. Tom's plan was simple—he would work four days of overtime every month, as well as one double shift during the week.

Tom did the math and realized that at his overtime rate of $50 an hour, he could save $2,000 a month purely in overtime (40 hours a month x $50 an hour). Tom was also able to save an additional $1,500 from his base salary, giving him a total of $3,500 a month in savings. This would equal $42,000 a year.

Tom studied real estate investing. He learned to analyze properties, make connections with those who could find him deals, and secure financing to buy them. Tom learned how to manage rehabs. He would typically find properties that needed carpet, paint, and sometimes appliances, and he got good at finding the materials for these rehabs on sale.

Tom also found a good property manager to manage his assets so he could spend more time working at his job. Tom's plan was simple—he would work overtime, make more money, and use that money to buy houses. He would buy these houses making down payments of 25 percent and then pay for the rehabs to get them rent ready. Tom realized he would rather use his capital to buy more properties than to fix up properties he already bought. Due to this, he purposely sought properties that only needed "light" rehabs.

Tom focused on building his cash flow. He saw all the late-night infomercials full of yachts, bikini-clad women, and Ferraris that all promised he too could have that lifestyle if he built up enough cash flow. Now, Tom knew he didn't want to party, but it sure looked appealing to be able to quit his job and go sail on a boat all year. Because Tom was looking solely for cash flow, he would look for properties with a strong ROI, immediately upon purchase. Tom focused on finding single-family houses with high rent. Tom got good at this strategy and perfected it after many years of hard work.

Tom's typical deal would look something like this:

Purchase price = $100,000

Rehab cost = $10,000

Closing costs = $5,000

ARV = $115,000

Rent = $1,100

Down payment = $25,000

Total investment (down payment plus rehab and closing costs) = $40,000

Equity created (all-in cost of $115,000 subtracted from ARV of $115,000)

Mortgage payment ($75,000 at 5% over 30 years) = $403

Tax (1.25% of purchase price, $100,000) = $104

Insurance = $40

Property management (8% of $1,100 rent) = $88

Total Expenses = $635

Total monthly profit (not including maintenance, capex, etc. for simplicity) = $465

ROI ($465 x 12 = $5,580 / $40,000) = 13.95%

As you can see, Tom was getting a very solid return on his money, nearly 14 percent in year one! Tom watched as his rent increased by about 3 percent every year. This led to seeing his cash flow grow, along with his ROI. Tom swelled with pride as he shared his story in real estate investment meetups. He was outperforming even his own projections.

As mentioned earlier, Tom was able to save $42,000 a year through hard work and living below his means. This meant Tom was able to purchase one investment property every year. At the end of 16 years of hard work (year one was spent just saving for the first down payment), sacrifice, and delayed gratification, Tom owned 15 single-family houses.

After 15 years of seeing consistent 3 percent rent growth, Tom's houses were averaging $1,665 a month in rent. This meant his average cash flow had increased. It was now ($1,665 - $680 =) $985 a month! Tom's expenses rose slightly because his management fees increased along with his rent.

With an average of $985 a month, Tom's 15 houses were bringing in $14,775 a month, before accounting for maintenance, vacancy, and other expenses. Tom was very proud of himself and what his hard work had accomplished. Fifteen years of sacrifice had produced nearly $15,000 in gross monthly cash flow.

Investor B: Mastery Mike

Mastery Mike was an entrepreneur who built a business buying distressed debt. Mike would find businesses that made loans to borrowers. Some of those borrowers would default on their debt, and Mike would buy the right to collect on that debt. After contacting those who had defaulted, Mike would arrange for the asset to be collected, or a new payment plan to be worked out.

Due to the fact Mike was working for himself and had no previously established path to follow, he found himself often looking for new, improved, and more efficient ways to do things. Mike learned how to talk to people, solve problems creatively, and evaluate assets quickly. He became good at picking out patterns that would lead to successful outcomes for himself. He also built relationships with those who would be likely to send him opportunities to buy distressed debt.

Like Tom, Mike realized the impact real estate could have on his family's future and decided it was worth pursuing. Just like Tom, Mike realized he would need to change his spending habits. Mike made the commitment to himself, his family, and his friends that he would begin working overtime and living below his means. Also like Tom, Mike was able to save $3,500 a month from his business. This meant Mike could save $42,000 a year, the same amount as Tom.

Unlike Tom, Mike did some research before he jumped in and started buying properties. Mike saved up for an entire year and was able to put $42,000 in his savings account. Before getting too excited and buying his first property, Mike sought the advice of a more experienced investor, Wise William.

When they met, William asked Mike what had made him successful with his distressed debt business. Mike thought long and hard about it. It was an interesting question, and one he had never slowed down to think about. After much thought, Mike told William the secret to his success was his ability to purchase debt at prices much lower than he could recover from the borrower. Mike realized all the tricks he had used to get defaulted borrowers to start paying again, or repo the assets and sell them, were what made him an effective businessman. Furthermore, Mike realized that knowing where to find the distressed debt in the first place was a major contributing factor to his success.

After speaking with William, Mike realized he had built up a very useful skill set that would be wasted on real estate. Mike knew the power of real estate to build wealth long term, but he also wanted to find some way to combine his valuable skill set with the power of real estate. Because Mike had already faced challenges like this when first building his business, he was comfortable looking at things from a new perspective, and taking a path less traditional.

After much thought, Mike decided he would buy real estate in a manner more similar to buying distressed debt than he had previously considered. When Mike bought debt from a lender, he would front cash for the right to collect debt. This debt was often secured by assets worth more than the amount Mike paid for the right to collect it.

The value in that asset was in its potential. Mike's sales, business, and creativity skills are what allowed him to take that potential and make it something real—and profitable. After much studying, learning, and seeking, Mike realized there was a way to buy property using similar methods to those he developed in his business.

Mike decided he would look for distressed houses, much as he looked for distressed assets in his business. He did some research and discovered there were several ways to buy properties like this. Tax liens, auctions, foreclosures, out-of-state landlords, trustee sales, hard-money lenders that had to foreclose on their borrowers, beaten up houses on the MLS—there were tons of ways to find real estate that was not performing for its owner, and was therefore worth much less to the owner. This was the same way Mike was used to finding distressed debt!

Once he decided where he would get the deals, Mike realized he needed to find ways to get the assets performing again. Buying distressed debt was only good if you could improve its value by improving its condition. Mike began studying this, too. He learned there were people out there that could work on the properties he bought and get them in better shape, improving their value and putting equity into Mike's new business.

For single-family homes in bad physical condition, Mike would need a contractor. For multifamily homes with bad tenants or low rents, Mike would need a good property manager with a plan to improve the NOI (net operating income). For properties with old, undesirable floor plans, Mike would need to find someone to help him move walls and create new space. For properties missing bedrooms or bathrooms, Mike would need to find people to help him get permits and add the space the properties would need to bring them to their top value.

None of this scared Mike, as he knew he had done it before, and many other investors were doing the same thing. Mike knew he was onto something, and decided to write down his business plan. Just like buying distressed debt, Mike knew he wouldn't be able to obtain financing to buy those assets that were in the worst shape. The whole reason he was getting them for pennies on the dollar is because they weren't worth anything to a lender!

Mike looked at his financial situation and made a decision. He knew it might cause him to start off slower, but he decided he would save up enough money to be able to buy distressed property for cash. Once it was purchased, he would use his cash to get the property in better condition, improving its value. Once the property was improved, Mike would finance it, recover as much of his initial capital as possible, and repeat the process. Mike knew this model would work, because it was already something he was doing in his distressed debt business.

Once he had his plan in place, Mike got busy saving money. He also told his friends and family what his plan was so they could keep him accountable. At the end of year one, Mike had $42,000 saved up, just as planned. This wasn't enough to buy anything, and Mike faced ridicule from those he had shared his plan with. Many people told him it had been an entire year and he had done nothing, and mocked him for talking such a big talk.

But Mike continued on. At the end of year two, he now had $84,000 saved up, quite an accomplishment! Mike faced even more ridicule as it had now been two whole years and still, nothing. At the end of year two, Wise William gave Mike a call to ask how things had been going. Mike told William he had $84,000 saved up and was eager to get started. William told Mike to start getting the word out to agents, wholesalers, and bird dogs that he was looking for a property he could pay cash for in the $50,000–60,000 range. Mike did just that.

About two months into year three, Mike found his first deal. An agent called him saying one of their investors had started a project and ran out of money, and the investor needed to sell—quick. The investor was racking up debt to their hard-money lender and the property was in danger of being foreclosed on. Mike asked the agent for the numbers, and the agent provided them:

Purchase price = $52,000

Rehab cost = $32,000

Total costs for Mike = $84,000

Closing costs = seller paid

ARV = $110,000

Rent = $1,000

Note that this is a rent that is 10 percent lower than Tom was getting ($100), and the ARV was also $5,000 less. Mike purchased the property, conducted the rehab, and rented the property to a tenant. Mike found a portfolio lender that would allow him to refinance after owning the property for four months. Four months after purchasing, he refinanced the property with a bank that let him borrow 75 percent of the appraised value (the ARV).

Amount financed = $82,500

Closing costs = $5,000

Net capital recovered = $77,500

Down payment/money left in the deal = $6,500

Mortgage payment ($82,500 at 5% over 30 years) = $443

Tax (1.25% of purchase price, $52,000) = $54

Insurance = $40

Property management (8% of $1,000 rent) = $80

Total expenses = $617

Total monthly profit (not including maintenance, capex, etc. for simplicity) = $383

ROI ($383 x 12 = $4,596 / $6,500) = 70.7%

Just like Tom, Mike proceeded with this plan for the next 15 years. Unlike Tom, Mike's plan produced a compact effect that changed the entire landscape of his real estate investing.

Because Mike was using the BRRRR method, his portfolio grew at a much different rate from Tom's. Tom's portfolio grew in a linear fashion. Each year, Tom purchased one house. He saved the same amount of capital, he purchased the same priced house, and he made the same cash flow. Tom's portfolio grew in a linear, and predictable, fashion.

Mike's portfolio grew much differently, because Mike was able to use his capital much more efficiently. After refinancing his first house, Mike immediately bought another and repeated the process. After he refinanced that, Mike bought a third house. Because he could refinance every four months, Mike was able to buy three houses a year with the same capital he saved in year one. The following is an illustration of how Mike's portfolio grew. For simplicity's sake we will leave out rent growth and asset appreciation until the very end, just as we did with Tom:

- Year 1—Nothing
- Year 2—Three homes.

Remember, while Mike was purchasing three homes in year two, he was also still working and saving money. This allowed him to have more capital to invest in real estate each year than the year before. As Mike was able to save $42,000 a year, he could purchase one additional house every two years than he could before (assuming he is buying houses at an average all-in price of $84,000).

Year 3—Three homes
Year 4—Four homes
Year 5—Four homes
Year 6—Five homes

Year 7—Five homes
Year 8—Six homes
Year 9—Six homes
Year 10—Seven homes
Year 11—Seven homes
Year 12—Eight homes
Year 13—Eight homes
Year 14—Nine homes
Year 15—Nine homes
Total—84 homes

Now, before going any further, I want to make a few quick points. No, I don't expect everyone to want to own 84 homes. I understand that may not be practical—I'm just illustrating a point here. And, yes, those numbers are accurate. Pairing the BRRRR method with finding an area to invest in that has the right price points, inventory, and rents that work for you, would allow you also to replicate Mike's numbers. Also, I gave Tom 16 years whereas I only gave Mike 15. Mike's numbers would have ended up even more impressive given that last year, but I wanted to give Tom an advantage to help drive my point home.

Let's dig a little deeper into Mike's portfolio after 15 years of hard work and BRRRR magic. Assuming Mike's rent increased at the same rate as Tom's (3 percent annually), Mike's average rent per property would have gone from $1,000 to $1,480.

$1,000 x .03 = $30

$30 x 16 (years) = $480

$1,000 + $480 = $1,480

This meant Mike's cash flow would have increased from $383 a month to $854.

With 84 units bringing in $854 in gross cash flow, Mike would be looking at $71,736 in gross cash flow a month. This does not include all the cash flow he made during the 15 years he was building the portfolio. (If we had included that cash flow, Mike would have ended up with even more than 84 houses at the end because he would have had more capital with which to buy them.)

Assuming that not even one of Mike's properties appreciated over that 15-year time span, Mike would have accumulated an average of $21,000 a property ($84,000 all-in price, plus $5,000 closing costs = $89,000. ARV of $110,000 – $89,000 = $21,000) in equity.

84 properties x $21,000 = $1,764,000 in equity.

As you can tell, these are conservative numbers (for both Tom and Mike). The real estate market goes through ups and downs, but it's always trended upward due to inflationary pressures. Tom and Mike would also have more than likely received raises during these times, and would probably have found ways to get better and better deals the longer they invested. We always get better at things through repetition.

It stands to reason, Mike would have done much, much better than he did in this hypothetical story—but even if with conservative assumptions, he did very well. Let's compare Tom's final numbers with Mike's.

Tom's Final Numbers:
    Number of properties—15
    Gross cash flow—$14,775
    Total equity in properties—$0

Mike's Final Numbers:
    Number of properties—84
    Gross cash flow—$71,736
    Total equity in properties—$1,764,000

An Analysis of the Results

First off, it is obvious Mike's strategy outperformed Tom's. I tried very hard to keep all the variables as consistent as I could between the two investors, and it's very apparent which strategy was superior. While I'm sure many of you assumed the BRRRR strategy would prove to be the better model, I wanted to point out *just how much better the strategy is*.

Let's break down some of the differences between the two strategies, and highlight why Mike's produced such a radically better result than Tom's. I won't go over everything, but some of the big differences should be pointed out. That way, as you continue reading the book, you'll develop a better understanding for *why* BRRRR is better.

Mike's ROI Was Noticeably Better than Tom's

Tom's average ROI was about 14 percent. Mike's was about 71 percent. This difference led to Mike's massively larger gross cash flow. Tom was focused on building more cash flow, while Mike was focused on making his money work harder for him. This led to a very different final outcome for the two investors.

Mike was able to achieve such a larger ROI because of the way he structured his deals. By financing his properties after he improved them, Mike left much less money in each deal. This helped him in many ways, one of them being an increased ROI.

Lesson: ROI matters. We should all expect our money to work hard for us, just as we would if we had employees. The traditional method allows your money to be lazy. The BRRRR method forces it to work hard, and serve you better.

Mike's Capital Was Used Repeatedly; Tom's Was Used Once

Mike was able to save money and invest it. His investments brought him equity and cash flow, which is what he wanted. Tom was able to do the same (absent the equity part). What Mike did differently is what made the major impact. After gaining his equity and cash flow, Mike pulled money back out of the house to use again, while Tom left his money in the property to stay there.

Mike sacrificed cash flow in doing this. His loans were larger than Tom's and therefore his mortgage was higher. This led to lower cash flow in each deal. In spite of this, Mike made more cash flow in the end. Why? Because Mike used his capital over and over to continue buying deals that would give him equity and cash flow. He forced his money to work harder.

Mike found a good thing and repeated it many times. Tom found a good thing and got one shot at it. Mike made his money work harder for him by recycling the same money. Tom used his money once. Tom looked at money like a financial gift he gave to someone in need: a one-time investment. Mike looked at money more like how a business owner looks at employees.

Mike's money was like a construction crew he hired and trained for his construction business. He sent them on a job and when they had earned him a profit, he sent them on to the next job! He kept them working, and with each job they got better, faster, and more skilled. Mike's crew would get better and better with each job they did, making him more and more money in the process.

Lesson: Tom didn't make his money work or teach it to perform better. We should always have high expectations for our money. Money is hard to make and hard to keep! The "velocity" of our money makes a very big difference in the overall wealth-building game. We should always be looking for ways to improve it, and we should have high expectations for how to make it work.

Mike Avoided "Light" Rehabs and Bought Better Deals

Tom focused on light rehabs because he wanted to use less money for improvements and more for down payments. He was correct in understanding he'd be better off using the money to purchase more assets, but he was incorrect in the way he went about doing that.

By avoiding larger rehabs, Tom inadvertently ended up avoiding better deals. Rental properties on the MLS that don't need much work typically don't see as large of a discount. Why would they? Mike figured this out faster than Tom and was able to take advantage of it to grow his wealth faster.

Our first priority should be finding deals we can purchase under market value. This doesn't always include a major rehab, but it often will. Mike looked for deals and solutions to the problems that would have prevented him from buying them. Tom looked for an easy purchase.

Lesson: Every deal we buy should be for as much under market value as possible. Buying properties under market value is a foundational tenet to good investing and should be practiced as much as is practical. "You make your money when you buy" is one of the oldest and truest real estate maxims around. There is no substitute for buying a good deal. Focus first on how to find great deals, and wealth will end up finding you.

Mike Added Equity to His Deals

Mike realized larger rehabs led to better deals, which led to more equity. By adding equity to all his deals, Mike grew his wealth at a much faster rate than Tom did. In addition to this, Mike was able to recover much more of his initial capital when he refinanced than Tom did. This gave him more capital to buy more deals, and empowered him to end up with 84 houses, not 15.

At the end of 15 years of investing, this led to Mike having $1,764,000 of equity in his portfolio, while Tom had none. If Mike didn't like the thought of owning 84 single-family properties, he could sell them and use the equity to purchase a large multifamily building. Mike's equity gave him options.

Lesson: Equity grows your wealth, not just cash flow. Mike grew this much equity, and this is without any form of appreciation at all (not likely after 15 years). Look for ways to add equity to every single deal you buy and you'll watch your wealth grow quickly. Adding bedrooms, bathrooms, square footage, and other tricks are great ways to do that, which we will talk about later in the book.

Mike Sought Counsel Before He Started

Tom saw an infomercial and realized he wanted to invest in real estate. He wasn't wrong. Tom's decision made him a lot of money and set him up for a much better retirement. Tom wouldn't have regretted this decision.

Mike sought the advice of a wiser, more experienced real estate investor before he got started. He spent an additional year gathering information, and it led to the birth of a strategy that ended up making him noticeably more money than Tom.

Both Tom and Mike used strategies that made sense to them based on previous decisions they had made in life. Tom was a traditional guy, who took a traditional vocational path, and followed the traditional investing model.

Mike was an entrepreneur who was used to looking for creative solutions to problems and wasn't scared at the thought of doing things a little differently. Where Tom saw risk, Mike saw opportunity. This opportunity led to massive results over time.

Lesson: Fear is healthy. It can prevent us from making mistakes and sometimes protect us. But as an emotion, we can't just follow it blindly. Like a sign on the beach that says *caution: high tides* can cause dangerous conditions, we should take note of the warning and look to see if the ocean is at high tide. If it's not, we should enjoy a great day of surfing. If it is, we should wait until the tide goes low. If we can't tell the difference, we should educate ourselves before jumping in.

Don't assume when you feel the emotion of fear that it's justified. Dig deeper and explore whether or not you should be obeying it. Oftentimes our fears are based on past experiences that have nothing to do with the question we are facing now. When you're unsure, surround yourself with facts, wise counsel, and educate yourself. Mike would have lost out on an immense amount of wealth if he didn't take the time and effort to work through his fears first.

Mike's Volume Was Noticeably Higher

Mike bought way more houses than Tom. 69 more (and in one less year! With one additional year Mike would have had an additional ten homes). Even though Mike's cash flow was lower than Tom's, the sheer volume of it produced much more income. This is one of the benefits that comes with more volume.

Mike was able to produce much more volume with the same amount of capital Tom was using. Mike just used it more efficiently. By repeating this process, year in and year out, over a 15-year time span, Mike was able to produce a vastly superior result, through vastly superior volume.

Lesson: Volume amplifies your results, both positive or negative. When you are losing money, volume can cause you to lose a lot more. When you are making money, you can make a lot more. Use volume as a tool when you've found a good thing, but only once you've found a good thing. Move slowly until you know the process you're using is leading to the result you want—then you can step up your volume.

Key Points

- The BRRRR model outperforms the traditional model in every relevant statistical category.
- There are two ways to add value to a property: buy at a low price (buying equity) or add value through the rehab process (build, or force equity).
- BRRRR increases your ROI by lowering the investment basis left in a deal.
- BRRRR builds wealth faster by increasing the velocity of your money.
- BRRRR increases efficiency by returning more of your capital to you and maximizing leverage.
- Mastering each element of BRRRR will make you an overall better investor in general.
- Mike's ROI was nearly 71 percent vs. Tom's 14 percent ROI. BRRRR made a huge difference in the end results of the two investors' portfolios.

PART TWO

Buying Great Deals

CHAPTER TWO
Buying Under Market Value

How many millionaires do you know who have
become wealthy by investing in savings accounts?
I rest my case.

—ROBERT G. ALLEN

As we just learned about in the hypothetical story of Tom and Mike, buying right is important. "Buying right" is a phrase used in real estate that simply means "buying an investment property at a price that makes it a good deal." This is an entire book written to teach you one thing: how to make more money in real estate. Buying right is the single most important thing you can do if you want to accomplish just that.

Learning to buy right and find great deals is what allows all the rest of BRRRR to work. Because it's so important, we are going to spend a lot of time going over how to find great deals, how to pay less for them, and how to get the very most out of everything you buy. Excelling at this area of real estate is what will open the doors to put everything else you learn into practice.

To simplify this as much as possible, we are going to consider "buying right" to mean paying as little as possible for a deal but still being able to get the owners to agree to sell to us. To inexperienced investors, this means lowballing 100 sellers a month and hoping something sticks. To the experienced investor, this means targeting sellers in some form of distress who are more likely to work with a buyer who isn't going to pay top dollar. By narrowing in on those most likely to be attracted to our offer to buy their property, we increase our odds of finding a "win-win" situation.

The Three Forms of Distress

What does this mean? If you want to be a successful real estate investor, you need to get good at targeting people in distress. Now, there are three kinds of distress we target as investors, and we are going to touch on all three at different times in the book. They are:

1. Market distress
2. Personal distress
3. Property distress

Market distress is when an entire market, economy, or area is in a rough time. Think of 2010 when the housing crisis was at its peak and there were "for sale" signs on every four to five houses in some markets. California, Nevada, Arizona, Florida—lots of different markets were in such distress that savvy investors could throw a rock and hit a deal. This is the easiest time to find deals, but the one you have the least amount of control over. If you rely on market distress, you will spend the majority of your time waiting and not investing.

Personal distress is how professional, full-time investors target deals. It's how most wholesalers find deals. Personal distress is when the owner of a property is in some form of distress in their personal life that is affecting their finances. Examples would be a divorce, a lost job, a death in the family, trust sales, sudden medical expenses, etc. Personal distress is the best form of distress to target if you want to find deals with the highest margin. It is also the most difficult. Finding those in personal distress involves a large amount of time, energy, and focus devoted to creating and developing relationships with professionals who are likely to come across people going through tough financial times.

Property distress is when the property itself is in such bad condition that its value is affected. Properties that need large amounts of work to be livable are a form of property distress. Examples include leaking roofs, foundational problems, significant pest problems (termite damage), obsolete floor plans, etc. Property distress is the form of distress that involves the most work, but it is also the easiest form to target and the one you have the most control over finding. As a BRRRR investor, this is the type of distress you will typically find yourself targeting the most.

Once you learn the three kinds of distress, you can start evaluating which of these three is best suited for your personality, risk tolerance, and skill set. For example, if you're great with people, networking, and building relationships, you'd be best suited to target personal distress. By letting your entire network know you're looking for people in trouble who need a quick sale, you're more likely to find great deals before someone else does.

If you're busier, working a full-time job, or have other time commitments, property distress might be a better option for you to target. By having an agent search for properties that need a lot of work, you can focus on making money in other ways while your construction crew or rehab team takes care of the problem (the work the property needed) that allowed you to buy it at a discounted rate.

If you know yourself well enough to know that you don't want to learn investing, don't like risk, and just want something easy to dump your money into that won't take much of your time, you may settle for the fact market distress is your best bet. If this is you, saving money consistently and waiting for the next crash may be your best bet.

No matter which method you feel is best for you (or if you want to use all three!), understand that buying right is where everything starts. Buying properties below market value will open up the rest of the doors we talk about in the book.

Rules of Thumb

Before we dive right in, there are a few basics we should cover first. Nothing I do in real estate investing is all that brand-new or innovative. The majority of it has been done many times before I even thought of it, by many different people. These people who have gone before me have recognized patterns in their process that led to success. These patterns have come to be known as "rules of thumb," and are now practiced by many successful investors all over the country.

I'm going to share a few of these rules of thumb that apply most consistently to the BRRRR strategy. Learning them will shorten your own learning curve, as well as help you analyze potential deals much faster, giving you time to spend on more productive activities.

The 1 Percent Rule

The 1 percent rule is a very simple maxim that states if a property will rent for 1 percent of the price you paid for it, it's likely to cash-flow positively. This is a very important metric for us as BRRRR investors are those looking to keep properties as rentals, not sell them as flips.

To put it simply, if a property will rent for $1,000, and you paid $100,000 for it, it meets the 1 percent rule. A $200,000 house should rent for $2,000, and a $150,000 house for $1,500. Houses that meet these criteria tend to cash-flow stronger than properties that do not. This is most important when considering what area you want to start looking for deals, which deals to look at, and what price you can offer to the seller. If the area has a high percentage of 1 percent properties, you're more likely to have success there.

Please note, a property doesn't *have* to conform to the 1 percent rule in order to cash-flow positively. There are many factors that go into whether a property will make you money every month. Some properties have HOA (homeowners association) fees, high property taxes, extra insurance required, etc. These are all variables that you wouldn't be able to take into consideration using only the 1 percent rule.

Additionally, I've found the more expensive a property is, the less likely the need to conform to this standard. A $500,000 property would not need to rent for $5,000 a month in order to cash-flow positively, whereas a $50,000 property would need to be really close to $500 a month in order to make money. The 1 percent rule tends to apply more strictly to lower priced properties—which is where most investors operate.

Lastly, keep in mind it's a general rule, not a hard-and-fast rule. "Buying right" is something that is nonnegotiable. The 1 percent rule isn't. In times like now (2018) interest rates are at historical lows. Money is very cheap, and therefore mortgage amounts are abnormally low. This means you can borrow more money and collect less rent than normal but still cash-flow well, all because your mortgage expense is exceptionally lower than usual. This gives you more slack when it comes to not meeting the 1 percent rule, but still being able to make money.

In general, I've found a property can rent for around .08 percent of the purchase price and usually still be profitable. Because the 1 percent of the rent is easier to calculate in my head than .08, I find myself just using the 1 percent rule and digging deeper into properties that get "close" to it. The purpose of the 1 percent rule is *not* to justify a purchase that doesn't make sense (we don't buy every 1 percent property). Its purpose is to help you decide if looking deeper into a property's financials is a wise use of your time. The 1 percent rule is a *preliminary* screening procedure meant to save you time.

When I'm choosing a market to invest in, I look for areas that have lots of properties that meet the 1 percent rule. I know if I can find an area like that, I am much more likely to find success.

75 Percent of ARV

This isn't so much a rule of thumb used by all investors, but it is a metric I use personally when determining what to pay for a property. This rule states that I want my total expenses for a property (acquisition plus rehab) to add up to 75 percent of what the property will appraise for when I'm finished. It is essentially saying I'm willing to pay 75 cents on the dollar for what I buy.

If you're curious where I came up with the 75 percent number, it wasn't by coincidence. I've found that most banks are willing to lend at a 75 percent LTV (loan to value). We will discuss more about LTVs, what they mean, and why they are important in *Part Five: The Refinance Process* of this book. For now, understand that if I can hit this metric, I'll be able to recover 100 percent of the capital I put into a deal once I refinance it.

This is always my overall goal. I want my money to be working hard for me, which means I need to get it back after I invest it so I can put it to work again. This is not an easy goal. I have to look long and hard for deals that will meet this standard. That ends up being a good thing, as it forces me to step up my game in the other areas of investing—most notably "buying" and "rehabbing."

How Properties Are Valued

Understanding how properties are valued is extremely important in real estate investing. If you understand what impacts a property's value, you can know what to manipulate in order to make your property worth more money.

The first thing you should understand is that single-family properties are valued differently than multifamily properties. Single-family properties (anything less than five units) are assumed to be bought for the primary purpose of having somewhere to live. Lenders (the force behind deciding how a property will be valued) know the vast majority of buyers for a single-family home are buying it to live there, not as an investment. It's important to remember this because we as investors look at these properties from a different perspective.

Since single-family homes are assumed to be bought for the purpose of a dwelling place, they are valued in comparison to other single-family homes. When appraisers are assigned by lenders to give a professional opinion on the value of a single-family home, they compare the property to recently sold properties that are nearby and similar in size and makeup. We call the homes they use to compare the subject property to "comparables," or "comps" for short.

If you want to know how your single-family property will be valued, you look at the surrounding homes and find the "comps" that are closest in size, number of bedrooms, and condition. This is what an appraiser will be looking at when determining the value of the property you purchased.

Multifamily properties are different. Multifamily properties are assumed by lenders to be purchased for the purpose of running a business. Lenders know multifamily properties are bought primarily for the purpose of making money, so they are valued as a business.

Without me taking too much time to explain, just know that multifamily properties are valued based on the amount of profit they generate, not what other nearby multifamily properties sold for. If you want to increase the value of a multifamily home, you increase its profitability. If you want to increase the value of a single-family home, you improve its condition to compare to other, more valuable single-family homes nearby.

Tricks for Understanding and Increasing a Property's Value

First off, it's important to recognize that appraisers in different areas use different formulas to determine the values of single-family homes. They are all still comparing them to other single-family houses, but they give weight differently depending on certain aspects of a home. For example, a California-based appraiser is much more likely to give more weight to the proximity and condition of a home than to the square feet of the home.

In other areas, like the South, appraisers are more likely to use the price per square foot of a home than the condition it's in. Understanding your area, and how homes are valued there, is a terrific way to make sure you are adding as much value as possible to the properties you buy and rehab.

A large chunk of my rental portfolio is in the Southeast. Because of that, I've learned the number of square feet in the properties I buy plays a major role in the overall value of the property when my rehab is finished. If I want to add value to a property that is undersized, adding square feet to the floor plan of the property is the fastest, cheapest, and most efficient way to do that.

The reason is because in the Southeast many appraisers will look at the average price per square foot for other properties in the area. They will take that number (let's call it $100 a square foot) and multiply it by the overall number of square feet in the home (say, 1,100). This would give them a number of $110,000. They would then make their adjustments, up or down, based on the condition of my property compared to other nearby properties. If my property was in worse condition, they would adjust down from the $110,000. If my property was in better condition, they would adjust up.

Understanding how properties are valued gives me an advantage when looking for how to make my property worth more. The more knowledge I gain, the more tools I have in my tool belt to help me make better decisions. The better decisions I make, the more money I'll end up making, too. Throughout this book, I'm going to show you ways to maximize every level of the BRRRR process, increasing the money you can make at each step.

Finding Property Deals and Analyzing Them

As I mentioned before, the most important step in the entire investment cycle is finding a great deal. There is no substitute for it, and if you learned how to do just this one thing well, you'd probably do great with investing! Finding great deals is priority No. 1 if you want to BRRRR successfully.

Before you can find a great deal, you need to be able to recognize one. Every investor needs to know what they're looking for, and only then can you know where to find it. I highly recommend writing down your criteria and sharing them with other investors. I know my own criteria very well and share them with everyone I know. My criteria are simple and logical. I look for three things in a deal.

1. To be all-in for 75 percent of ARV.
2. To cash-flow positively.
3. To be in an area that won't cause me a headache.

Now, these criteria might seem oversimplified, but take a deeper look and you'll see why they work so well for me.

1. If I want to be all-in at 75 percent of ARV, there needs to be a significant amount of equity in a deal before I'll even look at it. This weeds out marginal deals and prevents me from talking myself into a mediocre deal just so I can say I bought something. It protects me from making bad decisions and ensures I have a built-in safety net in case something goes wrong with the rehab or the ARV.
2. If I need my property to cash-flow properly, I won't be spending much time looking at anything that isn't in a 1 percent rule area. This saves me time and energy.
3. If I'm avoiding headache areas, I'll also be avoiding a lot of long-term bad investments. Investing is more fun when you're not constantly frustrated with evictions, destroyed properties, and late rents. I also end up buying in areas that appreciate faster than the surrounding neighborhoods, so I can refinance several times over the period of time I own the property and reinvest the money I pull out.

Because I know what I'm looking for, I also end up knowing where to find ideal properties. I spend very little time analyzing the vast majority of properties that other investors waste their time looking into. The more I know what my target looks like, the quicker I realize it when I see it. You should do the same.

Knowing what you're looking for in a deal comes first, but you still have to be able to analyze a deal in order to know if it makes sense to buy. In my experience, the No. 1 factor that prevents investors from building wealth is the fear of what could go wrong. The more fear someone has, the less likely they are to take the steps required to move forward. We can't learn if we aren't moving forward.

If you want to overcome fear, get good at analyzing deals. As Brandon Turner (the bestselling author of *The Book on Rental Property Investing* and *BiggerPockets Podcast* host) says, "Overcome fear with math." Math won't lie to you. It's not subjective. Math won't confuse you or leave you feeling disillusioned. What Brandon is really saying is this: If you're feeling afraid of the deal, get better at understanding what the deal is with concrete numbers and the fear will disappear. Understanding how to analyze a deal will take so much of the fear and uncertainty out of the decision. When I talk to would-be investors about what holds them back, almost every one of them tells me the same thing: a laundry list of fears or concerns they have about what could go wrong. When I ask these same people what they have done, learned, or studied about how to handle those problems, they almost never have an answer.

The solution is simple. Learn to analyze properties and you'll find yourself feeling much better about the decision to be made regarding whether or not you should buy. The best way to get good at analyzing deals is through practice. Repetition (and practice) builds mastery!

When you first start to analyze properties, there are two things you should focus on. Not coincidentally, they are the same top two things I consider in my own criteria! The first is how much you are buying a property for under its value (how good the deal is). The second is if the property will cash-flow positively or not.

To know how far below value you are buying a property for, you need to understand a few things. The first is comps. Learn how to find comps and compare them to the property you're evaluating. Other people like agents, appraisers, and wholesalers can help you with this. You can also do some of this research yourself using listing portals like Zillow.com or Realtor.com.

The next thing to understand is rehab costs. Learning how to estimate rehab costs is really beneficial. Talking to contractors, handymen, and other investors is a great way to build up your confidence in this area and know if you're overpaying. You want to see the projects from their eyes. If you're using the BRRRR method, you're very likely to be doing significant rehabs. Learning how to estimate rehab costs is a skill that will come in handy.

The last thing to learn is being able to determine whether or not a property will cash-flow. My favorite method is what I call "the napkin method." You are basically taking the five different inputs involved in just about every purchase, and quickly calculating them by writing them down on a piece of paper—or a napkin.

The five inputs in deals are:
1. Rent
2. Mortgage
3. Tax
4. Insurance
5. Property management fees

We'll talk more later in the book about how to calculate these numbers more accurately. For now, I would recommend creating a "baseline" in your mind for an average amount of each one. When you look at enough homes in a specific area, you start to get a basic idea of what they cost to own. This basic idea becomes the "baseline" you will use to help recognize a deal that stands out.

For instance, if you're looking at houses between $100,000 and $120,000 in an area, and you look at enough of them, you'll start to recognize patterns in the numbers behind them:

- Rents may average $1,000–$1,200
- Mortgage amounts may be around $450–$550
- Taxes may be about $100–$125
- Insurance costs may run about $40–$50
- Property management fees at 8 percent would be about $80–$96

If you use all conservative numbers in these estimates, you could come up with a baseline to add up either in your head, on a calculator, or on a piece of paper (or a napkin, of course). If you continually do this often enough, you'll start to find patterns in the way the numbers read. Once you recognize these patterns, a good deal will stand out immediately. *That* is what you're looking for.

The *only* way you get to this point is by repeatedly analyzing deals over and over and over. Those who can make the fastest decisions are those who have the most experience. Just like new quarterbacks struggle in the NFL because they don't have much experience reading defenses yet, new investors will struggle because they haven't analyzed enough deals.

Commit yourself to analyzing several properties a day, five days a week. Do it until you feel you know the result before you even run the numbers. Once you get to that point, you'll find your confidence skyrockets and your fear of the unknown decreases significantly. We want to commit to mastering real estate. You can't claim to be a master of something until you can anticipate what is likely to happen before it does. In this specific circumstance, you want to be able to anticipate which deals will pencil out and which won't *before* you make the time to analyze them thoroughly.

Still don't believe you'll ever be able to do this well? Compare it to other everyday chores you do without even thinking about it. As you walk through the grocery store, you recognize a good deal when one of your staple food purchases is on sale. The reason is simple: When you're used to looking at something over and over, your mind remembers what falls within the pattern of normalcy for that item. When a sale occurs that is outside the "normal" pricing, it immediately catches your attention. Real estate isn't any different. Maybe you just haven't been looking at it as much because it feels more intimidating.

Rockstars Know Rockstars—Finding Talent to Help You Find Deals

Once you know what you're looking for and how to recognize if it's what you want, the next step is to find people to help you do it. A person alone can only do so much, but by leveraging others whose goals align with yours, you'll find that your success will start to come much, much faster. Rockstars help you accomplish as much as you can in as short amount of time as possible, compared to painstakingly going at it alone.

Rockstar is a synonym in the world of real estate for someone who is really, really skilled at their job. There are many musicians in the world, but there are very few rockstars. If other people can help you succeed fast, a rockstar can help you succeed at "ludicrous speed!" They are the cream of the crop, masters of their profession, who are equipped with life-changing talent and often have already endured years in the crucible of real estate investing. Having just one rockstar in your corner can make you immensely successful. One of the core principles of your business practice will be to find, attract, and work with as many rockstars as possible.

When I look to buy in a new area, my first priority is to find my "Core Four." The Core Four are the four people I need to invest in any market, any time. These are the people who will be running my business for me, making me money, and helping me become successful—all while returning the favor. They are my "Dream Team." Even if you're looking to invest where you live, you'll still need a Core Four. The following are examples of what it looks like to have a rockstar at each position.

Agent

A rockstar real estate agent would be a top producer, the type who knows everybody and is well liked. They are the agents who find deals before anyone else, know how to negotiate the best, and have the brightest minds. They have the most talent on their teams, the best mentors in their corner, and they demand excellence from everyone around them. Rockstar agents have the best referrals because they only work with top lenders, contractors, handymen, and property managers. These agents are never hurting for business, don't lower their commissions, and know real estate like the back of their hand.

Rockstar agents got to where they are because they know how to close deals. They've found the right people who can fix problems when they arise, and they have very low tolerance for people who don't. Rockstar agents are usually very resourceful, knowledgeable, and creative. These are all traits you want working for *you* when it comes to building your wealth. Finding a rockstar agent should be your first priority, because they can help you find the rest of your Core Four.

You'll recognize a rockstar agent because they aren't bending over backward to win you over. They are professional, courteous, and helpful, but they have a confidence in their process that won't take a second place to a newer investor. Rockstar agents want to educate you on the process, but also get right to the point. If you want to work with an adept agent, you'll need to be comfortable following the process they have in place. It's there because after hundreds of deals, they've learned the best ways to secure them.

Lender

A rockstar lender is one who doesn't throw in the towel easily. They have access to the most loan programs, and when a loan doesn't work, they know how to go find one that will. Rockstar lenders know how to help you repair your credit, how to find ways to manipulate data to get you better rates and terms, and can solve problems when they arise. They are tenacious, resilient, and they hustle! Finding a stellar lender can open up financing doors for you that a regular lender cannot.

Rockstar lenders became that way because great agents brought them clients. They understand customer service and the need to go the extra mile. A rockstar lender won't say "no" without proposing an alternative solution. When you find the right lender, ask them about the best agent they know when it comes to finding investment property, or other lenders they know that do the kinds of deals you need. If they can't do the kind of deal you need, a great lender will know someone who does.

The best way to find a great lender is to ask top-producing real estate agents who they recommend. If the agent you're speaking to works with a lot of investors, they are more likely to know lenders who will do loans for investors. Tell your agent you want to buy properties with them, but you need financing, then ask who they know. If they don't know of anyone, ask them who they can talk to who does! If your agent simply won't make an effort to find you a lender, look for another agent who will.

When you do find a rockstar lender, they often have too much business to handle on their own, and have hired team members or employees to help them keep up with demand. For many of those inexperienced in real estate, this can feel uncomfortable or off-putting. Try to remember it's a good sign if your lender is doing so much business they need help. At the end of the day, this is a business transaction, and if you don't always speak to the main lender on every phone call that's okay as long as the transaction closes.

Contractor

Rockstar contractors may not look like what you think at first. They may not answer your calls right away or be the best communicators. That's not what makes a great contractor, at least not for an investor. An ideal contractor for an investor is someone who understands what needs to be done, how to do it, and how to save you money on it. They are a contractor who understands your business goals, not just their own. These are people who can tell you what the best plan of action for your property is before you even look into it.

Rockstar contractors get the job done inexpensively and correctly. These are the people who know when they can save you money with tile they found on sale, or can make repairs to existing structural components when an average contractor would make you go buy new materials. These contractors are always looking for ways to make themselves money by saving you money. They understand your needs.

Great contractors can communicate with the city for you to get permits approved and can provide you with recommendations that other contractors wouldn't think of. Great contractors know the best roofers, HVAC services, plumbers, electricians, and more. They are concerned about your bottom line, but they are also concerned about their own. Knowing a rockstar contractor can open up doors for you to buy deals that you couldn't even consider without them.

Property Manager

A first-rate property manager is someone who knows the areas you're investing in. They manage many rental properties in the area you're investing, and they have a large sample size of properties they've learned from. These people know which areas work, and which do not, and they will share that information with you if you let them.

Rockstar property managers likely own properties themselves, and that's why they got into property management. They have access to the best handymen or repair crews because they have been looking for them for their own properties. They can be an excellent source of referrals for you, and they can also oftentimes be an underutilized deal source. These property managers know other investors who want to sell before anyone else does. They are the ones managing those properties!

Top-rate PMs tend to want to take care of your problems without getting you involved, and are better at handling them than you would be yourself. They are more experienced than you, more connected than you, and more knowledgeable than you. When you find the right project manager, they will teach you more about investing than you could hope to learn, and they make you better just from being around them. You know you have found a rockstar project manager when your first inclination is to call them when a new deal comes your way.

Rockstars Play with Rockstars

When you're a rockstar, and you know you're an actual rockstar, you don't waste your time playing with mediocre bandmates. The best will always surround themselves with top talent and demand everyone put in equivalent effort. They search for the best drummers, the best vocalists, best guitar players, everything.

In my experience, top-level talent only works with loyal and honest clients. If you aren't someone who's serious, they are going to figure that out pretty quickly. If you aren't someone who's honest or fair, they'll know that, too. If that happens, you'll likely find yourself kicked out of the concert and listening from the parking lot while everyone else rocks out. In the world of real estate investing, that can end up costing you a *lot* of money.

Don't let that happen! If we already know rockstars play with rockstars, start working on becoming one yourself! Everyone asks me: "How do I get the best to work with me?" The answer is simple—become someone worthy of working with them. Agents are in this business for the same reason you are: to make money! So are lenders, contractors, property managers, and everyone else. Too many investors think it's okay for them to make money, but expect everyone else to serve their needs for free. This kind of thinking will never get you anywhere but frustrated. Top talent expects to be paid for their work and they aren't shy to admit that. If you are too worried about what someone else is making, you're not focused enough on the role you're supposed to be playing in your business.

If you want the best to work with you, start acting like you're also the best. Learn to give value first. Learn to find what these rockstars need in their business or their life and bring that to them. Take the attitude of the servant first, putting your fears behind you and instead focusing on proving to them why it's in their best interest to help you. I know this sounds counterintuitive, but it's the best thing I've done to help grow my own business.

Now, if you are reading this section and think it's bad advice, my guess is you probably trusted the wrong person in the past and got burned for it. Don't make the mistake of trying to prove yourself to mediocre or below average talent. That is the fastest way to get taken advantage of.

Practical Advice for Proving Your Value to Top-Level Talent

If you're looking for some easy ideas for how to bring value to the Core Four you want to surround yourself with, here are a few that worked for me. What I've found is before I could learn what others need, I had to first learn how their job worked. Once I figured that out, it became apparent how I could help each person. Trying to bring value to someone before you recognize their business model is an exercise in futility. But, taking some time to walk in someone else's shoes will help you find the best way to assist them.

Agents
- Agents live by referrals. If you can send an agent business you will

be making them money, and that is going to lead them to be very loyal to you and make them very happy.

- An easy way to send referrals is by talking to your friends about real estate and sending the serious buyers to the agents.
- Start an online blog, meetup, discussion group, or chat room and send interested buyers to the agents you want to make a good impression on. This will help people remember to send you deals, as well as score you points with agents.
- Remember to only send serious buyers to the agents. Sending them "referrals" who have no intention to buy but instead only want a free education is a great way to prove you bring work without pay—not the reputation you want.
- Communicate openly with your agent. Tell them exactly what you'd like them to do, and share your thoughts. Agents want to help you, but they can only do so if you know what kind of help you want. Take it from me, an agent: This one is big.
- Give them great reviews online. Giving your agent a great review on Facebook, Zillow, Yelp, or Google can earn you some major brownie points.
- Call your agent's boss and tell them how great they are. Find out who supervises them and give them a great review.
- Ask them what they need in their business, and help them find it. If they work with a lot of investors, they may very well need a solid handyman to fix dry rot, or a great roofer who doesn't overcharge. If you can give them a referral they need, you're likely to get to the top of their list when the next great deal comes along.
- Give them bonuses. Yes, I know to an investor this idea seems painful, but think about it—I often buy houses for $40,000 that are completely trashed. How much is my agent making on this? Giving them a bonus to at least help them make a decent amount of money is a great way to stay in their good graces.

Lenders
- Lenders also want referrals. Send your friends their way.
- Online reviews. This works for lenders, too.
- Let their boss know you appreciate their hard work.
- Introduce lenders to websites like BiggerPockets.com. Many lenders don't realize there are entire communities of people out there who

are looking for investment properties and need a lender.

- Check in with them once you've introduced them to BiggerPockets and see if they've gotten any clients. It never hurts to remind someone what you've done for them.
- Give them great references to rockstar agents. This is how lenders get their deals. If you do this, they'll love you for it.
- Give them a shout-out on social media. Let everyone know how great they are by tagging them in a nice post, and make sure they see it, too!

Contractors

- Pay them on time. Seriously. Just do it. You have no idea how much this means to a contractor.
- Pay them in a way that isn't a pain in the butt for them. I've found wire transfer to be the easiest.
- Don't ask them to work for free. If you want additional work done, ask them how much more it will be, and make your decision accordingly.
- Don't micromanage. Nobody likes that.
- Don't beat them up over little things like $10 off the paint quote. They'll remember and they'll return the favor.
- Ask them questions. Some contractors are willing to do certain jobs but don't enjoy it—things like laying tile as opposed to laminate. If it doesn't matter to you, have them do the laminate instead so they know you have their back.
- Ask them what work they are doing and what they are contracting out. They can give you better prices on the work they do themselves. It puts them in a bad position when you want them to reduce the price significantly for work they are subcontracting to someone else. They won't feel comfortable negotiating someone else's money.
- Don't ask them to bid jobs if you're not serious, and if you do, pay them for their time. Sending someone to bid a job when you weren't likely to buy the property and not paying them is a great way to let them know you are not a rockstar.
- Send them referrals, when practical.
- Send them leads for people they can hire. Contractors are *always* looking for new employees, and often frustrated with it. If you know of a hard worker who is dependable, let them know.

Property Managers

- Send them referrals. (Are you noticing a pattern here?)
- Ask them what investors do that makes their job harder, and try to stop doing it.
- Read the actual management agreement and address the issues you see *before* signing a contract with them. Don't be that person who throws a fit when you're charged for something you didn't bother to look at first, then blame them for it.
- Don't call them incessantly over unimportant things. Property management is a low-pay, time-consuming job. They have to be very careful with their time. Show them you respect that.
- Ask them about properties before you buy them. Get them involved in the process and rely on their expertise early on.
- If the house doesn't rent for what you thought it would, don't automatically blame them. They can't control the market.
- Reply to them in a timely fashion like you'd want them to reply to you.
- Find other investors and introduce them to the property managers! They are always looking to grow their network.
- Find out if they are licensed, and if they are, let them find you deals. This is good supplemental income for a lot of them.
- Tell them what you need, so they can be on the lookout for you. Communication here is also essential.

Finding ways to bring value to others is one of the most important business skills you can learn. Considering that one good property can bring you hundreds of dollars in monthly cash flow and tens of thousands of dollars in equity, it becomes apparent just how much money you can lose by not treating people well. In business, there is a popular maxim: "Your network equals your net worth." Relationships bring and build business.

Understanding the "rockstars know rockstars" concept is the first step in finding good talent to help you accomplish your goals. If you want to work with the best, you need to be the best. Finding a rockstar is better than finding a deal, because they can bring you *many* deals. The search for talent should be No. 1 on your list when looking for great deals in the acquisition stage of your investment cycle.

Using Wholesalers to Find Deals

Wholesalers weren't mentioned as part of the Core Four because they typically don't provide as much value as an agent. They do, however, play a very similar role. A wholesaler is much less likely to provide you with necessary partners like contractors, vendors, property managers, etc. With that being said, a good wholesaler can find you incredible deals, while a bad one can cost you a lot of money if you're not careful.

The term "wholesaler" is used to describe someone who puts a property under contract (hopefully at a good price), then assigns the right to purchase that contract to someone else for a fee. Wholesalers make their money from the person they are assigning the contract to (you, if you are using one) in exchange for the value they are providing in a good house already under contract. In some states, the rules for wholesaling are different than others. If you're considering a career in wholesaling, be sure to consult a legal professional before taking on the endeavor.

A typical wholesaler would target people in personal distress, usually through marketing methods like direct mail, SEO-based websites, driving for dollars, word of mouth, or targeting out-of-area owners. Once they find a motivated seller, the wholesaler determines what a good ARV would be and tries to put the property under contract for a price significantly less than that. If they are successful, another investor will pay the wholesaler for the right to purchase that property, landing themselves a great deal in the process.

Since we are talking about the "buy" portion of investing, it's important to note how the "buy" process works. Brandon Turner has an acronym he uses to describe the process: LAPS. LAPS stands for lead, analyze, pursue, and success. It details the process of finding a deal and closing on it successfully. You start with a lead, you analyze the lead, you pursue (make an offer on) the lead, and if your offer is accepted, you negotiate and close on it (success). At each stage in this process, you are eliminating a serious amount of work from the previous.

You start with a large number of leads; you analyze the best ones, cutting out the rest. Of those you analyze, you offer on the best of those. For those you offer on, you close on a smaller percentage. The majority of the work is done at the "top" of this funnel, with less and less work done as you move your way down. Wholesalers are doing the first three stages of LAPS for you. They are pursuing leads, analyzing them, making offers, and putting them under contract. When you buy from a wholesaler, you only have to complete the last portion, close (for success).

Good wholesalers provide great deals. They've already done the work to find the property, researched the numbers, and negotiated the contract. If you're lucky, you can step right in and take the deal over. While some investors don't like the thought of paying someone else the "assignment fee," I would advise you to consider how much money and time you would have spent to find that deal, research it, and put it under contract yourself. Odds are, you are saving way more than you are spending when you buy a great deal from a wholesaler.

Finding good wholesalers is similar to the process for finding your Core Four. You build up your reputation, build up the value you can bring to others, and make it known you are looking to buy properties. By finding other people who know reliable wholesalers, you're likely to find good ones yourself.

The biggest risk you take when buying from a wholesaler is you are buying without representation. In these transactions, you don't have an agent representing you, and neither the seller nor the wholesaler have a fiduciary duty to your interests. None of the parties in a transaction like this are licensed or supervised by a governing party. This can become confusing when you are used to purchasing a property with all the inherent benefits of agent representation, especially if that's what you're used to or expect.

I once bought a deal from a wholesaler that ended up having 30 percent less square footage than was advertised. I never considered checking the tax records myself to make sure the numbers I was given were accurate, because I was used to buying through an agent who had already verified this info. If I had used a real estate agent, there would have been legal consequences to this situation as the seller had misrepresented the property. Since I didn't, there was nothing I could do but learn from my mistake.

A bad wholesaler can cost you a lot of money from what they don't tell you. Your property could be in a flood zone. It could be infested with termites. There could be serious zoning restrictions, or no public water/sewer/garbage. The property could be in a historic district with permit restrictions or it could be less square footage than advertised. There are countless uncertainties when buying from a wholesaler, and the less experience you have, the less of these questions you'll know to ask.

One way to recognize a bad wholesaler is by verifying the validity of their comps. A wise person once told me, "How you do one thing is how you do everything." The point being, if someone is honest in one area of life they likely will be in others. If a wholesaler is being dishonest in one area of their business, they will likely be dishonest in the rest as well. Because comps are one of the first things a wholesaler provides you with, they are one of the easiest ways to judge if the wholesaler can be trusted or not.

When wholesalers are advertising the deals they have under contract, they will usually include a brief amount of information to get the buyers interested. Most of the time they'll provide you with a purchase price, pictures of the house, rental comps, and purchase comps. Of all this data, the information most important to you is the ARV comps. This is the piece of information you're putting the most stock in when deciding if you want to purchase the property.

An honest, skilled wholesaler will provide you with accurate and conservative comparable properties. Their reputation will matter more to them than the money they might make off of a quick sale. Now, not every wholesaler you meet who gives you inflated comps is necessarily dishonest. They may just be unskilled or uneducated on how to pull accurate comps. Either way, you don't want to buy from these people!

When you're first doing business with someone, you should verify everything they tell you or provide to you with someone else. Wholesalers are no exception. You want to mitigate your risk as much as possible when dealing with new business partners. Trust, but verify. A great method to mitigate your risk when buying from a wholesaler is to get other members of your Core Four involved in the process. If you're considering buying from a wholesaler, find a trusted investor, agent, or property manager with experience in the area you're buying to look over the information you're considering. Running numbers doesn't help you if the numbers you are running are inaccurate. Have your favorite agent look at the comps the wholesaler is providing, as they are more likely to have a better understanding of values of properties in that area.

Do the same with your property manager. It's best to get as many eyeballs on a deal as possible until you know the values yourself, and even then I sometimes have others look them over! The more people involved and giving you their opinion, the more layers of protection you have, and the more likely you are to see things others missed. The one thing to keep in mind with this is you don't want to get others involved if you aren't bringing them business. Don't ask someone to look at deals all day long if you're not also helping to make them money. This is why bringing value to others is so important—it frees you up to ask for value from them.

I really can't stress this enough. When you are looking for a deal, you are searching for a "lead." A lead is any contact that could turn into a sale or lead to a desired result. If we can't find and convert leads, we won't make money and won't be in business for long. The best agents are the best lead generators and lead converters. This is true for the best investors as well.

How BRRRR Helps You to Pay Under Market Value

BRRRR itself is really nothing more than a system designed to help you maximize the efficiency at which you produce wealth through real estate. By learning to master it you can find yourself isolating its components and breaking them down to find ways to do better in each area. Of the five components of BRRRR, buying is by far the most important and influential when it comes to building your wealth.

It's important to understand that simply using the BRRRR method is no guarantee you'll do any better than using the traditional method. Driving a Ferrari is no guarantee you'll get to your destination quicker than driving a Honda Civic—but it sure has the potential to help you do it! If you want BRRRR to work correctly, you *must* be buying deals under market value. If you're not doing this, BRRRR isn't much help.

The whole goal of BRRRR is to buy a property at a discounted rate, then make it worth more before you finance it. There are really only two numbers you need to get right to make this all work, but getting them right is paramount.

1. The amount of money you put into a deal (typically the acquisition and the rehab).
2. The amount the property is worth when you're done (ARV).

If you get those two numbers right, you can BRRRR successfully. There are three components to these two numbers. The amount you purchase the property for, the amount you spend to fix it up, and the ARV. Of these three components, the one you will have the most control over is the price you pay for the house. With this being the case, the price you pay for a property is the single most important contributing factor to whether you have a good deal, great deal, or bad deal.

I'm going to be sharing strategies I've learned, both through my investing career and real estate agent career that have led to me finding deals and paying less for them. I've accumulated several strategies that all led to finding good deals, and found that combining several of them in the same deal is what led to me finding a great deal. Whether you use these strategies individually or combine them, knowing them is important.

If all you have is a screwdriver in your tool belt, the only problem you can solve is a loose screw. The more "tools" we have available to ourselves, or the more options we have to fix a problem, the more problems we can fix! As real estate investors, we think we are targeting houses, but what we are really targeting is problems.

Deals come from distressed situations, and distressed situations are problems looking for solutions. When you're a real estate investor, what you're really targeting is a problem an owner can't fix. Almost every great deal came as a result of some investor having the ability, desire, and plan to fix someone else's problem. Money was made as a result of this. If you want to make wealth in real estate, learn how to fix other people's problems and you will find that wealth finds you.

Cash Offers Are Stronger

It's a well-known fact in real estate that cash offers are the strongest offers. This is where we get the phrase "cash is king." You don't need me to tell you that cash offers are stronger. Nearly all of us have heard some story, or experienced it ourselves, when an offer to buy a house was beat out by an "all-cash offer."

I don't just want to tell you to "go get cash and you'll get better deals." Anyone can do that. I want to show you *why* all-cash offers are better, where their strength comes from, and how you too can harness that strength to work for you. Once you understand why cash offers help you so much, I'm going to share different ways you can raise cash or make all-cash offers (or their equivalent), even if you don't have the money in your bank account. There are lots of ways to do this!

The first thing you should understand about why a cash offer is stronger is to understand that it's better for the person *selling* the home. Now, take a minute to think about it—to the person selling their home, why would they care whether the cash came from you, a bank, a hard-money lender, or an alien? It really doesn't matter to the seller where the money comes from, just that they get it.

So why are cash offers "stronger"? It's because they come without contingencies. Contingencies is a fancy real estate word used to describe the way a buyer can back out of the deal and still recover their earnest money deposit. We get these words from the language of the purchase contract. Most contracts read something like "The buyer will buy this house *contingent upon* the home passing their inspections." If the buyer finds something during their inspections they don't like, they can exercise their inspection contingency to back out of the deal.

Now, there are several kinds of contingencies in most purchase contracts that can be exercised, but every contract contains three main ones. These are the contingencies that the escrow period orbits around. They are the:

1. **Inspection Contingency**
   - The period of time to order and perform inspections
   - Buyer decides if he or she wants to move forward, back out, or renegotiate
   - Buyer can ask for repairs, a financial credit, or reduction in purchase price

2. **Appraisal Contingency**
   - The period of time to order an appraisal
   - This is the bank's way of ensuring you aren't overspending on an asset that will become theirs if you foreclose
   - Appraisals "at value" or "above value" have no problem
   - Appraisals "below value" will usually require the buyer to make up the difference in the purchase price and appraised value

3. **Loan Contingency**
   - The way the buyer can back out of a deal if something goes wrong with the loan
   - The longest contingency period, because lenders take a long time[1]

Now, you'll notice, every one of these contingencies exist to benefit

---

[1] In California, a standard loan contingency is 21 days, meaning a buyer could be in escrow for 21 days and then back out of the deal and still recover their deposit, leaving the seller high and dry.

the buyer. They are designed to protect the buyer's interests and their deposit, allowing them to recover it if something goes wrong. If a buyer wants to make their offer more competitive, they will typically shorten the length of time they have to exercise these contingencies, or in some extreme cases, remove them all together.

One of the main reasons cash offers are stronger is because they come without the financing contingencies. A cash buyer doesn't need a loan contingency, because they will not have a loan. They also don't need an appraisal contingency because there is no lender requiring an appraisal. A cash buyer would have the option of including an appraisal contingency, but it wouldn't be required.

To a seller, this is very appealing. The loan and appraisal contingencies make up two-thirds of the way a buyer can back out of a deal! With no worries about a low appraisal or a loan falling through, sellers can feel much more confident the deal is actually going to close. This makes a cash offer stronger than an offer contingent upon financing.

A cash buyer would still have the option of including an inspection contingency, and most of them do. Inspection contingencies exist in case a property has more damage than the buyer accounted for, and the deal becomes less desirable than originally thought. One thing to keep in mind is that the worse condition a property you are buying is in, the more you will need to replace, and the less important a home inspection becomes.

I'm not advising you as a cash buyer to waive your inspection contingency, but I would advise you to consider eliminating it in some cases. If you know you are going to be tearing a house down and replacing the majority of it, and it's a great price, consider making your offer stronger without raising your purchase price by making it an "as is" sale. Waiving the inspection contingency if you weren't planning on using it anyway is a great way to do that—making your all-cash offer even stronger.

A typical real estate escrow period of a transaction in most areas is around 30 days. This is the period of time in which the inspections are conducted, appraisals are ordered, the loan is approved by underwriting, and title work is conducted to ensure a clean certificate of title. Most of this work is done in the first half of that 30 days. In most cases, only the loan approval is still needed after that.

By eliminating a loan, you can significantly shorten the period of time needed to close escrow. In fact, if you can get your inspections done in seven days the only thing holding you back from closing sooner is the time it takes the title company to provide you with title insurance. Now, every region is different, and some regions have unique things that need to be done that may take more time. All things considered, assuming you get a clear certificate of title and the inspections come back like you thought, there is no reason why you can't close on a property in ten days or less.

I routinely do this. Because I am looking to pay as little as possible for a property, I make my offer stronger in more ways than just the offer price. By significantly reducing the amount of time I need to do inspections and making the title company aware that we want to close in ten days, I can write all-cash offers to the seller, with little or no contingencies, for ten days or sometimes less.

Now, this may seem unrealistic to you. Surely it creates more pressure than a 30-day escrow would, and your initial thought may be that a ten-day close is reckless. But let me ask you, if I can get everything done that I need to get done in ten days, what is the point in taking more time? If I can make my offer more enticing to the seller, *without* having to pay them more money, and it won't hurt me, why wouldn't I do that? This is one of the reasons why all-cash offers are stronger.

You may also be thinking you wouldn't care about a shorter escrow period if there was that much money on the line. To you, the money matters more than the time or certainty does. I can understand that perspective, because I share it! However, you (if you're reading this book) and I are not like everyone else. We are investors. We think like investors, and not everyone thinks like us.

Consider that many sellers don't look at a home like an investment. To many folks, a property that is useless (in terrible condition, not renting, etc.) is nothing but a drain on their resources and an anchor holding them back from moving on to the next phase of their life. Consider that we are seeing a diamond in the rough, while many sellers just see the rough.

Understanding how other people see will help you a great deal in business. In this case, many sellers are dealing with emotional trauma, frustration, and a sense of hopelessness trying to get rid of a property that won't sell. Oftentimes they have already been in contract, sometimes several times in a row, and can't seem to close. This can happen for many reasons and is very frustrating to those not familiar or conditioned to the process of buying/selling houses!

Most houses that fall out of escrow do so because the buyer found something during the inspection period they didn't like. Others, because the loan wouldn't go through. Maybe the buyers had bad pre-approval letters, maybe there was a condition of the property that came up during underwriting and the underwriters rejected it. There are tons of things that can go wrong, but the end result is always a dejected, frustrated seller who had their hopes up when they went into contract and found themselves crushed when they fell out.

My goal as a buyer who wants to "buy right" is to find these sellers when they are at a point where they are about to give up, and swoop in as a savior able to close the deal. By waiving the contingencies that would allow me to back out (which I don't need as a cash buyer), I present myself and my offer as someone much more likely to actually close on the deal. To someone who's been let down several times in a row, the feeling of relief I can bring them by actually closing is worth more than the potential for more money other buyers brought them that never materialized into more.

In short, cash offers have a much higher probability of closing than offers contingent upon financing, and that is why they hold such a strong reputation in the world of real estate. Many agents know a cash offer is "better," but don't really understand why. If you understand the why, you can replicate all the benefits of a cash offer—even if you don't have the cash.

Cash offers carry a reputation as being more serious, stronger, and a sign the buyer is solid. By making all-cash offers, you are sure to stand out from the rest of the pile, should other offers be made. There is a psychological edge to an all-cash offer because it takes the sting out of a "lowball" offer price. Should you offer significantly less than the asking price, it won't be received as offensively if the offer is all-cash, because all-cash offers are expected to be lower. This can play a positive role for you as well.

For those who want to mimic the strengths of an all-cash offer who don't have the cash, consider other options like private money or hard money. While you will pay interest for private money, and more interest for hard money, this can still be okay if the deal is good enough. Getting funding from these financing sources doesn't require an appraisal or loan approval in most cases. In cases where loan approval is needed, these types of lenders can usually get it to you within the period of time you're doing your inspections. With this being the case, you can eliminate a loan contingency and an appraisal contingency, which makes your offer just as strong as a cash offer, but without the cash!

If you find yourself having trouble saving or finding cash for a deal, but find a deal first, this can be a great option for you. Some investors write their offer as not including financing, even if they are using hard money or private money. Double-check with your agent or an attorney before doing this in your state, but know it is an option for you to BRRRR, even if you don't have cash yet.

Cash Offers Open Doors to Buy Homes that Aren't Eligible for Financing

One benefit to offers without financing I don't hear spoken about nearly enough is the fact that some houses are in such bad condition they simply do not qualify for financing. Some of the best deals I've ever bought fit this criteria. This one strategy alone opens doors for you to buy properties that 90 percent of your competition cannot. By eliminating competition, you increase the strength of your own position. When there aren't many buyers, the few out there wield more power!

This is the same principle I talk about in *Long-Distance Real Estate Investing: How to Buy, Rehab, and Manage Out-of-State Rental Properties* when I discuss looking for areas to invest in where there aren't a lot of other investors. By targeting areas that are being ignored by institutional investors, hedge funds, and the "Top Ten Lists to Buy Real Estate" that are all over the internet, I can increase my likelihood of finding better deals by decreasing the number of competitors.

I picked this strategy up after listening to Warren Buffett talk about one of his investment strategies: "Be fearful when others are greedy, and greedy when others are fearful." I realized it's wiser to zig when everyone else zags sometimes, and I started looking for opportunity where other investors were not. This same principle applies to making all-cash offers.

The majority of investors are not all-cash buyers. Saving the cash is hard. Finding people to borrow from can be hard. Getting pre-qualified for a loan is much easier and candidly *feels* safer. When you're investing less initially, it's easy to trick yourself into thinking you're making the conservative, safe choice. For this reason alone, if you can get to the point where you are a cash buyer, you will have successfully elevated yourself over the majority of your competition in an area.

Will this help you? When someone wants to use a loan to purchase a home, the lender gets a say in the condition of the property. Remember how those using a loan are required to get an appraisal? That's a condition of the lender, designed to protect the lender's interests. The lender has a similar interest in the condition of the property. If a lender lets you borrow against a property in terrible condition, then has to foreclose on you, how will they sell the property to recover their investment?

Most lenders have a standard that a property must be in "livable condition." This standard varies from area to area, but generally speaking, there are minimum conditions that must be met for a home to be in livable condition. A few common examples of this would be:

- The home must have a roof without holes.
- The home must have appliances like a stove or oven.
- The home must have flooring.
- The home must have plumbing.
- The home must have working electrical.
- The home must have windows.

How does this help you? It means as an all-cash buyer, you can purchase certain homes those with loans cannot. Many homes will not be eligible to be purchased with financing. These leave the seller with limited options: sell for cash, give away, or seller finance. In situations like these, you as an all-cash investor have a huge advantage. If you have the ability to buy a property that the majority of your competition does not, you can offer much less for that same property and still get it under contract!

What I love most about this is how well it fits with the BRRRR strategy. The majority of BRRRR success stories were properties that were purchased significantly under value and rehabbed into better shape. All-cash offers allow you to pay significantly under value for properties that can only be bought with a cash offer. These two qualities married together can produce big results—much bigger than either would be isolated on their own.

When you are able to make all-cash offers, aim your sights on properties in such bad condition that only a cash offer could buy them. Tell your agent that's what you're looking for. Tell everyone! By targeting properties that only a few can buy, you will be avoiding the crowds who are all going for the same houses and finding the deals others are scared of or don't have the ability to act on. Use what you have to your advantage!

Example of a Real-Life BRRRR

I'm not the only investor to use the BRRRR method! I've included two examples here of other investors who bought income property, improved its condition, and then later refinanced to recover their capital and reinvest it later. The first is a story of an investor, Derek Clifford, and his duplex.

Derek is a California-based investor who invests long-distance for cash flow. After Derek identified Indiana as the market he wanted to start investing in, he decided he would make a trip out there to meet people and start interviewing potential team members. Derek, being a wise man, started reaching out to BiggerPockets members in Indiana and sending them the following message: "We're headed for Indy, calling all PMs [property managers], brokers, lenders, contractors, and wholesalers. We are looking to build a portfolio. Let's talk."

Derek found people that eventually put him in touch with a reputable wholesaler. As he looked through the wholesaler's portfolio, his attention was drawn to a duplex listed for $32,000. Derek was able to negotiate the price to $27,500 and purchased the property after finding it needed about $25,000 worth of work to be made rent-ready. The ARV for the property was projected to be $80,000.

Derek's final numbers looked like this:

Purchase price—$27,500

Rehab total—$37,000

All-in—$64,500

ARV—$80,000

Loan amount after refinance at 75% LTV—$60,000

Rents—$695 a side for $1,390 total

Cash flow after financing—$225 a side for $450 total

Now, you'll notice Derek's rehab ended up being about $12,000 more than he anticipated. Even with this being the case, Derek still only left $4,500 in this deal. In addition to adding a little over $15,000 in equity to his net worth, Derek is seeing a yearly return of $5,400! Since he only invested $4,500, he will recover 100 percent of his capital before the first year is over. How is this possible? Derek bought right. By buying so far under market value, it didn't matter that his rehab went over budget. He still made incredible money and recovered everything he put in the deal very quickly.

Script for Agents (all-cash offers on distressed properties)

Hello, my name is _____ and I wanted to know if you had a second to talk.

I am a real estate investor and your name came up when I was asking for the best real estate agent in the area. I was very impressed with your reputation and wanted to know if you were currently looking to take on new clients.

Great! A little about me and what I'm looking for—I'm a buy-and-hold, cash flow investor who lives in _____. I'm looking for all-cash offers on properties that need significant work—the more the better. I target properties that need new roofs, have water damage, renovations that were started but not completed, etc.

I'm looking to buy them, fix them up, and rent them out when I'm finished. My ideal house would rent for somewhere around and be worth around when finished. I can offer a 10–14 day close, seven-day inspection period, and strong earnest money deposit.

I'd like to know if you could look for properties that meet these criteria and send them, and only them, to me when you find them. Is that something that sounds like it falls within the scope of what you do?

Great! Another way you could help me would be if you knew any reliable and experienced contractors, lenders, or property managers I could use to help me with this process. That would help me a ton and allow me to buy more deals faster. Is that something you have experience with?

Awesome! I'm very excited from this conversation. Let me know what more you need to know about me and what I should know about you. If everything looks good, I'll be excited to start working with you!

Why Mastering "Buy" Is the Most Important Part of Real Estate Investing

So far in the book, I've alluded to the fact that "buying" well is the No. 1 part of being successful in real estate investing. Now, I'm going to dive deep into this topic and explain why, as well as some of the common pitfalls investors fall into when they try to dig themselves out of the hole they created when buying incorrectly. Many have tried to fix a bad buy through throwing money at it, but I've never seen anyone pull this off successfully.

You Make Your Money When You Buy

As I mentioned before, this is an age-old maxim in real estate. What's obvious is the fact you *can* make money when you buy. Buying a property for a great price is a great way to make money. The point of this saying is a little deeper, however. What it's trying to convey is that fact that you *can't* make money through a rehab, or a superhuman real estate agent, or some extremely creative financing trick. Too many people who overpay for a property try to get cute in a way to save the deal, and it rarely ever works.

Let's look at Sucker Sam, for example:

Sam was a newbie investor who just got done signing up for a guru course where he spent $15,000 to learn how to analyze a property and put together a direct mail campaign. After nine months of consistently following the process, Sam had yet to put a deal together. Although he'd had plenty of opportunities, Sam was unable to negotiate with sellers in a manner that could put a house under contract.

Sucker Sam was bad with conflict. He didn't like upsetting people, and always felt guilty about offering the price the numbers told him he should offer on a property. Because of this, Sam was never quite able to make a compelling offer to convince distressed sellers to sell him their home. Now, Sam didn't have enough knowledge of making offers so he shouldn't have been doing this; it wasn't his strength. But because Sam had taken a guru course, there was no one to tell him this.

After nine months, an additional $10,000 in postage, and the $15,000 he had spent on the guru program, Sam was getting desperate. The anxiety was starting to creep in as Sam was realizing he was soon going to have to start cutting into the capital intended to buy the property he was looking for. Sam could feel it every day, closing in on him, panic knocking at his door. He imagined his friends all calling him a fool for spending so much money with no result. Real estate had sounded so promising!

Every night when Sam would go to sleep, he would kick himself for getting pushed around by sellers and promise himself he would do better tomorrow. Every tomorrow, Sam just fell into the same cycle.

Finally, one day, the panic became overwhelming. Full of emotional instability and a cloudy mind, Sam decided he was going to buy something and "make it work." Rather than addressing his problem with not being able to stand up to sellers, Sam found the best deal he had out of his list, then put the property under contract for about 90 percent of ARV.

Now, Sam was a sucker, but he wasn't stupid. Sam knew this was not a price that would work according to his numbers. In order to talk himself into this deal, Sam told himself he could push the ARV significantly higher. This was easier than reducing the price he was offering because it didn't involve conflict! Also, Sam decided he would flip the house, rather than use the BRRRR model he had originally intended, because it would be easier than trying to recover his money on a refinance.

Sam looked at comps and could see there was an argument to be made for prices rising in the area. He then looked at a neighborhood across town and saw there were higher-priced homes in that neighborhood that had had extensive renovation work done. Then, he told himself that during the rehab phase, if he did a more extensive rehab, prices would continue to climb and the longer he waited the more money the house would be worth. After going over these facts over and over in his head, Sam was able to convince himself this was a good buy, and in a worse-case scenario, he would just break even.

The plan was to close on the house, do a complete remodel, and then market the home as if it was one of the more expensive ones in the nicer neighborhood across town. During the remodel, Sam would bank on prices to continue to rise, and if he found the right buyer who fell in love with the place, surely they would spend a little over market value to get their dream home. If he could create a bidding war, it could happen right? To save a little extra, Sam determined his real estate agent would just have to take a reduction in their commission. If everything came together perfectly, Sam could still make some money.

Sam talked to a few top-producing real estate agents who all told him the house would not sell if he listed it at the price he wanted to. Sam, who felt he had no choice, continued to interview agents until he found one that told him what he wanted to hear. The inexperienced agent (who was really starving for business and not very good) also agreed to Sam's demand they reduce their commission. The agent didn't have much choice, as they hadn't sold anything in months and would pretty much say anything at this point just to get a deal.

Sam had convinced himself he could make his money through a rehab process. He also believed he could make money through "creative," slick sales practices. He bet on the fact he could make money through appreciation, and he bet on the fact a good Realtor would agree to work for discounted rates, as well as the fact he could tell the Realtor at what price they needed to sell the home. Sam backed himself into a corner by paying too much for the home, and found himself doing everything he could to salvage the deal after that, in all the wrong ways.

It did not go well for Sam. The first thing Sam found was the contractors who had been referred to him were contractors who specialized in working for investors. They were not experienced or suited for a high-level remodel like he had in mind. Things quickly went awry. The contractors did not choose high-end materials like Sam wanted, and did not do a good job tying the project together. Countertops did not match cabinets, and the backsplash did not match anything.

Furthermore, the contractors did not think to replace items like interior doors, the exterior door, the deck in the backyard, the landscaping, or the fixtures in the bathroom. They did not install recessed lighting or replace the electrical outlets. The inexperience of the people Sam hired to do the kind of job he really wanted set him back significantly, and only increased his holding costs. Sam ended up paying much more in interest, taxes, and insurance while waiting for the rehab issues to be corrected.

In order to try and save even more money, Sam elected not to repair or replace anything that wasn't cosmetic. Sam wanted the house to make a great impression and did not want to allocate funds for repairing dry rot, roof leaks, or termite damage. Sam readjusted his budget and told himself he was saving money.

While waiting for the rehab to be finished, Sam missed the peak selling season. By the time the home was finally ready to be sold, it was December, and most of the home buyers who were in a desperate bind to find a home had already bought or renewed their rental leases. Sam lost his opportunity for a bidding war, and in addition to that, he lost the majority of home buyers. With significantly less people looking to buy a home during the holidays, Sam's long shot to find a buyer to fall in love with his home and overpay for it went out the window.

Unfortunately for Sam, this was just the beginning. Once the project was completed, the agent had no idea how to market the house appropriately. Because Sam had sliced the agent's commission so much, the agent didn't pay to get professional pictures taken, have marketing materials made, or advertise the home much at all. Instead the agent used the three-P method: Put it in the MLS, put a sign in the yard, and pray for an offer. Sam was getting what he paid for.

Sam's home sat for a long time without getting much action. When he did get a showing, the feedback was all the same, "beautiful home, priced too high." When his agent approached him about a price reduction, Sam refused, insisting the agent work harder to sell the home. Sam pointed out that homes across town in similar condition were all selling without a problem. Sam's agent was unable to articulate effectively that these homes were not comparable properties, and was afraid to do so because the agent knew they had told Sam they could sell the home at this price to get the listing.

Sam had failed to take into account that the homes across town were in a vastly superior school district, with much lower property taxes, and were much closer to the freeway. To buy on Sam's side of town, buyers would have to drive through 15 to 20 minutes of traffic just to get to the freeway on-ramp. The special assessment taxes in the place where Sam had bought added so much to the monthly payment that it made sense to pay more for a property on the other side of town and still save every month. An experienced real estate agent would have told Sam as much, but he had chased all of them away in his effort to save money he hadn't made yet.

Sam watched as his holding costs grew and grew. To add insult to injury, one month after buying this property, Sam received a call from an extremely motivated seller begging for someone to buy their property. It would have been a killer deal, but Sam's money and resources were all tied up with the project he already started. Sam lost the deal he had been looking for the whole time because his money was tied up in the deal he'd forced.

When Sam finally got an offer, his house had been on the market for 60 days and the offer was for significantly less than Sam listed it for. Sam did the math and saw that even with his discounted commission to the agent, he would still be losing a good amount of money. Sam desperately wanted to turn it down, as he didn't want to lose, but he was smart enough to realize that waiting for a higher offer would just cost him even more in the end as his carrying costs were continuing every month.

Sam had no choice but to accept, as his agent was unable to do anything to get the offer any higher. To add insult to injury, during the escrow process, the buyers ordered inspections where they found significant dry rot, termite damage, and roof damage. The buyers threatened to back out and Sam's agent had no idea how to find a solution for everyone because he didn't sell many homes and was inexperienced in this kind of situation.

As a result, the buyers demanded the work be done by a licensed professional of their choosing, but on Sam's dollar. Of course, the buyers chose the most expensive company in town to do the work, and Sam had no choice but to pay. He made a brief attempt to get his rehab crew out to give an estimate instead (which would have been much cheaper) but they had already moved on to their next job and were so unhappy with the way Sam had treated them during the initial rehab that they refused to return his calls.

Sam was screwed, and he knew it. When the deal finally closed, Sam had lost a significant amount of capital. When he sat down to debrief and figure out what went wrong, Sam realized he had somehow found himself trying to flip a high-end luxury product in the wrong neighborhood, surrounded by miserable non-talent—all when his initial goal had been to purchase a cash-flowing property at a great price and BRRRR!

How did this happen? Well, Sam made a lot of mistakes, and each mistake compounded the others. But what was Sam's biggest mistake that allowed all the others to happen? It's simple. Sam tried to find ways to make money other than buying his property at the right price.

Learn from Sam. You don't want to be a Sam. Dejected, forlorn, with his confidence shaken, Sam found himself trolling the forums of Bigger-Pockets and other online blogs, spouting his bitterness and pessimism everywhere he went. A Johnny Appleseed of negativity, Sam may never take another shot at investing again!

Lesson: We can avoid Sam's fate by following the first rule of real estate, and the most important element of BRRRR. *You make your money when you buy.* Do not be fooled, enticed, or tempted into trying to make something out of nothing. Do not try to find creative ways to talk yourself into a deal when the numbers obviously don't add up. Don't stray from your original goal if it was to BRRRR when the numbers don't work.

The Correct Money Mind-set

Sam ended up in a real estate pit because he didn't want to admit he should not be the one negotiating with clients on the phone. It wasn't Sam's fault that he wasn't great with conflict or negotiation, but it was 100 percent his fault that he didn't find a way to build his business around that deficiency. Sam made a whole chain of bad decisions, all in a row, to try to cover up for one bad decision he made in the beginning. If you set your sights to make your money when you buy, this won't happen to you.

One way I've learned to avoid getting into this same pickle Sam found himself in is to change the way I look at investing. All of us, whether we realize it or not, have ways we look at things like money, real estate investing, and success. We all operate under subconscious beliefs that guide our emotions, and our emotions guide our decisions. Challenging the way you look at something can have a profound effect on the types of decisions you make.

For instance, most people look at money like it's made to be spent. Money is something we earn, then consume. When we adopt this mindset, it feels it's unfair to hold ourselves to a budget. Our subconscious rebels against the concept because we believe it is our "right" to spend that money, and enjoy what it brings.

I've learned to look at money like it's a seed for me to plant. My seeds are used to produce more seeds, as my money is used to produce more money. I have told myself the purpose of earning money is to invest it, and spending money is really just eating into my future. This attitude helps me not to feel entitled or discouraged about not being able to spend what I make.

I want you to challenge the way you look at using the BRRRR strategy to build wealth through real estate. Our goal with BRRRR is to buy something significantly under value, add value to it somehow, then recover as much of that value as we can. I like to think of the process as pouring as much water into a bucket as I can, and then trying to keep as much of that water in the bucket as I can. When I'm done, the more water I have in that bucket, the more water (or money) I'll get back at the end when I refinance.

In my analogy, the bucket is the property, and the water is the amount of equity you are creating in it. You can add equity by buying under market value, and you can add a little bit of equity through rehab hacks (which we'll discuss in detail in *Part Three: The Rehab Process* of the book). Every other part of the BRRRR process takes water out of your bucket.

Sam's mistake was thinking that he could add more water to his bucket at every level. Sam didn't add much water when he first started, and he knew he needed more. So he tried to add water through making it a fancy rehab. He tried to add water by pushing up his ARV way beyond what the numbers were telling him. He tried to add water by selling the property instead of refinancing it. He tried to add water by cutting costs on his team and using the cheapest agent he could find.

The goal with the rehab and the refinance is to limit the amount of water that spills, not to try to add more water. When you're finished with your project and ready to refinance, the bank will be keeping 20–30 percent of the "water" (or equity) in the deal. This is because they are only letting you refinance 70–80 percent of the ARV. This is some serious spillage! Knowing this, you need to have a whole lot of water already in the bucket if you want to make sure you have enough left over when you empty that bucket.

Sam learned the hard way that he couldn't add any water to the bucket after he bought the property, and he didn't add enough when he first bought. Don't make that same mistake yourself. If you buy a property for $60,000 with an ARV of $100,000, you've added $40,000 of water to the bucket. If your rehab is $20,000, you've just taken half the water out.

Don't think that means you can avoid a rehab! If you don't rehab the property, it won't be worth the ARV of $100,000. What I'm saying is, spending more on the rehab isn't going to add more water to the bucket. It's more than likely just going to take more out. In this example, when you're finished, you'll have spent $80,000 to own an asset worth $100,000. When the bank lets you refinance but keeps $25,000 of that water (the amount they keep as equity in the property at a LTV of 75 percent), you're left only losing $5,000 of capital. Not a bad price to pay for a newly renovated property that cash-flows positively.

If you adopt the mind-set that every purchase is adding water to a bucket and you *will* spill water throughout the process (the rehab, closing costs, rent advertisement costs, the bank keeping equity, etc.) you will quickly realize that the goal is to add as much water as you possibly can to that bucket in the very beginning, and then try to walk as smoothly as possible while carrying it to the finish line. The smoother you walk (the better you learn to handle the BRRRR process and keep costs low), the more water you'll have at the end, and that water is your wealth!

Positioning Yourself Safely for Market Corrections
Wise investors plan for market cycles. Just as a market can skyrocket, it

can also plummet. Sometimes it creeps down, but more often than not it crashes down—suddenly and violently. If you were buying property in 2008, it looked like the party was in full swing and the music was never going to stop; then the record scratched, the lights came on, and we could see clearly that a lot of the party members weren't in great shape or positioned to exit safely. The market crashed.

We buy right because we want to make money, but also because it's the best way to ensure you don't lose money, or at least not as much money. Buying right helps protect you against market corrections and preserves your capital for when the market does something you weren't expecting. None of us can predict the future. Making sure you only buy great deals is a smart way to protect yourself in case the future makes a turn you weren't anticipating.

Remember, if the more equity we get in a deal is the equivalent of putting more water in our bucket, then a market correction is like punching a hole into the bottom of that bucket. As property values drop, the equity in our property drops as water leaks out of the bucket. The faster you can sell or refinance the property, the faster you can plug that hole and stop losing water.

If you don't have enough water in the bucket when you start, you will run out of water before you can sell or refinance. This will really hurt you because you can't refinance a property that is worth less than you owe on it. If you don't owe anything, this will mean you'll be pulling out less money than you anticipated. If your plan is to sell a property before values drop too far, you'll find it much harder to sell in these markets and you may end up losing money here too.

Don't get fooled into thinking that the real estate market is always rising. Make sure you have a healthy amount of equity built into the deal *from day one*. The amount of equity in a deal is the first metric I look at when a deal comes my way. If the market continues to rise, you'll make more money. If the market turns on you, you'll have more time to sell before you lose money, and more money left over to start buying again when the market hits bottom!

Buying Right Gives You the Option to Flip or Hold

As mentioned earlier, sometimes the plan changes and a property you intended to hold becomes something you want to flip. This isn't always necessarily caused by a real estate market turning around: There are lots of other reasons why you may choose to sell a property you intended to hold. The important part is you make the decision because it makes financial sense to do so, not because you made a previous bad decision and now you're trying to dig yourself out of a hole you created from paying too much.

Why would a BRRRR investor decide to sell instead? One reason might be they realized the rents aren't going to be as strong as they anticipated. If you realize the rents are going to be lower than you thought, it may make sense to reanalyze the deal as a flip and see if it's better to sell it for profit rather than keep it.

Another common reason to sell is to be prepared for a new opportunity you would rather use the money for. Sometimes banks make you wait a "seasoning" period (often four to six months in most banking institutions) before they'll let you borrow against a property. If a bank isn't going to let you pull your money out for six months, and you see the opportunity to get into a much better deal in three months, you may want to consider selling and recovering your capital to put into the next deal.

How can you know if you should refinance or sell? I advise investors to analyze whether the ROI you will get on a particular deal is as good as the ROI you can expect on your current deal. For instance, if you run the numbers and see you can BRRRR and achieve a 10 percent ROI, but you know you are averaging a 30 percent ROI on most other deals, you may want to sell that property and recover your money to put somewhere else that will give you a better return.

This becomes especially important when you are likely to add more equity to the property than you originally anticipated. If you thought you might make $30,000 on a flip when you first analyzed it, but end up looking at a possible $60,000 profit, that would cause me to look closer at the ROI on my cash flow. If I find that I'm going to cash-flow $300 a month, I can quickly see that $300 a month is a 12 percent return on the $30,000 I would have made, but only a 6 percent return if I'm going to have $60,000 in equity.

This would cause me to consider flipping instead. If done well, I would end up with more capital to put into future properties. Buying right gives me the option to look at things this way and lets me make the best financial decision. Changing dynamics, market values, and after repair value (ARV) lead to different strategies being more desirable.

When you buy right, you are adding value to a property. Selling the property as a flip allows you to realize that value immediately, while keeping the property as a rental allows you to realize *more* of that value but not right away, as you'll wait longer to get a payoff on a rental. In order to make the best decision for you, you need to look at all your options and see the big picture, but it sure is nice when you actually have these two options to consider because you bought right!

BRRRR Allows You to Pull More Money Out Than You Put In

The BRRRR model achieves such incredible ROI because of the smaller amounts of capital you leave in each deal. If things go well, you end up recovering much more of your capital than if you had used the traditional method and left less in the deal as equity. The more capital you pull out, the less you have in the deal, and the higher your ROI. Makes sense, right?

Well, if you buy right, you can do even better. It's not impossible to pull out more money than you put into a deal! In fact, not only is it not impossible, it's not even all that uncommon. I've done this on many of my deals, and it's one of my favorite things that happens in real estate investing. Pulling out more money from a deal than I put in is like getting paid to own cash-flowing real estate. Who wouldn't want that?

Now, if you don't have an investment basis left in a deal, you can't really have an ROI. There's no "I" in ROI if you haven't invested money! When this happens, I call it negative ROI. It doesn't mean you're losing money, it means you literally cannot use ROI as a metric because you haven't invested anything but time. You actually *received* money, more money than you even spent.

This only happens when you buy an incredible deal. Who wouldn't want to get paid to own a cash-flowing rental property? When you BRR-RR correctly and focus on buying right, this is not out of the scope of possibility. It *is* out of the realm of possibility if you are being lazy or taking the easy road and not pursuing great deals. This is possible using the traditional method.

In many cases, you will buy a property *expecting* to pull out more than you put in. The logic is all in the math. If you calculate your acquisition plus rehab to be less than the LTV rate the lender will give you, you will pull out more money than you put in—unless something goes wrong.

Example:
- You have spoken with a lender and been preapproved for a loan to value of 75 percent of the appraised value.

- You've checked the comps and they show a conservative ARV of $100,000.
- The property is in very distressed condition and listed for $55,000. You write an offer for $50,000 and it is accepted.
- Your repairs come out to a total of $25,000, making your total investment $75,000.
- The property is appraised for $110,000 once the work is completed.
- The bank lets you borrow 75 percent of $110,000, equaling $82,500 you can pull out of the property.
- The $82,500 you got back is $7,500 more than the $75,000 you put in. This means you are getting paid $7,500 *more* than you invested to own this property.

Now, of course, there are other factors to consider. You still want to make sure the property cash-flows properly, is in a profitable area, isn't expected to have significant problems later, etc. But the fact you can make money on an investment, before you even start earning cash flow, is an incredibly powerful wealth-building tool! Consider the long-term effects of what this can mean for your net worth and investing success.

Let's say you repeat the above example four times a year, for the next five years. That would give you $30,000 a year, times five years, equaling $150,000 more than you invested. Now, $150,000 is a great amount of money to get paid for owning an appreciating asset, but I want you to think about more than that. It's not just the $150,000, but what you could *do* with the $150,000 that really matters.

How many more houses could you BRRRR with that? What kind of returns could you expect on money like that? What if you were able to pull out more money than you put in with the houses you bought with that extra $150,000? How many more properties could you then buy with that?

You see my point. Every time you pull out more money than you put into a property, you end up with more capital to invest. Pulling out more money than you put in is a good money move. Doing it several times in a row is a lot of good money moves. These good money moves allow you to have opportunities to make more good money moves, which open up opportunities to make even more later.

This is how real estate is meant to be done! Wealth is built over a period of time where good decision after good decision is made, each decision opening up doors for more good decisions to be made. These ever-increasing opening doors are what lead to financial freedom and the ability to impact many, many lives. BRRRR is one of the best tools you can use to get you there!

Key Points

- Buying right gives you the option to flip the property or hold it. Options keep you from making ill-informed decisions.
- There are three main points of distress: 1. Market distress; 2. Personal distress; 3. Property distress. Most fixer-upper properties will be found by targeting property distress.
- If a property will rent for 1 percent of the purchase price every month, it is likely to cash-flow.
- If you are all-in for 75 percent of the ARV, you will likely recover 100 percent of your capital.
- Multifamily properties are valued based on their NOI and the capitalization rate of the area. You improve their value by improving their NOI.
- Single-family homes are valued based on comparable sales in the surrounding area. You improve their value by improving their desirability and condition.
- My three main criteria for buying a property are: 1. Equity in it; 2. Positive cash flow; 3. No headaches/bad neighborhoods.
- There are five inputs that go into analyzing most deals: 1. Rent; 2. Mortgage amount; 3. Tax; 4. Insurance; 5. Property management.
- Your Core Four is made up of a: 1. Deal finder; 2. Lender; 3. Contractor; 4. Property manager.
- Rockstars know rockstars. Get in touch with one rockstar and you'll meet others in their world.
- There are three numbers you must be able to crunch to know if a property will make money: 1. Acquisition cost (price to buy); 2. Rehab cost; 3. ARV.
- Cash is king. If you can put together a cash offer or its equivalent, it will be much stronger than competing offers.
- Look for properties that require a cash offer. You will find better deals by eliminating your competition.

CHAPTER THREE
How to Find Deals

*You can get everything in life you want if you will
just help enough other people get what they want.*

—ZIG ZIGLAR

So far we've touched on some basic ways you can find deals. These are the fundamentals of deal finding, and once you master them you are on your way to success. Success is important, but it's not all we want. We want mastery. I'm going to share some ways you can take these fundamentals and leverage them to produce success along with real estate mastery.

Remember, it's repetition that creates mastery. These methods were developed because time and time again I would use them, find out what worked and what didn't, and then adjust my technique to make it more effective. This happened because I embraced the BRRRR technique and committed myself to real estate investing. By putting the time in, I created systems and methods that would help increase my success, leveraging other people to save me time and make me money!

As you read these tips, make note of how this would apply in your own life, who you already know that could help with these, and what you can do to start taking action. "MINS" is an acronym that stands for "most important next step." Every one of these methods is something that will find you deals and ultimately make you money. If you want to be successful, get in the habit of asking yourself: "What is my most important next step toward executing this technique?" and write down the answer.

By breaking big tasks (e.g., finding an agent on a top-producing team) into smaller ones (search Zillow.com for top agents with teams, email the team leader, ask for agents to interview, then come up with a list of questions for the agent, etc.), you can make it much easier on yourself to come up with a strategy to start taking action. The "MINS" funnel is a great way to go about doing this.

The following are some of my tried-and-true techniques for finding deals. As you read them, ask yourself what you can do to start applying these techniques today. If you're not ready yet, make a list or bookmark this page so you can come back to it when you're ready to start looking for deals. Remember to break these tasks down into smaller, more manageable tasks when it's time to get started.

What's your most important next step?

All About Agents

Having an agent looking for deals for you is great. Having several is even better. By seeking out multiple agents, you'll be able to tap into different networks with sources that you can use to find great deals. Sometimes they even specialize in certain types of real estate so you can expand your knowledge by expanding your network. And when you expand your knowledge, you'll create better wealth-building opportunities for yourself.

Some agents can find you a condo, others multifamily property, and others single-family property. There may be some agents who network with investors and hear about deals before they hit the market, while others network with attorneys and know about sellers in distress due to divorce or death.

There are tons of agents out there who have different specialties. What's important is to understand that diversifying the people you talk to will increase the reach of your network, and increasing the number of connections you have will help you find more and more new deals. Doing both puts you in a much stronger position.

The thing to understand about networking isn't that you're "finding more people." It's that you are connecting with people in your sphere of influence, who have their own unique sphere of influence as well. Networking is gaining access to new spheres and making them a part of your own. The more of these "spheres" you can work yourself into, the more likely you are to start finding what you want. This is how you create an army of people advocating for your success.

For those who don't work in real estate professionally, the whole "agent-with-a-team" thing can seem confusing. Every agent sets their teams up differently, and when you are on the outside of a transaction looking in, it can be hard to understand what the point of the whole team thing even is.

The idea behind a "team" is an agent who is doing so much business they can't keep up with demand. Rather than turn business away, or worse, do shoddy work, agents will hire people to help assist them and their clients. This starts off small, with hiring admin help, and can eventually grow to, you guessed it, a full-fledged team. Some agents end up hiring other agents to work with their buyers (we, as buyers, take up the most time, flake the most often, and make the least amount of money for the agents) and eventually even their sellers.

The reason I prefer an agent with a team is because I am much more likely to find that the things I need are already in place. The first is, if an agent has so much business they needed to hire staff to keep up, they are much more likely to be a top-producing agent. Top-producing agents not only have more connections, but usually have more experience. Experience matters in the world of real estate. You can build that experience for yourself, and you will, but why wouldn't you want to leverage other people's experience as well?

Remember how I said repetition builds mastery? Well, top-producing agents who sell a lot of homes get more reps in than agents who don't. This doesn't guarantee they'll be better, but it does make it much more likely that they'll be more skilled, more experienced, and better equipped to help me. Typically, the more someone does something, the better they get at it. Real estate sales is no exception.

The next reason I prefer an agent with a team is because if an agent is a top producer, they are usually talented, and talent draws talent. Rockstars know rockstars, right? If this is true, talented agents are likely to only select talented agents to be on their team. This increases my odds of getting a tenacious, knowledgeable, talented person working on my behalf. These are the kinds of people I want to surround myself with to help me find deals and to teach me more about real estate in their market.

The third reason for the team-clad agent is because of the network they provide. I'm desperate to get connected to the contractors, lenders, and property managers of a top-producing agent who works with investors or invests themselves. The problem is, the agent who leads the team likely doesn't have the time to take on new clients, especially an investor client who is going to be needier than a traditional client.

By finding an agent with a team, and working with one of their buyer clients, I can often tap into the network of the top-producing agent without needing to work with the agent personally. I often tell the buyer's agents I work with to go ask the team leader for questions they don't have the answer to, or for referrals I need that they can't provide.

There are several examples of this, but some of the more common things I ask them to do is to ask the team leader . . .

- Who on the team has a lender that will work with investors?
- Who can provide a good handyman referral at the next team meeting?
- Who do they know that can introduce us to wholesalers with good deals?
- Who is the most experienced person in the office at finding great comps?
- Do they know a rockstar appraiser we can talk to when we are unsure of the validity of comps?

You get the idea. By working with an agent with a team, I am more likely to find a talented buyer's agent to work with me, more likely to get the experience of the agent who started the team, and more likely to find resources that will help me put together the pieces I need to be more successful. This is one more way you can leverage someone else's talent, experience, and network to help you achieve your goals.

Calling Team Leaders/Brokers to Ask for Top Talent

Of each technique I'm sharing in this section, this might be my favorite. This method allows you to leverage the knowledge and experience of one of the top talents in an entire market center/brokerage, and use them to save you massive amounts of time while increasing your odds of success in a big way.

Every real estate brokerage has someone who runs the office. Different brokerages call this position by different names, but essentially they do most of the same jobs. Sometimes they are referred to as team leaders, brokers, sales managers, office managers, etc., but they are ultimately the person who knows the agents in the office and helps keep things running smoothly.

Now, because these positions are in charge of making sure the office stays profitable, they are usually compensated based on the performance of the office, or at bare minimum, the overall success of the office. This means these people have a lot of "skin in the game" since they are tied to the performance of the office as a whole with regard to their own personal success.

People in a position like this are much, much more likely to know who's a rockstar and who's just a groupie in their organization. These are the people who keep the books for the office, look at the sales statistics, and know who the top producers are. They are often tasked with keeping the top producers from leaving and trying to train up the bottom-rung performers.

What I do to capitalize on this is simple:

- **Step 1:** Google the names and numbers of real estate offices in the area I want to invest in.
- **Step 2:** Call and ask for the team leader, owner, or office manager.
- **Step 3:** Explain my goals to the person I talk to, and ask who from the office they would recommend I work with.
- **Step 4:** Write down the names and numbers of the recommendations.
- **Step 5:** Start calling these agents (likely top producers with experience working with investors, since that's what I said my goals were) and interviewing them to find out who I like the most.
- **Step 6:** Start working with the agents who seem like a good fit.

I know this seems really simple, but it is so easy—and incredibly effective. I'm cutting out all the non-producing agents in the office and only getting the names of the top talent, and not only that, but they are much more likely to have experience working with investors, which is exactly what I wanted. Also, I received the information from the one person in the office with the most to lose if it doesn't work out.

If you think about it, this is the same technique we use when analyzing deals. We don't want to look at every deal; we only want to look at the ones most likely to fit our criteria. Makes sense we would use those same principles when searching for someone to find us deals, right? This is a prime example of how mastery in one area of real estate increases your performance in others. Because I learned how to find deals, I put together rock-solid techniques for finding deal finders, using the same techniques.

All the Ways to Find Agents

I've discussed the benefits of having a top-producing agent in your corner. Now let's dive in to seeking agents out. Here are three best practices to finding the right agent for you.

Find Agents through Other Investors

This method can be tricky but when you pull it off it's easier than it seems. The hard part is finding an investor that trusts you enough to provide you with their agent's info! When someone is in a "scarcity mind-set," this can prove to be a challenging task. If you want to find agents through other investors, your best bet is to learn to bring value to them first.

Understand when you are asking another investor for an agent they recommend, you are asking them to give up a potential deal that could have gone to them to go to you instead. Understandably, many investors won't feel comfortable with this situation. But others will.

The first thing you should keep in mind when asking another investor for an agent recommendation is to make it clear you won't ask for deals to be brought to you before them. The goal isn't to poach deals from other people, it's to be next in line when a deal comes their way and they don't have the funds to buy it. If another investor sees you as a threat, it doesn't make sense for them to share their resources.

The next thing to remember is it only makes sense to ask someone for a favor after you've provided value to them. Value doesn't have to be monetary: It can come in many different forms. Value can be provided through friendship, encouraging words, resources of your own they might need, or sharing your knowledge. Sometimes value can be provided through helping them with an area in their business they struggle with that is your strength. No matter what it is, look first for ways to provide value to someone else before asking them for anything.

If you feel like the investor has really good resources you'd like to benefit from, consider paying them for any deal you buy from one of their contacts. If you know up front you'll be paying the other investor $2,500 when you close, you just need to underwrite that amount into the offers you make and ensure the deal still works. It can be easy to focus on the fact you "shouldn't have" to pay someone else $2,500 for a deal they didn't bring you, but is that in your best interest? If you are going to make $45,000 in equity, would it make sense to lose that to save $2,500?

Investors who have established talent already working for them in a specific marketplace can be incredibly powerful allies to have on your side. You should always, always, always look to make friends with these people when getting into a specific market. Just remember that you are their competition, and if you want them to help you, you should be offering to help them first. Becoming someone who is well known and well liked makes it much harder for others to tell you no. Learning to do this can make you a lot of money.

If this is an area you feel uncomfortable with (or even if you're already good at it) I would recommend you read Dale Carnegie's classic *How to Win Friends and Influence People*. This is a book with detailed examples and information on just how to make yourself more likable and make it much easier to get what you want from others. Many of the techniques work incredibly well in the world of real estate investing.

Finding Agents through Lenders/Contractors/Property Managers

Once you find a rockstar member of your Core Four, you are often that much closer to finding the other three members as well! Real estate investing is a niche market. It does not represent the majority of real estate sales—it is actually the minority. This means that those of us who make our living or work in this niche know many of the others. It's a bit of an underground world where the same people rub elbows.

Because it's such a small world, the lenders who make their money working with investors often know the top-producing agents who bring them those leads. If you find a lender who can work with you, there's a good chance they can put you in touch with an agent who can help you find the deals and walk you through the process. Finding one lead will often open up doors to more leads, and so on and so forth.

The same goes for contractors. If you are lucky enough to find a contractor with experience working with investors, they probably work mostly with investors. This means they are likely to know the agents those investors work with. It's the agents who are opening the lockboxes to let them in the houses so they can give their bids, the agents who are recommending them to investors, and the agents who are checking on the work for those who are flipping houses and want the progress monitored.

If you find a contractor who's good at working with investors, you're likely to find good agents as well as other investors. This can work especially well if the contractors themselves are experienced investors or dabble in it. Consider sharing investing knowledge with contractors who want to learn more about what happens on the investing side compared to the labor side. Making yourself valuable to them will give them incentive to do the same for you and your business.

Lastly, if you find a property manager that does a large amount of business or manages a large number of properties, you are likely to have just found yourself an incredible resource for finding great deals. Property managers like this network with the people who are likely to bring them deals. Top-producing agents who work with lots of investors are a huge source of deals for them.

Property managers sometimes do invest themselves, but their main goal is to find houses to manage. If they can put you in touch with someone who can find properties for you to buy, they can generate income for themselves by managing that property. This creates an incredible and powerful incentive for them to put you in touch with these people, and if they don't know any, to go find some. I can guarantee you property managers (if they are good) have more contacts than most others in the investing world. If they want to find top-producing agents for you to use, they will find them.

Understanding how things work at a "big picture" level can help you solve a lot of your "small picture" problems. Knowing that property managers are motivated to help you find people that can get you deals is a "big picture" piece of information. Learning how to let them know you want their help connecting you with agents is a "small picture" solution. Mastering the BRRRR process will force you to learn the "big picture." Once you get the big picture, the smaller, more manageable steps become clearer.

The more repetitions you get with "small picture" tasks, the better you get at executing them at a high level. The better you get, the more effective you'll become, and this will lead to you achieving success. With time and experience, you'll also be building your roster of rockstars who can help find and service deals. Eventually, you'll have a booming business generating leads without having to do any work, and that's the goal, right? None of this happens without repetition, and your repetitions will be severely limited using the traditional method instead of the BRRRR method.

Finding Agents through BiggerPockets

This one really isn't a surprise. At least, it shouldn't be. If I look at all the agents I work with, the one I work with most is someone I found through BiggerPockets.com. If you want to find agents more likely to be experienced working with investors, going to a source known for educating only investors would make a whole lot of sense. There is no location better for this purpose than BiggerPockets.

The key to using BiggerPockets to find a good agent is to find an agent who also invests. Too many people make the mistake of finding a traditional agent and expecting them to provide results in a niche market like investing. It doesn't work.

BiggerPockets educates more than a million investors. This means there will always be "vendors" hanging around looking to get business from these crowds. Oftentimes these are wholesalers looking for investors who want to invest in real estate but don't have the guts, time, or determination to learn it for themselves (obviously that's not you, because you're reading this book teaching you how), but it's not only wholesalers! I've found lenders, handymen, and agents all on the same website.

Many times these people actually found me! If you edit your profile to say exactly what you're looking for, the right vendors know to introduce themselves. If you are active on the forums asking questions or on the marketplace stating what your needs are, these vendors can find you and check out your profile.

And remember that people you connect with have a network of their own, meaning even more connections for you. If there is one thing I've learned about real estate investors, it's that they like to talk. Tons of research goes into every decision we make, and most people love to sound smart and share this knowledge with others. By simply making friends and asking questions, you're likely to get your answers (and learn about more things than you ever expected to) from talking to them.

Wholesalers

Wholesalers are one of the trickiest methods to finding deals but can also be one of the best. They are a "high risk high reward" option, and if you're new to investing you should highly consider using a real estate agent to help you with your first several processes before using a wholesaler. For those with more experience investing, wholesalers can still be risky in that the word "wholesaler" is not an official title. They are not licensed, not insured, not governed by any formal body, and not under any legal or ethical obligation to look after your interest. If you plan on using a wholesaler, please check with your local laws or legal counsel to make sure this is a good move for you.

Wholesalers are simply people who find a deal, put it under contract, then assign the right to buy that property to someone else by switching the contract to their name. They make their money by finding motivated sellers, negotiating a deal, then finding motivated buyers to assign that deal to. Imagine them as a person who goes to Macy's ahead of you, finds the items that are on clearance, then guards them until you arrive so no one else can buy them. They are paid for finding you a deal on something you want to buy.

While you definitely want to proceed with more caution when using a wholesaler than an agent, that doesn't mean you should avoid them. A good wholesaler can get you a tremendous deal with very little from you! Wholesalers' jobs are to find incredible deals and assign them to someone else. This means those that are good at it become highly specialized in that one aspect of the business, get tons of repetitions with it, and therefore are much more likely to master it.

What does this mean for you? It means you can get yourself connected with someone who does all the hard work of finding you a great deal so you don't have to. It also means you're much more likely to find a great deal that won't involve a significant rehab compared with the MLS (using an agent) for a deal. Remember how I mentioned the three kinds of distress? That applies here.

Agents are more likely to find "property distress," meaning a big rehab. Wholesalers are more likely to target "personal distress," meaning a deal with less rehab. As far as the third method, market distress, you're not as likely to need a wholesaler, as the market itself will usually be providing you all the deals you need.

Although wholesalers can get you incredible deals, there's no guarantee that they know what they are doing or that the information they are providing you with is accurate. Remember, they are not licensed and do not owe you a fiduciary duty of responsibility. The biggest risk with wholesalers is inaccurate information, or in some cases, a complete lie.

Most wholesalers sell their deals by providing evidence supporting their claim that the property is a great buy. This evidence usually comes in two forms—comparable property values and estimated rehab costs. With a bad wholesaler, these numbers will be off. Trusting bad numbers can lose you a lot of money.

Using wholesalers to find deals is one of my all-time favorite ways to get great buys, but it's also the one method I've used that's burned me the most. I've had cases where wholesalers provided me with inaccurate information regarding the square footage of a house, the number of bedrooms in a house, and the tenant's record of paying their rent on time. I've also had cases where they didn't disclose that the property was in a flood zone or was not zoned for the addition the current owners had constructed.

In the end, there was no one to blame but myself for not confirming all this information. I share it with you not to scare you, but to shed light on the reality that if you buy from a wholesaler, proceed with caution. That being said, wholesalers have provided me with some of the best deals I've ever bought.

The most important thing to consider when looking for a wholesaler is to find one that's *credible*. This is where their reputation becomes so important. My advice is to look for credible, trustworthy people and only get wholesaler referrals from them. I always ask if the person referring me to a wholesaler has worked with them in the past. If so, I ask how the experience went and verify the accuracy of the information. As a general rule, I only want to work with wholesalers who have assigned contracts to someone I know who speaks highly of them.

If you're going to make an effort to look for wholesalers (which is a good idea), I strongly recommend you only go to experienced, knowledgeable, strong investors for referrals. My best referrals have come from a property manager who bought properties from them himself, an investor who bought from the wholesaler he recommended, and a contractor who bought houses himself. All three of these were experienced investors who knew what they were doing and could vouch for the validity of the wholesaler, and it worked out great every time.

For newer investors, keep in mind there is a lot a real estate agent does to help you in a transaction other than finding you the deal. In many ways, this is actually the least important of the services they offer. If you aren't extremely confident in your abilities or skills yet, consider waiting to look for a wholesaler to add to your roster until you've got a couple of transactions under your belt.

Alternative Methods of Finding Deals

In addition to the methods I've given you so far, there are several other miscellaneous methods many investors use to find deals I can share with you. While they aren't as common, they are still effective and worth learning. These are the "other" methods investors use to find deals that aren't talked about as often but still produce big results.

Direct mail: Many investors do the work of a wholesaler and look for off market deals by mailing out "I buy crappy houses" type cards. These cards state you are looking to buy houses in any condition and usually spell out what you can offer (cash, quick close, no Realtor fees, no closing costs, etc.). The idea is to find interested sellers and convince them to sell to you without finding a Realtor first.

The key is to find a motivated seller who doesn't care about getting top dollar, doesn't know they could, or values a quick and easy sale over the final dollar amount they'll receive. Many times these are people with houses in terrible shape who either don't want to go through the hassle of putting it on the market with a Realtor, or are too embarrassed for someone to see the house in its present condition. Finding a seller like this can be a big score for you. The successful direct mailers will tell you success is achieved through—surprise!—repetition. Sending a wave of direct mail isn't likely to get you a result, but sending several waves, consistently and over time, is much more likely to work. Most sellers aren't likely to call you the first time they see your mailer. However, after seeing it over and over and realizing you're a serious business and not a gimmick, they are much more likely to give you a call and see how much you'll pay for their house.

Direct mail is simple to do. You can Google popular direct mail designs and get a free phone number through Google so you don't have to use your personal one to receive the calls. There are also services that provide cards for you, and will even mail them out to lists you provide them. Then, there are companies who provide these lists! In addition, there are companies who will answer the phones for you and take messages from the sellers, and you can see how it's possible to create an entire business where you do nothing but take the pre-screened calls from a system that has done all the work for you.

SEO: Search engine optimization is a phrase used to describe getting higher results via a search engine. When it comes to investors, this usually means creating a website stating you buy crappy houses, then looking for ways to get that website to rank higher than others in online searches. The goal is to show up higher in a search when someone Googles "sell my home in Wichita" or "fast home sale Denver." Distressed sellers will often search for a solution to their problem online, and you want a presence there where they can easily find you.

When done correctly, sellers will end up at a landing page of yours where they fill out a form giving their contact information for you to follow up with. A landing page is a web page designed to prompt the visitor to fill in their personal information in hopes of being contacted—or being provided with your information so they can reach out to you. Having a good website will allow these sellers to find you and either provide their info for you to follow up or reach out to you directly.

This works similarly to direct mail, but rather than sending letters, you're making yourself available online. Combining these two methods is a common tactic used by professional wholesalers to find motivated sellers. If you are looking for a similar result, you should be combining them as well. Consider companies like Lead Propeller or InvestorCarrot to provide you with ready-made websites intended to increase your SEO and create better conversions on your landing page.

Personal networking: A highly effective and often underutilized method is to let everyone know you're looking to buy houses. Telling people these houses can be in any condition or situation is important so they don't avoid sending you the ugly or embarrassing ones. This is a free and simple method that allows you to capitalize on those you know best and are most willing to help you achieve your goals.

Better yet, you don't even have to talk to strangers! Some of the best deals I've ever heard of have come from this method. Let your relatives, friends, coworkers, parents on your kids' baseball teams, *everyone* know you buy property in any condition. If you make this a habit and commit to it daily, you'll find deals start filing in.

Professional networking: Similar to personal networking, but different in the sense it involves connecting with people you don't know yet. The key is to find people who are more likely to come across distressed sellers than the average member of society would be. Examples would be divorce attorneys, probate attorneys, bankruptcy companies, and morticians/funeral homes.

Make a list of these companies and follow up with them regularly. Similar to what makes direct mail work, you want to continually remind people you are looking for those with a property to sell and you can help them out of a bind. This is a simple and easy plan for success, but has one of the highest margins of success that I've ever seen.

Whenever you meet someone, ask what they do and show interest in their chosen vocation. When you sense this person may be likely to come across someone who needs to sell a property, ask for their business card and tell them you'd like to stay in touch. Add these people to a database and follow up with them regularly by phone, email, social media, or text messaging.

You can use a CRM (customer relationship manager) or a spreadsheet to organize the data. Some CRMs can be purchased for under $35 a month that will organize, systematize, and remind you who to follow up with and when. Many also provide a way to take notes so you can track conversations and get quick reminders before you follow up with your next call.

It's not super important what you say during these calls: What's important is how often you connect with these people. Your goal here is to stay top of mind so they don't forget about you when they hear of someone going through a short sale, foreclosure, or a trustee sale. This is the exact same system I used to become the top Realtor in my office in my first year of full-time work. I created a list of people likely to know someone who would need to sell their house, and I stayed in touch with these people regularly. Use these same principles to grow your investment business and you'll see the same results!

Auctions: Many investors find deals at auctions, and there are many different types to choose from. Typically, we think of auctions as being on the courthouse steps as an auctioneer calls off addresses of homes for sale and excited investors hold up numbered paddles to indicate their interest. This *is* how some auctions are conducted, but it's not the only way. These are typically foreclosure auctions where banks are trying to sell properties to the public before taking them officially on their books (at which point they would become REO, or "real estate owned").

Foreclosure auctions like this can provide great deals, but also can be incredibly risky. Most of the properties are sold with no contingencies, cash only, and very little opportunity, if any, to conduct any due diligence. Investors who purchase property this way should be extremely experienced with a high tolerance for risk and a solid team of assistants to do title and background research regarding what they are buying. This is a fast-paced environment with little margin for error, and very few soft places to land if you make a mistake.

Luckily there is more than one way to buy property at an auction. I myself have bought properties at online auctions where sellers of property replicate the process of bidding on a property auction style, but the process takes place over several days. This gives the potential buyers more time to do research and make sure it's an investment they are comfortable making. This also takes away the emotional pressure of making a very big decision, very quickly, with limited information.

Looking for online auctions to buy investment properties can be a good way to find deals, especially if you have a solid contractor you can depend on. I've found that the majority of online auctions are selling very distressed properties that need to be cash-only sales. Having a contractor that gives you fair prices and quality work is a must to succeed in this environment.

When I bid on houses like this, I have an agent do all the work for me. They look up the comps, get me an ARV, bid for me, and watch the other bidders to see if we've been outbid. If the agent isn't compensated by the auction site, I pay them directly. If they are compensated by the site, I will pay the difference between what the auction site is compensating them and 3 percent of the purchase price. This way my agent is motivated to do all the work I need done and I don't spend too much time on deals I'm not likely to win.

Tax liens: Buying properties that owe taxes to the state or county is another form of finding deals many investors don't pursue. While the process varies by region, there are similarities in the general technique. Generally, you are buying the right to foreclose on a house by paying the money they owe in taxes to the government for them. By paying their lien, you are compensated by the government with the right to take the house (the item being used to secure that lien).

This is similar to buying a non-performing mortgage note (for more on this, consider reading *Real Estate Note Investing* by Dave Van Horn). Essentially, the government entity that is owed the taxes has decided they will never be able to collect or that collection isn't worth the trouble. They are selling off the right to take title to the property to anyone who will pay the taxes owed by the current owner. Not a bad way to find yourself in a great deal.

The caveat here is there are different laws that govern how this works in different areas. Some areas give the owners a certain period of time to pay you back the money you paid the government for them, and if they pay it back on time they can keep the property. Other areas have a time limit before you can actually take over the property. Knowing these laws are essential to having success with this strategy, but the strategy itself is a pretty solid and underutilized way for investors to find great deals.

Driving for dollars: Driving for dollars is a method of finding real estate that is hands-on and simple. Just like the name implies, you simply get in your car (or bike, motorcycle, or moped) and look for obviously distressed properties. When you find one, you write down the address and make a note to look up the owner's information. Then, you call or mail the owner and tell them you want to buy their property. Pretty simple, right?

When driving for dollars you want to look for signs that a property is being neglected. This creates a situation where you are far more likely to find an owner that is more motivated to want to sell it. Some signs of obvious neglect are:

- An overgrown lawn
- Newspapers piled up in the driveway
- Neglected landscaping
- Dead grass
- Boarded-up windows
- Rotting wood
- A roof with plants growing on it
- Broken windows

When you see signs like this, make a note of the address. Then find a Realtor or title representative with access to public tax records and ask them for the owner's name and mailing address. Sometimes you can find these owners on social media and reach out to them there. If you can't, mail them a letter expressing your interest to buy their property, or better yet, drive to their home and deliver the letter in person.

Receiving a letter in the mail can be annoying for the recipient but delivering a letter to someone in person puts a face to the name and lets them know how serious you are. Many deals are put together on the foundation of the rapport the buyer is able to build with the seller. Meeting someone in person is a really good way to build that rapport faster.

Bird dogs: *Bird dog* is a slang term for someone who goes and looks for deals for you. Similar to the way a bird dog looks for a bird (the goal of a hunter), your bird dog will be out there on your behalf, looking for you and doing the things you're unable or unwilling to do yourself. What makes a bird dog successful is how much grit and determination they possess.

A bird dog is a great resource to use if you know you don't have the time, patience, or skills to find deals yourself. And actually, bird dogs use many of the techniques I've described in this chapter. Have them read this and find out which areas they think they'll be most successful at and have them start working on those techniques first.

The important thing to know is there are people out there who are so hungry for success they'll do what it takes to find it. These are the people you want to surround yourself with, and grow together. The best partnerships are those where each partner is bringing a different piece to the table, and together you make the full puzzle. And to show your appreciation, you could offer your bird dog part of the deal. Some pay them for their time or give them bonuses when they find a deal. Others use some combination of the three. If you know you have the money, ideas, and resources, look for someone who can provide the time and you could create a great partnership!

Key Points

There are so many ways to find deals when it comes to real estate. In my opinion, most investors don't have the success they want because they go about pursuing a deal the wrong way. As you consider these methods, don't feel like you need to use every one. Instead, think about which of these methods works best for your personality, skill set, and abilities. In business, it's always best to double down on your strengths. Once you find a method that works for you, I encourage you to pursue it with tenacity, intention, and perseverance. Master the methods you know work for you, seek help from those who can do the work you can't or are unable to do, and watch as success is a natural by-product of that!

- Use multiple agents to find you deals.
- Use agents on large, successful teams.
- Call team leaders and ask who their top talent is for working with investors.
- Find agents through your Core Four.
- Find agents through BiggerPockets.
- Use wholesalers to bring you deals.
- Use direct mail, professional networking, personal networking, auctions, driving for dollars, and bird dogs to find you deals.

PART THREE

The Rehab Process

CHAPTER FOUR
Rehabbing Like a Pro

A successful man is one who can lay a firm foundation with the bricks others have thrown at him.

—DAVID BRINKLEY

If buying right is the most important thing you can do to make money in real estate, getting the rehab right is the second most important part. Buying a property right ensures you'll have lots of equity in the deal. That means a lot of water in the bucket. Doing a rehab right means you won't spill much of that water, and in some cases, you can actually add more water to the bucket through the rehab.

With this being such an important part of the BRRRR strategy (and investing in real estate overall), I'll go into depth to explain how you can run a great rehab, find great people to do the work, and add value to your property through the process. Like most things, we are going to start at the result we want to end up with (getting good work done, quickly, for a good price) and work backward.

In this chapter we'll cover how to find all the pieces of the puzzle, how to find the right people, how to organize and understand the information you'll be collecting, and how to "hack" your rehabs. At this stage you should start seeing patterns in how you find a great contractor in the same way you find a great deal finder. This is a great example of how a skill you developed in one aspect of BRRRR will help you in others, and how success tends to compound on itself to build more success in your business.

Finding a Rockstar Contractor/Handyman

In my personal investing career, I've had to build teams in several different markets throughout the United States. Having had to find my Core Four in four different markets has given me a lot of experience (and frustration) when it comes to learning what works, what doesn't, and why. Now that I've repeated this process several times over, I've gotten a pretty good idea of what to do when I move to a new market and need to find and build a whole new team.

Whether you're starting this process in the city you live in or the other side of the country, you'll find the process is exactly the same. Finding talent is finding talent, and it doesn't matter where you are: Talent always acts the same. Teaching yourself how to recognize talent, treat talent, and attract talent is what will make your job as an investor easier and more enjoyable. Understanding that surrounding yourself with talent will create success, rather than trying to do everything yourself, is crucial.

How I Found My Most Recent Contractor

In 2017 I was excited, discouraged, and frustrated. From 2013 to 2016, I had been buying property in Arizona with moderate success. I had a team in place, a terrific agent, and a rockstar contractor. My contractor was so good, and so affordable, that I actually started looking for work for him to do that I didn't even need. I honestly realized if I had him put in granite countertops and tile floors, for the few thousand dollars he charged me, it was worth skipping on a year's cash flow to add so much more value to my properties and increases in future rent.

I began adding bedrooms onto properties and learning how to see these properties from a contractor's point of view. When I added bathrooms to properties, I could see how they had to draw up schematics for the plumbing, electrical, and windows. This experience helped me see the importance of hiring an outstanding contractor, and gave me a newfound appreciation for them and the impact they could have on my business.

Everything was going great, except for one thing. Arizona had become too expensive to find, buy, and hold property! All I could do was flip, and that wasn't really my goal. My goal was to build up a portfolio of single-family houses and hold them for years. As I continually looked for the kinds of deals that would provide me the ROI I wanted, my discouragement grew while my success rate plummeted. Arizona home prices had climbed too high.

Around this time, I found a wholesaler in Florida who was finding good deals. This wholesaler put me in touch with a lender who would underwrite me, and just like that, I had the two toughest pieces to my investing puzzle handed to me. It was just that simple; I was back in business.

I knew I could get started investing in Florida and find deals good enough to dive in. While the deals were great, my process wasn't. Not yet at least. I didn't have a rockstar contractor or property manager yet. It was apparent that not having a great contractor was costing me a lot of money, at least compared to the Arizona guy I had. I set out to make it a top priority to find one. I started off doing the same things I had done in California and Arizona—looking for agents, talking to other investors, and networking with property managers. I found a few contractors that were pretty good, but no one that was great.

When I realized I needed more contractors to choose from, I went to my property manager and told them I needed bids for all my rehabs. For every single house I bought and needed to fix up, I told them I wanted five contractors to provide bids on each job, and I would pay them $50 a bid.

To some, this might seem like a waste of money. Spending an unnecessary $250 per job seems imprudent on its face, but I knew one great contractor would save me ten times that on the first job they worked on. Over ten jobs, it would be one hundred times that. Not only did this technique end up saving me money, it also saved me the time of having to send copious numbers of emails to other people asking for contractor referrals.

By having my PM do it for me, I got myself out of the job! All they had to do was go to the list of vendors they had and sent five new ones to each job. This gave me five new bids for each project, five new contractors to talk to, and new opportunities to find my next rockstar. Previously, I had been taking as few as two bids. Upping my number to five increased my odds dramatically.

It wasn't long before I found a contractor with a professional demeanor whose prices were coming in way below most other's. It wasn't just that he was the most inexpensive because several other contractors were close to his prices. It was more the impressiveness of the whole picture. His bids were delivered in a professional-looking manner, exactly how I had requested. When I reached out to him and discussed rehab options, he was always weighing the pros and cons of each option and trying to find a solution that was best for my situation, not just easiest for him.

I immediately loved this because it's the same method I use with my real estate clients. When I'm representing someone, I ask a lot of questions to learn the most about their situation, weigh the available options, and use my experience to provide them with the best solution for them. I know my stuff, so I do this boldly and confidently. This contractor approached me the same way. He shot down my ideas he knew wouldn't work, he supported the ideas that would, and he presented me with options I hadn't considered.

This was what I needed! I'm a decently smart dude, but my goal is to always surround myself with people smarter than me. This contractor was clearly smarter and more experienced than me in the area where I needed him to be—my rehabs. Why was he so good? He was also an investor and used these same principles in his own investing.

It was at this point I realized I should start targeting members of my Core Four that were also investors. This became a game changer. By surrounding myself with experts in their field, real rockstars, who also invested themselves, I began to grow my business exponentially. Not only were my jobs getting done well, but I was *learning* incredibly fast from these people who knew more than I did. In fact, I learned so much I can now write a book about these topics without ever having had to swing a hammer at one of my properties. Not even once.

Everything was going great and I was able to scale my portfolio at a rapid rate. But just when I hit full swing, some bad news came crashing down. My contractor called me, told me he was sorry, but that he was firing me and would no longer work on my projects any longer. Just like that, all the work I had done to find a rockstar, train a rockstar, and work with a rockstar was gone. In one phone call.

I'll be honest. My initial reaction was to say "You'll regret this one." Luckily, I was getting effective coaching at the time and was learning all about how we need to bring value to others before we can expect them to bring value to us. This caused me to stop in my tracks, take a deep breath, tell the contractor I'd call him back, and hang up. I took a day to think about what I was going to do and say, and called him back the next afternoon with a clear head.

The first thing I asked was "Why?" in a non-accusatory manner. I genuinely wanted to know what I had done. It turned out I hadn't done anything at all! The contractor was smart and had two sets of crews: One was reliable, well paid, and easy to work with. This was the crew they would send to do jobs on primary residences where customers would pay more for a better overall experience. The other crew that he was using on my jobs was newer, less experienced, and less reliable. He could pay them less, and use guys from the "good" crew to supervise their work to make sure it was done well. By organizing things this way, he was able to keep his costs super low and pass those costs on to me. The problem was, it was guys from this crew that were causing him all his problems. All of his headaches, but very little of his profits, were coming from this aspect of his business and he realized he had to make a tough business decision and dissolve that side of the business. That's why he had fired me.

Once I heard the story, I was sympathetic of his situation. I had no idea any of that was going on and I realized he was probably losing money for quite some time just trying to keep my projects going. While listening to him talk, I realized I had the solution to *his* problem, and could provide expertise for him, just as he had for me with rehab solutions.

At Keller Williams Realty, we get good training about how to find, recognize, hire, and train talent. This is where I get a lot of the tactics I use to build up teams in my real estate investing business. I explained the whole philosophy of "rockstars know rockstars" (RkR) to the contractor. Turns out, the contractor was getting his hire leads for his crew from the other guys on his staff. The same guys that did shoddy work, were unreliable, and full of issues, were recommending their buddies to come work for him! Because this contractor was growing so fast and taking on so many new jobs, he wasn't paying as much attention to who he hired. Because he didn't have a position to hire/train/supervise these guys (he was just using workers from the other side of his business), no one was accountable for their performance! It was zero surprise to me why he was having trouble with his team. Some small changes in his hiring process produced some very big results in his company, and two weeks later he called me up and said he'd love to start doing jobs for me again with his crew that was running much smoother.

Now this is a really neat ending to what could have been a disastrous story! These are all skills, concepts, and ideas you can replicate in your own business and have the same success.

Recognizing Patterns to Success

After having put teams together in several markets, I learned a lot. Through the process, I was able to see what consistently worked, what never worked, and what was worth trying that either did or didn't pay off. As I look back, I realize I was recognizing patterns in my process that led to successful outcomes. Isolating the actions that brought me success allowed me to replicate those actions, and repeating them led me to perfecting them.

The BRRRR process allows you to get the repetitions you'll need to accomplish the same. Whenever you finish a project or complete a goal, it's a great idea to "debrief" the process. This simply means looking back at what you did and making notes about what went right and what went wrong. Debriefing helps you recognize what you did successfully so you can repeat it.

Look back at all the most important parts of your investing world. Where did you find your best deals? Where did you meet your best team members? Who taught you the most? Find the answers to these questions, then start asking yourself what patterns emerge from the answers. Once you see them, immediately start looking for ways to implement these "patterns of success" to the different areas of your business. You should experience a much shorter learning curve and get better results that flood in much faster than before.

Recognizing that rockstars know rockstars gave me the idea to start having a really good property manager get referrals for me to interview, rather than do it myself. This led to an excellent contractor, which allowed me to buy more deals, which put me in touch with even more rockstars. If you embrace this concept, you can expect to see the same results.

Make Top Priorities a Top Priority

When I started investing in Florida, I quickly realized I needed a top-talent contractor to take me to the next level. I was losing money on every deal I did with mediocre talent. This motivated me to come up with the plan to have my property manager get me at least five bids for each project so I could increase the number of people I was interviewing.

Truth be told, there were hundreds of things I could have been doing instead. There's *always* something that can be done that will take up our time. Scrolling through Zillow, reading inspirational Instagram quotes, perusing Yahoo News reading real estate articles—you get the point. In this instance, I was able to recognize what my top priority should be and actually make it my top priority. This led to me getting the result I wanted much faster and my business growing much quicker as a result.

Take a second and ask yourself how many things you do in a day that give you zero result. Clearing your unread email list to zero, scrolling through Facebook, responding to text messages from people who bring you no value, watching TV shows that do nothing to help you achieve your goals. Every day we waste the majority of our time. Why not make an effort to have at least one priority, one that you make a priority and pursue every day in the middle of all that wasted time?

It's easy to get seduced by the false notion of productivity that "checking items off a list" can provide you. In reality, doing one or two things right will have a much bigger impact than 100 things, if those one or two things are a priority. Understand what your priorities are in your business, and watch your business grow.

Recognizing Talent

In my first conversation with this Florida contractor, I realized he was talented. He knew what he was doing, had good ideas, and shared the vision I had for what we could accomplish. I knew what I was looking for, what I needed, and what it would look like when I found it. Because of this, I recognized immediately the contractor as someone I wanted on my Core Four.

Understanding what talent looks like, making an effort to find it, and recognizing it when you see it are crucial to learn in real estate investing. You can't do everything yourself, and even if you could, it wouldn't be long before you felt burnout from all that work. Finding talented people to help you achieve your goals should be a top priority for you. If you don't know what that looks like, then you found what should be your top priority.

Below is a table that demonstrates what talent looks like and how it acts. Whenever I'm considering if I should have someone on my Core Four hire someone for my real estate team or get into business with someone, I ask myself what side of the column they fit in on this table. If they aren't on the left-hand side, they aren't someone I want to be committed to! Take this table, burn it into your brain. Take a picture to make as the home screen on your phone. Learn it! Understanding this will help you immensely in your business.

NON-TALENTED TEAM MEMBERS	TALENTED TEAM MEMBERS
Require pushing	Push you
Don't fulfill your needs and end up making you do aspects of their job	Fulfill your needs as a by-product of succeeding in their role
Don't know what they want and aren't looking for the answer	Know what they want, what it looks like, and how to find/achieve it
Don't associate with rockstars and repel rockstars	Demand to work only with rockstars
Cause problems	Find solutions
Don't know why your bar is set so high	Continually look for ways to raise the bar
Do the bare minimum	Look for ways to overachieve and earn more of your trust/business

Finding talent is no easy feat. It will require a significant amount of work and it will cost you quite a bit. However, the price you'll pay to work with mediocrity or worse will cost you so much more in the long run. When I hear about newer investors who started with a promising future but soured on real estate investing, most of their stories are the same. They had a bad experience with a member of their team and decided real estate investing was just too hard.

When I ask where they found the team member, the answer is almost always that it was some form of a referral they did not work hard to get. An investor they didn't know well recommended them, or they got their number from a property manager they weren't even using, or it was the first name in a Google search. When you don't put the time and effort in on the front end to find high-quality candidates, you'll pay for it on the back end through shoddy work, lackluster results, and a terrible experience.

When you consider how much there is to gain from investing in real estate, do you really want to risk losing all that because you were too lazy or scared to make looking for a talented team member a priority? Think about this carefully. You, the person reading this, really don't even need to learn how to invest in real estate at all. Theoretically, if you found a rockstar for every member of your Core Four, you could just follow their advice and direction, let them do their thing, and watch as your net worth and passive income grows on its own.

Isn't that incredible? If you found a rockstar agent who was a guru at finding great deals, a great lender who was funding them, a top-notch contractor to get them rent-ready, and a rock-solid property manager who tied all the pieces together, you could literally know nothing about real estate investing and you would still become very wealthy. Why? Because talent on your team is more important than you knowing everything—or knowing anything, for that matter!

Surrounding yourself with talent is that important. Therefore, make finding talent your priority. Talk to other investors about what they like about their team, and what they don't like. When you find someone who is hungry for your business, ask them questions to find out what level of experience they have and what they can offer you. Continually look for talent and you'll put together a rockstar team, not to mention thriving business.

Finding Team Members Who Also Invest

If you want to make the talent search easier, take a bit of advice from me—start looking for team members who invest themselves. Agents, lenders, property managers, and contractors who also invest have an advantage over those who just work with investors. Allow me to elaborate.

If your team member invests, they are much, much more likely to understand your needs. A property manager who does not invest understands property management and most likely only that. They understand rent collection, finding market rents, tenant screening, and scheduling repairs. They understand bookkeeping, advertising, and communication. They understand all the things that go into managing a property, but that doesn't mean they understand investing.

It's not your property manager's job to understand ROI. It's not their job to look for the cheapest and best handyman, or to network with deal finders. It's not your property manager's job to know the value of the properties you're buying or the process for securing permits within the city you invest. However, if you find a property manager who invests themselves, they are much, much more likely to understand all these things, and more.

When a team member of yours is also an investor, they are much more likely to have looked at the job from *your* eyes, not just their own. They are way more likely to know your needs and anticipate them. Compare them to a general contractor vs. someone brought in to do a small part of the job. The floor guy understands how to put in the floor. He knows what he'll need and shows up to do his job with his materials in order to perform his role. He can see his small perspective of the big picture.

The general contractor (GC) understands the entire job. He knows when the painter is coming and when the appliances are going in. He knows when the demo work is being completed and when the baseboards will be ready for installation. The general contractor can move the schedule of the floor guy for after the appliances are installed so the floor isn't scratched, or before the baseboards are put in. The GC can see the big picture, and therefore can anticipate the needs of the floor guy.

When you hire someone to be on your team that also invests, you are hiring someone who is much more likely to see the project from the perspective of the general contractor. Like you, they've done this before. They are more likely to know not to schedule the appraisal until after the property is cleaned and prepped. Or to make sure the contractor makes certain repairs necessary for area-specific guidelines or legal requirements. They can see things you'll miss, and assist you in ways you may not have known you needed.

They are also much more likely to be able to refer you to better people, because they might be using those same people. Or, better yet, they may *stop* you from taking a referral from someone they've used in the past who did bad work. People on your team who invest themselves are more likely to know what you need, and that can lead to a much better experience for you. Newer investors often don't know what they need, and haven't learned to communicate those needs to others. They may not even know what is fair of them to ask for.

Having someone who has done what you're doing for themselves is a huge asset to your business and can help you learn much quicker than if you tried to do everything yourself. One of the very first questions I ask anyone I'm considering working with, partnering with, or trusting with a role in my projects is "Do you invest in yourself?" If there was one question I care about more than anything else, it would be this one.

Bringing Value First

This is something I can't stress enough. Before you ask anyone, for anything, ever, you should make it a habit to offer something to them first. Every time. When my contractor told me he couldn't work with me anymore, my first impulse was to lash out. Thankfully, I didn't. Instead, I had trained myself to learn to give value first, and that training kicked in before I sabotaged the entire situation with my pride.

When I asked my contractor what his problem was (why he couldn't take on my jobs anymore), not only did I show him I cared as a person, but I also received information from him about his situation that allowed me to help him. That transfer of information was really important. Without that, I would never have been able to offer him the business advice I had learned from Keller Williams about rockstars knowing rockstars, and he never would have been able to hire better crew members. This would have left me without a contractor and starting from scratch. Not ideal.

I can't tell you enough how many great relationships I've built from learning to bring value first. I'll share a secret with you—if you find a rockstar, and you don't bring value first, you don't have a shot of working with them. Rockstars know their value and know what they can do for your business. They know just how valuable they are. If you're not showing you can be valuable to them as well (it doesn't have to be proportional, it just has to be something) they aren't going to waste precious time, effort, or energy on you.

I can pretty much guarantee this as a fact because I've found myself ascribing to this same principle as well. As I've grown into the role of a top-producing real estate agent and an authority on real estate investing, the number of people who have reached out for "a little of your time" or "a quick cup of coffee" has grown exponentially. If I went to coffee with even half the people who have asked, I'd never get any work done. I'd stop being a top-producing agent, stop sharing information on real estate investing, and soon enough not even know what to talk about anymore.

My point is, I have to pick and choose who I can spend time on, and that becomes a skill in itself. Is this a serious buyer/seller? Will they be loyal to me or are they just getting my advice to relay to a different agent? Is this person just looking for my personal agent as a referral instead of learning how to find their own? Is this another agent wanting to learn my secrets, or a potential partner to help me grow? Will this person help me achieve my goals, or just want to fulfill their own?

It can be exhausting trying to learn how to know what everyone else's motives are or who is the best investment of my time. So how can I tell? The easy answer is: those who want to give me something in return when they first reach out to me are 1,000 times more likely to gain my trust and confidence. I can't see into someone's soul, but I *can* see if they are reaching out to offer me something, and that gives me good insight into what I can expect from a relationship with them. (By the way, I don't like the taste of coffee, so that's not a great way to reach out to me.)

Rockstars won't settle for less. If you haven't learned to bring value to someone else, start learning that right now. The secret to working with talent isn't something I shared in the talent section, but I'll share it here. The secret to finding talent is to *be* talent yourself. Act like talent and you'll draw it. Look at the table in the talent section. Ask yourself if you fit in as a talented person. If you don't, you'll repel talent, not attract it.

One of the best people I've ever met when it comes to bringing value is Derek Clifford (same person in the BRRRR example mentioned previously). Derek heard me on the *BiggerPockets Podcast* episode no. 169 and realized we lived close to each other. He heard I was an out-of-state investor and realized he wanted to get to know me better because he also wanted to invest out-of-state. Derek lived a few hours away and wanted to "pick my brain." Derek went about things the right way by prefacing our meeting and letting me know how he could add value.

When Derek showed up at my office, he explained how much he respected me and what I did. He told me exactly what help he wanted from me (which isn't unusual), but then he did something smart. Derek asked me what *I* needed in my business, and how he could help. I told Derek I was having a hard time finding lenders to refinance my properties, and that was a big hindrance (it still is). I then told Derek I was a new real estate agent and needed to find clients to help buy or sell properties. Derek promised he would get to work on helping me, ended our meeting, and drove back home.

Two weeks later, Derek emailed me a list of banks in the areas I invested that would work with investors. He then provided me with notes from the conversations he had with each of the bankers, including the interest rates, terms, and underwriting requirements. Derek showed he had put hours into solving my problem and made it a priority. Furthermore, Derek let me know he had taken a request up the HR chain at his company to let me do a "first-time home buyers class" at a lunch break there, and had been handing out my business cards and talking about me with his coworkers, referring me as an agent.

This, my friends, was impressive. Do you think Derek was likely to get my help and attention after that? Not only that, but I ended up selling Derek's investment property for him and managed a full rehab on it beforehand without charging him anything. Now Derek is being primed to take over my single-family residential portfolio and will be in charge of organizing, running, managing, and growing it.

Derek is a prime example of the *right* way to approach someone. It's paying spades for him now. If you want to learn how to find talent, learn to approach them with the intention of bringing value to them first. Derek is probably the most talented person I've ever met when it comes to bringing value to others first, and he's going to be immensely wealthy someday because of it. If you want to be successful, learn to be like Derek. Bring value first.

Finding Contractors through Networking with Other Investors (and Others)

With contractors being such a crucial foundational piece to the success of your real estate investing business, it would make sense to network with others who are likely to have used the people you need and can vouch for them. If you can get another investor to recommend their contractor, it can be a quick and easy score. Unfortunately, it's difficult to be able to pull off.

Much like the section in Chapter Three where I write about finding agents through other investors, you'll use the same principles when looking for contractors. While the principles may be the same, the technique can be slightly different. Understanding a few key tricks to get another investor to share their contractor with you can make your job easier and save you time.

The most effective way to get another investor to share their contractor with you is simple, but can be hard to accomplish. The secret is to make them like you. When someone likes you, they are much more likely to do things that will help you—even if it means hurting them. Becoming likeable is one of the fastest ways to becoming successful. In many ways it's more important than being smart, hardworking, or experienced. Likability makes everything easier.

When another investor shares their contractor with you, it can have a negative effect on their business. They may need the contractor to work on one of their projects and they are busy with yours. You may give that person's number out to other investors and the contractor can get exponentially busier. The fact is, when someone shares their rehab team with you they are taking a risk. Take this idea and consider times when you helped someone else out. Usually we only help someone when it doesn't inconvenience us, or we are feeling particularly benevolent that day. When the weird kid in the cafeteria forgets their lunch, we may know we "should" give them half our sandwich, but we rarely do. When the popular kid forgets, the other kids are clamoring to be the one to share. The popular kid may even get to be picky about who they allow to help them! This is because being likable gets you further than being unlikable. I'm not saying this is fair, or that it's right—just that it is.

Consider also that you may approach this logically and determine that if you have something to give them, they will want to help you. This is true, and it's certainly better than relying on someone's goodwill to help you. Having something to offer is better than having nothing, but it's still not as powerful of a motivator to get help as being likeable is. There is a secret to "likeability": When someone sees a part of themselves in you, they may be more likely to want to help you.

For those who are less emotionally driven and not as likely to care how much they like you, you'll need to take a more practical approach. Find ways to scratch their back if you want them to scratch yours. Understanding what drives or motivates someone is a wise way to learn how to get them to help you since different people are motivated by different things. Some people prefer the emotional gratification doing a "good deed," while others may be more drawn to more practical reciprocation that will help their business grow.

Herein lies the rub. Keller Williams teaches their agents (of which I am one) top sales practices performed by businesses worldwide. One of these rules is that "Information makes people think, emotion makes them act." When I first heard this, I disagreed with it. As an investor, I believed I was making my decisions based on numbers (which I associated with information) and not on emotion. It wasn't until I worked as an agent for about a year before I realized I was wrong.

I found that when I presented deals to my clients that were *extremely* good deals, they would sit and ponder it, go over it in their mind, and agree it was a good deal. They would come back and tell me it was a great deal, but they weren't sure. When I would show them a move-in-ready home, priced at the top of the market, but beautiful inside, they would go nuts and I'd be trying to calm them down and get them to look at the numbers again. When they found a house like this that they liked, they immediately started looking for a way to justify it. I started to notice they would use information as a weapon to help justify the decision they had already made in their minds.

- "Well, it's closer to work right? That will save on gas."
- "It was recently renovated so we won't have to replace anything."
- "We could always just add on to the backyard later if we wanted."
- "Weren't you saying you wanted to work more overtime anyway, honey?"

The fact is, emotions drove their decision, not information. Information was only used to *justify* the decision they had already made. They had it all backward! Now, why am I talking to you about sales techniques taught to Realtors? Because it teaches us something about human nature, and this is something we can use to our advantage when finding other people to give us their contractor referrals.

I, as an investor, believed I was not acting on emotion, but rather logic. I came to find out I was wrong. For me, finding a house that hit my numbers made me so excited *it would create an emotional response within me that drove me to take action*. I was still being driven by emotion, I just didn't realize my emotions were tied to the numbers. You want to learn to *harness* your emotions to make you a better investor, which I'll explain later in this book.

Using Handymen in a Rehab to Save Money

While there are many definitions of what constitutes a "handyman" vs. a "contractor," it can be boiled down to that a contractor is licensed, and a handyman is not. I'm sure there are other, more subtle distinctions, but for the premise of this book we don't need to dive into those. What we need to understand is this: Sometimes using an unlicensed handyman can save you a lot of money over using a licensed one.

Are there pros and cons to using each? Of course. Are there potential ramifications to using a handyman over a contractor? Sure could be. I'm not a lawyer, so you shouldn't take this as legal advice. Only you can know what's best for you. What I *can* tell you is many investors use handymen instead of contractors, and this often saves them a great deal of money. If you want to know the legal ins and outs of this situation, please consult an attorney.

Should you choose to use a handyman, you need to understand they are not all created equal. Some can do minor things like unclog a sink or put up shelves, while others can lay tile and hang drywall. I refer to this distinction as a "skilled handyman" vs. a "non-skilled handyman." Skilled handymen can do jobs very similar to, or even the same as, a contractor, but often won't charge you nearly as much.

Now, if you're doing a full-on, gut-job remodel, you probably want to avoid having a handyman do the work. Too much risk here. If you're doing smaller jobs like having a backsplash installed, putting a vanity in a bathroom, changing light fixtures, or doing outdoor landscaping, a handyman may save you loads of money. Understanding the scope of your work will be key when deciding who you should hire.

Handymen can be cheaper for several reasons. The first and most obvious is they aren't licensed and don't have to pay licensing fees like a contractor does. The next would be they may work for a contractor during the week, and are available after work and on weekends to pick up "side jobs." This can be an extremely economical way for you to find skilled labor at a fair price. The final way they can be cheaper is they don't have the overhead of a fancy contractor. No big brand-new truck, expensive warehouse, or marketing costs. It's just them and their reputation. If you're going to find a skilled handyman who doesn't market themselves, you're going to need to find them through word of mouth.

This is where networking through other investors or members of your Core Four becomes vital. You may not be able to ask for a handyman who can remodel your entire house, since this isn't typically something a handyman can do. Asking others if they know of a person who can lay tile, install appliances, paint, or repair water damage will be a better way of approaching this. The more specific you are on what your needs are, the more likely others will know someone who can do that job for an affordable price. When you use handymen, you will get a better value (usually) but have to do much more of the legwork yourself. That's the trade-off.

But if you do hire a handyman, there are several things to do to keep them happy and wanting to work for you for years to come. The first being paying them on time. This may seem obvious but let me explain. Rehab guys are often in a position where they are providing a service to someone they don't see and possibly never met. In addition to their time, this service often also costs them money. Paying for materials, tools, and sometimes labor to help them are all things they have to do before they get paid by you. This means that you paying them promptly means a lot to them. Not doing so is a great way to get them to ignore your calls or put your jobs at the bottom of their priority list.

Another thing to avoid is sending them back to do the same job twice. A lot of investors or landlords don't understand how anyone else's business runs, just their own. This can be problematic. When you send someone back to a job site they have already finished, they end up getting behind on their other work, and paying someone else to help them, without collecting additional revenue. This is bad for business.

If the handyman doesn't do the job right, you may have no choice but to send them back. This isn't your fault. What you want to avoid is not being clear about what you wanted in the beginning, so you're forced to send them back to finish what you never detailed you needed done in the first place. It is your responsibility to be abundantly clear what your expectations were from the start. This is why I recommend having a detailed scope of work with everything you want done made before any rehabbing. It clears up any confusion that the person you hired to do the work may have had, and it absolves you of any responsibility if they fail to finish the job. Sending someone back to a job site to finish up when you made the mistake is bad for the relationship and can lead to them cutting ties with you, after you worked so hard to find a reliable handyman.

The final thing to consider when working with a skilled handyman is that the majority of the time these people are skilled labor, and not necessarily skilled businessmen. Now, of course, this isn't the case with every person. But in my experience it is most likely the case, and with this I've learned there are some things I need to do when working with handymen that I don't have to do when working with contractors. An example is that the handymen I've worked with aren't organized and don't know how to run their business very well. This is because they don't like running a business (that's why they work for someone else, only get found through word of mouth, and don't make as much money). If you want to have a good experience with this kind of partnership, you need to help a handyman to help you.

What I mean by this is you may need to handle the aspects of what they are doing that don't involve using the tools or doing repairs. Things like timelines, scheduling, etc.

Now, when I hire a handyman to say, put in the floors, I ask them how much money they will need and how much time they will need. Once they give me the answer, I ask them if they accounted for materials not being delivered on time, employees not showing up, dump fees to haul off old material, tools, etc. It's often the case they did not account for these fees and didn't realize they needed to.

If you're going to use a handyman, you need to do so with the understanding that you are taking on the role of general contractor, and you are hiring them as a subcontractor. You can't hire a handyman to do a job and expect them to also be able to manage the logistics of that job. When you find one that can do this, that's great. In my experience, there aren't many of them and I usually need to teach them. Skilled handymen can save you a lot of money, but what they cannot save you is time or headache. Understand this before you go into the deal, so you don't end up feeling frustrated or falling behind.

How to Receive Bids from Your Contractor

When it comes to working with a contractor, many investors deal with anxiety, stress, and worry. In my experience, these are all signs of uncertainty. When you don't know how an experience is going to go, your brain deals with it by creating anxiety. This anxiety is meant to cause you to go look for the answers you don't have. If you don't have an escape route planned for a fire, and this was brought to your attention, you could feel anxiety. This anxiety would cause you to come up with a plan (anxiety is the emotion that makes you act). Once you had the plan, you'd be safer, and you'd be better off.

We get into trouble when either A) we don't allow our anxiety to push us to action, or B) there is no action we can take because the situation is out of our control. Situation A occurs with people who fall into analysis paralysis; they continue analyzing deals or asking "what-ifs," but they never do anything, so their anxiety never goes away. Situation B occurs in circumstances like when I'm representing a client buying a house. They feel anxiety during the escrow process because they don't know how it's going to turn out.

Whenever we feel anxiety, we should ask ourselves if it's Situation A anxiety or Situation B anxiety. If it's Situation A, we should come up with a plan. If it's Situation B, we should push it out of our mind or find someone who actually has the authority or ability to address the issue and put them in charge of it. Doing this will let our brains know the situation is being addressed and let the anxiety go away.

When it comes to investor's anxiety over contractors, this is a Situation A type anxiety. Many times, if we break down what causes the anxiety, it is a result of several unanswered questions. In my experience, these questions are often the same for every investor:

- How do I know my contractor will do a good job?
- How do I know my contractor won't steal my money?
- How do I know I didn't overpay?
- How will I know what to do if the contractor doesn't finish on time?
- How will I know what the contractor is actually doing?
- How will I know if I would have got a better deal from someone else?

These questions are the foundation of where the anxiety comes from. Basically, it is the "not knowing" that causes the anxiety. This wouldn't be a problem except for the fact that anxiety is a killer of progress. For most of us, when we feel nervous we stop moving forward. We recognize it as a defense mechanism designed to prevent us from making mistakes or getting hurt. In real estate, this means we are trying to avoid losing money. The problem is, we also end up avoiding making money when we do this.

So should we ignore anxiety? Absolutely not. Should we blindly follow it and freeze every time we feel it? No. I'm saying we should examine it, find out where it's coming from, and consciously decide if it's a Situation A or Situation B type anxiety. If it's Situation A, we put together a plan to move forward in spite of it. I want to share with you my method for receiving bids from a contractor that is designed to bring more clarity to the relationship.

With clarity, many of the questions that caused anxiety get answered.

With clarity, anxiety goes away as we now "know what we don't know." If we can remove our anxiety, we can remove a lot of the hindrances to our success that were slowing us down.

The key to covering your bases with the contractor is all in the way you have them present you their bids. Normally, a contractor is going to present you their bids in the way that is most convenient for them. If they are lazy, it's going to be on a piece of paper. If they are trying to inflate their prices, it's going to be in a very professional manner that is also vague and general. No matter how they do it, it's usually in the way that's best for them. We want this done in the way that's best for us.

The key to having a bid work for you is to make it as specific as possible. By requiring the contractor to write their bid in a manner that makes them justify every expense, you can see exactly what you are paying for, and how much you are paying for it. This alone takes away massive amounts of uncertainty, simply by requiring the contractor submit an "itemized bid." The following is an example of how an ideal bid would look:

ACTIVITY	SCOPE	QTY	RATE	AMT
Plumbing	Repair sewer lateral, re-run plumbing to kitchen, repair leak in laundry room, dig up line in backyard, and add larger pipes.	1	$7,500	$7,500
Electrical	Install new electrical panel.	1	$1,900	$1,900
Demo	Tear out kitchen countertops and appliances, remove laminate/carpet and flooring throughout house, tear out old shower stalls, and remove light fixtures.	1	$1,500	$1,500

Paint	Paint interior of home two-tone color of clients choosing. Repaint exterior of home to include pressure washing, sanding, and proper prep work.	1	$3,500	$3,500
Flooring	Install laminate flooring throughout home, tile in kitchen and bathrooms.	1	$7,200	$7,200
Bathroom	Install new tile shower, low-flow toilet, vanity, paint, and flooring.	2	$2,500	$5,000
Kitchen Counters	Install granite countertops of clients choosing (labor only).	1	$1,300	$1,300
Kitchen Cabinets	Sand and paint kitchen cabinets. Install new hardware.	1	$1,100	$1,100
Appliances	Install new stove, microwave, dishwasher, and hood.	1	$1,000	$1,000
Roof	Replace roof with 30 year composition shingles.	1	$8,500	$8,500
Landscaping	Remove two dead trees in backyard, repair cracks in walkway to house, cut down weeds with weed whacker, and plant flowers around border of backyard.	1	$3,000	$3,000

Lighting	Install 16 can lights throughout kitchen, family room, and bathrooms. Install 6 light fixtures in exterior.	22	$50	$1,100
Misc.	Punch-list, caulking and taping, repair dry rot throughout exterior per pest inspection, and haul off garbage.	1	$4,000	$4,000
Total				$46,600

This bid is what allows you to see exactly what you're paying for and allows you to determine if you would like to move forward with the proposed scope of work or change it. Sometimes you can add additional items, other times you may ask to have items removed if you do not believe they are necessary or worth the price. Additionally, this gives you the ability to negotiate the price on certain items if you feel the contractor is charging too much, or at minimum ask them questions about why they are charging what they have.

I liken this process to ordering food at a restaurant. Imagine you are hosting a large banquet, and you know you have 50 people attending. Would you call the restaurant, tell them you have 50 guests, and tell them you want to provide food for all 50 without asking what kind of food they offer and how much it costs? Would you make plans to hold your event at this venue without ensuring the room was available for you to reserve?

This is what it's like for investors who don't know how to communicate with contractors regarding what they'll be paying or what they'll be getting out of their rehab. The fear of the unknown causes them to put off ever moving forward. You want your bid to look like a menu, where you have the option of adding items, removing items, and choosing the items you feel are a good value while removing those that aren't. Are your guests vegetarian? No sense paying for steak. Is your rental low income? No use paying for brand-new plantation shutters. The principle is the same.

Be aware that most contractors won't like this. Their goal is to make more money, and they do this by creating ambiguity and confusion through nonspecific presentations of data. They want to say, "I'll do the kitchen for $25,000, the bathrooms for $15,000, and the flooring and paint for $12,000." They don't want to explain to you how much each area will cost, or what they'll be doing. For many investors, they don't feel comfortable asking questions or digging deeper so they end up moving forward and "hoping" for a good solution.

We don't want to "hope" for anything. We want to plan. Without planning, and without knowing what to expect, uncertainty and anxiety are bound to follow. The good news is, you don't have to play by the contractor's rules. You can have them play by yours. Setting this up from the initial interaction is crucial when it comes to controlling the tone of the relationship and setting an expectation that will ensure your success. Don't feel bad about this either. If you are successful, you can bring them much more work. If you're not, they're stuck looking for new clients. If you do this correctly, you can meet their needs through the process of meeting your own.

Setting the bid up in this manner helps you out in another big way that I haven't mentioned yet. As you can see, when a bid is itemized you can see exactly what you are paying for within each line in the scope of work. While you can easily see what you're paying, this doesn't always mean you can know if that price is reasonable. The itemized list brings clarity, but if you're not experienced in estimating rehab costs, this doesn't necessarily help you.

One trick I've learned to determine if I'm overpaying for an item of work is to ask the contractor how much the materials will cost them for a job, then ask how many hours it will take for the labor. Once I have these two points of data, I can pretty easily tell if I'm overpaying or not. Here's an example of exactly how that works:

Let's say one of the line items in the scope of work is to replace all interior doors, and there are ten of them in the property. The contractor has given a price of $3,000 for this line item. You're not sure if this is a good deal or wildly expensive, as you have no experience with hanging or buying doors.

You start off by asking the two questions I mentioned. The contractor tells you the door hinges and screws will be a total of $100. Then they tell you it takes their subcontractor four hours to hang each door. This is enough information for you to figure out what's really going on here!

You see you are paying $3,000 for ten doors. You break this down to the price of $300 a door. You then see $100 of that is going towards materials. That means you are paying $200 a door in labor. The contractor told you it takes his subcontractor four hours to hang the door, you can see this comes out to around $50 an hour to hang the door. If you assume the contractor is making half of that and paying half to his labor, that would mean they are each making $25 an hour. Even as an inexperienced investor, we can still see that $25 an hour isn't an exorbitant amount. Neither is $50 an hour.

However, there is a little more to this story. It's entirely possible the contractor knew why you were asking and gave you an answer he thought would make him look better. If the contractor knows he's making $200 in labor per door, he could have been smart and told you it takes four hours just to make it look like you're only paying $50 an hour. How can you tell if that's accurate?

The answer is simple. You call another contractor and ask them on average, how long it takes one of their subs to hang an interior door. It's always a good idea to ask around and get multiple bids. If you've already done that, you have several other contractors to contact so you can get a quick answer to your question. Let's say you do just that.

The second opinion you get comes back different than the first. This contractor tells you his guy can hang a door in 45 minutes to an hour, and that is conservative. You ask him how much he pays his labor, and he tells you $20 an hour. You thank him for his time and let him know you may be in touch about the job (while telling him to send you an itemized bid if he hasn't done so already).

This new information has clarified a few things for us:
1. The "four hours to hang a door answer" was either a lie, or this contractor has unskilled employees. Both of these would be red flags when it comes to making the decision to hire him.
2. The contractor may have grabbed this number from thin air because he knew what you were getting at, indicating he's been in this same situation before with someone else. This is also a red flag.
3. The contractor may just honestly have no idea how long it takes his subs to hang a door, indicating he is inexperienced and not knowledgeable. This, no surprise, is also a red flag.

Now that we have this information, we can go back to the contractor and let them know we are confused. My typical approach is straight to the point. I call the contractor, tell them one of the competing bids said they can hang a door in one hour (a quarter of the time he said) and ask him if he purposely hires crummy labor, or if he's unaware he's doing so. I usually get some form of a justification in the answer, and if I let them go on for long enough, they'll stammer out that it's not always four hours, and sometimes they can do it in one or two.

I then ask him if it takes two hours to do it, and I'm paying $200 per door, why am I paying $100 an hour for something that does not require skilled labor to accomplish? Paying $100 an hour might make sense for a highly qualified plumber or electrician while working on a complicated problem, but it doesn't make sense to pay that to hang a door. At this point the contractor will admit they can negotiate with you on the price and you have a choice to make. Either you negotiate down the price, or you consider all the red flags you've already seen and you move on to another contractor.

This system is pretty simple, and in some ways might even be considered common sense, but many people miss it. The reason is because they don't get their bids itemized. This means it's much, much harder to break each item down into two pieces—labor and materials. If you can't isolate the labor cost, you don't have a number to divide the amount of hours into, so you can't figure out what you're paying per hour.

Can you see how this all becomes so simplified when we break down a vague, large, complex number (like $25,000 for a new kitchen) into a straightforward, specific, and simple number (the line item broken down into hourly rate, number)? Itemizing the bids you get from contractors will give you the control and insight to make the right decisions, and the ability to do this will remove many of the unknowns from the process for you.

Two Types of Contractors

Just like there are two types of handymen, there are also two types of contractors. I like to break them down into the categories of "investor-friendly contractors" and "primary residence contractors." The reason is simple. Each type has strengths and weaknesses to their models and learning to classify them quickly will save you time when making your decisions.

Some contractors have a skill set and business model that is suited to work with investors. These are the contractors who offer low prices and do thorough, solid work. They understand you're working with a budget, and they specialize in doing work that is "budget friendly." These are not the guys to install an indoor water feature or build a rock wall pool. They are the guys who can tile a shower and put up a wall to turn a loft into an extra bedroom. These types of contractors are used to working with investors and are experienced in finding ways to do jobs under budget and save you money.

Primary residence contractors are those who specialize in working on, you guessed it, primary residences. These are the contractors the average Joe hires to remodel the kitchen or do work on his primary residence. They are professional, usually wear uniforms, and have fancy software they use to give you your bids. Contractors like this are used to picky clients, and put a lot more time and effort into getting a very good feel for exactly what you want. They make you feel incredible, their work is great, and they usually get done on time. All for a price. You can't have both, honestly. If you found an investor-friendly contractor with all the strengths of a primary residence contractor, eventually they would get so good their business would grow to the point where you couldn't afford them anymore—then they'd be a primary residence contractor. Primary residence contractors are easier to find. They market themselves, understand SEO, and their companies have websites. Investor-friendly contractors are much harder to find, but they are much more useful to people like us.

Investor-friendly contractors may have teams that work for the primary residence contractors Monday through Friday, then pick up side jobs for them on the weekends or after working hours. From my experience, they work long hours, and need to make every hour count, so they aren't going to be answering their phone when you call them during the workday and they have a paint roller in their hand. They aren't going to check their email every day either, and when you do talk to them it's probably when they are on a job, so it's likely they won't write down what was discussed and may forget it without meaning to.

Understanding the challenges that come with working with most investor-friendly contractors allows you to put systems together to mitigate those challenges. Adjusting your expectations of them to reasonable levels allows you to maintain a positive attitude and have an enjoyable experience. Expecting to pay them like investor-friendly contractors but receive the service of a primary residence contractor is a mistake and will surely lead to disappointment that can have a negative impact on your business.

If you want to determine what kind of contractor you're interviewing, there is one simple question to ask: Do you often work with investors? If the answer is "no," odds are you are going to have a mini heart attack when you see the prices on their bid. If the answer is "yes," you should follow up with more questions to determine just what they mean by "investor." Their definition may be different than yours, and it's important to note that. You need to clarify if they have worked with landlords who own rental property who are looking to make it rent-ready as economically as possible.

Contractors who are experienced working on jobs like these are invaluable. Not only will you like their prices, but you'll also find they will have solutions to problems you thought you needed to fix yourself. Because they have experience working on these kinds of properties, they may know a cheap fix to the broken cabinets, or a way to sand and stain a bathroom vanity rather than buy a new one. These solutions can save you money, time, and headache.

I only work with these kinds of contractors, and I've learned to give them a lot of leeway on my jobs. I want them telling me what they think we should do so I can review my options to make the best decision. When they know how I think, they are much more likely to have already done some of the legwork when it comes to alternative solutions. This saves me time and presents me with alternatives I may not have looked into myself. I don't need to be the expert in everything to make money; I just need to know the expert. You don't need to have superpowers yourself if you've surrounded yourself with the Avengers!

Turning Your Bid into a Contract

We've already discussed several of the reasons why you want your bid itemized. I think you can agree this is a good system. I am about to propose something that makes it even better. Once your bid has been reviewed by you, your business partners, and your contractor, you can easily convert it into the contract with the terms stating what work will be done and what price it'll be done for. There are just a few small things to add and you're ready to sign and let them start working.

The first thing you'll need to add to the bid is the timeline for the job to be completed. This is something I always recommend, unless you're okay with the contractor taking an indefinite period of time to finish the work and you lose out on rent, not to mention lost opportunity from properties you could have bought after the refinance. There is a system I use to determine how long we should agree that a property will take to be rehabbed, or "turned," and it's worked very well for me so far.

Before I explain, I'll tell you that I came up with this system because contractors and handymen are notorious for going over the time they agreed to when they accepted the job. The problem is, there is really no penalty for them to take too long, but there is often a penalty if they get it done on time. This penalty for a timely finish doesn't come from you—it comes from the other work they had to turn down where the owner wanted it started before they finished on yours. In order to get that job, they likely had to pull people off yours to start over there. This means your job still gets done, but much slower. Throw in that people call in sick, one subcontractor messes up and that throws everyone else off, and a host of other problems and you can see why these jobs always end up taking too long.

My solution has been to ask the contractor how long they think it will take them to finish the project. I don't want them to feel pressured to agree to my timeline (which would always be aggressively short if it was up to me), I want them to give me a time they believe they can get the job done in. Let's say Carl Contractor agrees to finish the job in eight weeks. After I'm told eight weeks, I ask them again, "Are you *positive* you can do eight weeks? It's okay if you take longer, I just need to know up front so I can plan around it." Carl Contractor reconsiders and says nine weeks might be a better bet, just to be safe. At that point I would once again confirm nine weeks is a number he truly believes he can do, without much problem, and Carl Contractor agrees he can.

I then say, "Okay, Carl, I'm actually going to give you *ten* weeks to get this job done, and we've already agreed on the price for the job. Here's the thing, if you get it done in ten weeks, I'm going to add a bonus of 5 percent of the total job cost onto the last draw I send you. That's my way of rewarding you for doing a great job and hoping to build upon our business relationship for the future. Does that sound good?"

Carl, of course, is usually ecstatic about this. I then follow up with "But here's the thing, if you go over ten weeks, I'm going to subtract 5 percent of the total job cost from the last draw. And for every week above that, I'm going to subtract another 5 percent. I need to be very sure you're being real with me here, and not just telling me what I want to hear."

This is the moment of truth. Carl Contractor's reaction will tell me if he's been up front or full of crap this whole time. If Carl is excited and agrees to this request, it means he believes in himself and his numbers and is excited to earn a bonus. If he starts to backpedal, stammer, or make excuses, it may mean he was only telling me what I wanted to hear and had no intention of doing everything within his power to finish on time.

Can you see why I do this? I want to know if my contractor is serious, or if they are telling me whatever they can to get the job. I know that I will keep my word, and hold up my end of the bargain. I will pay the contractor what I agreed to pay him, and I will make sure he's paid on time. This means I expect him to keep up his end of the bargain. He needs to perform the jobs mentioned in the scope of work and complete them in the timeline specified. There are bonuses and penalties if he doesn't hold up his end, just like I can be sued if I don't hold up my end.

Once we've got these dates worked out, I spell out what the time frame will be on the bid we've agreed to. Then I put in a quick blurb detailing the bonus and penalty clause and I have both parties sign the contract. While I'm not an attorney (which means you should definitely check with one before signing contracts or going forward with advice from this book!), and I'm sure there are ways that are more likely to hold up in court should something go wrong, I've found that this is the cheapest, easiest, and most convenient way to create an agreement between yourself and a contractor. It spells out, very clearly, both parties' expectations as well as compensation and penalties should the contract be breached.

Creating a System with Your Contractor for Repeat Business

So far I've mentioned several methods of finding a rockstar contractor that have worked for me and my partners in the past. It's a lot of work to find one, but once you do, you're in a solid position within your business. In order to be more efficient and focus your efforts on finding deals or deal finders, you want to avoid looking for a new rockstar contractor on every job. Once you find one, it's important to keep them!

If you've established a strong relationship with your contractor and you know the two of you will be working together for the foreseeable future, the next step is creating a system the two of you are comfortable with. If you can systemize (this is a theme that runs throughout every part of BRRRR and will save you a lot of money in the long run) the way you interact with each other, you can create consistent expectations and a process that is repeatable, scalable, and profitable.

The first step to creating this system is establishing the way bids will be received over time. Getting your bids in the same way, every time, creates a level of consistency that allows you to evaluate the rehab numbers quickly and make good decisions expeditiously. In addition to that, it allows the contractor to make sure they aren't overcharging you, because it's easy for you to catch those numbers. This forces them to look for ways to bring value to you, not just collect large amounts of money!

Once you have this systemized, the next step is creating a consistency in the amounts you pay for the same jobs you see on the bid with every project. We want to establish a "base rate" that the contractor charges for certain jobs and ensure that base rate stays more or less the same on every job. Creating a base rate allows you to recognize immediately if a price is off and saves you time from having to look for a second opinion on every single line item, every single time.

An easy place to start with this is paint. Most contactors give paint estimates based on the square footage of the house (at least for interior paint; exterior paint has a few more variables involved). If the house is 2,000 square feet, and the contractor charges $2 a square foot, they would give you an estimate of $4,000 to paint the interior of your property. If you get used to this number, you can do some quick math in your head or your phone's calculator to verify this number is in line with what you've paid before and what you're on board with paying now.

Once you understand how a contractor determines what they'll charge you, you can work out a base rate for each job. This will leave you feeling in control and empowered in your interactions with your contractor. My advice is to start with the line items that just about every rental you will buy will need, and come up with a base rate for each one.

A few of the more common items involved on most of my rehabs are:
- Paint
- Flooring
- Shower and bathroom remodels
- Landscaping
- Dry rot repair

- Countertops
- Painting cabinets
- Removing trees
- Roofs
- HVAC installation
- Adding closets
- Hanging doors
- Installing slightly used appliances
- Installing ceiling fans
- Installing new vanities
- Installing new toilets
- Installing new light and bathroom fixtures
- Installing new baseboards
- Replacing windows
- Cleaning

These are certain issues I deal with on nearly every rental I buy because they come up time and time again when I'm going over the estimate with the contractor. Once I realized I was paying the same amount for the labor on a bathroom remodel, I came up with a base rate the contractor would charge me for a bathroom remodel and then just added the material cost to that. This was the beginning of how I learned to estimate rehab costs and it was a big help to my business.

For the items that frequently occur, ask your contractor how they came up with the amount they charged you for one of them. Let's take ceiling fan installation for example. You look at the bid and see they are charging you $200 per fan. You ask where they got that number from. They tell you a fan costs $125 at the store, and they have to pay someone to go pick them up and drive them to the site. Then, they have to pay this person to install them.

You can quickly see if the fan costs $125 and you're paying $200, they are making $75 in labor. If a trip to the store and back takes 1.5 hours, and it takes another hour to install it, you would just take 2.5 hours and divide that into the labor cost ($75 for labor divided by 2.5 = $30 an hour). This is a very competitive cost for you! Now, if you're smart you realized they only have to make one trip to the store and back to buy several fans, so if they are installing four, only one of them would take 2.5 hours. The rest would take about an hour. The difference in these amounts is how the contractor is going to make money for managing the project. The rest of the money would be going to the person they hired to do the work for them.

You can repeat this same process and logic for all the other items you are likely to come across on your deals.

How much will they charge to demo and retile a shower?

How much will they charge per square foot for labor to install flooring?

How much will they charge to install granite countertops on a standard kitchen?

Asking questions like this forces you to understand the contractor's point of view. Once you understand it, it allows you to come up with a solution that works for both of you. Remember, you are the business person in this agreement, they are the labor. They may run a business, but odds are they don't understand the big picture like you do. If you can help them become more successful, and help yourself in the process, you can ensure a steady stream of deals coming in that will make both of you money and keep both of you happy.

Upgrade Hacking

"Upgrade hacking" is a term I coined in my last book, *Long-Distance Real Estate Investing*, used to describe how to get maximum value out of your rehab by being wise and looking for ways to add value for less money. At its foundation, upgrade hacking is a way of learning to take advantage of certain parts of the rehab process so you can use better, higher quality, or more expensive materials without having to pay as much as you normally would.

In order to upgrade hack successfully, you want to look for opportunities in the rehab process to maximize your value without having to pay full price for it. There are times when using expensive materials will cost much more than makes sense (like tiling an entire house). There are other times when using top-of-the-line materials will make a huge impression for not much money (like tiling a shower or a small bathroom floor). Learning to spot opportunities like this during your rehab can give you an edge over other investors and help your property appraise for top dollar.

The reason most investors miss these opportunities is they don't understand how real estate works. When we lack knowledge, we resort to fear. This fear often compels us to do everything we can to save money, because this feels safe. It is too simple to assume saving money is the only way to increase your profits, and the wise investor learns to see the big picture. Oftentimes, spending more on a rehab in strategic ways can provide a big return on your investment when it comes to the value of your property, or to the vacancy costs associated with waiting to find a tenant. Our goals as black belt investors should always be to achieve the highest ROI possible, not just to save money.

My perspective is to think deeper than just "paying less money is better." Obviously paying less money is a way you can create value in a rehab, but it's not the only way. Remember, we are trying to fill a bucket with as much water as possible. That water is the equity we get in a deal. Equity is the difference between what you put into a property and what it's worth. This means there are two ways to grow it. You either put less in, or you make it worth more.

Upgrade hacking is all about making a property worth more, for less money than it would normally cost. It is a mind-set of looking for ways to get the most value for the least money, and it involves an understanding of how properties are valued as well as an understanding of what materials cost. When we marry these two pieces of information, we are able to look for relatively cheap ways to add value that wouldn't have been apparent to us if we weren't educated.

Common Upgrade Hacks

Upgrade hacks will help you in several ways. When you add up all these different ways they can equal big results. When we look at the most common ways upgrade hacking makes you money, it boils down to four things.

1. Better materials are used in your project
2. Less vacancy
3. Higher rent
4. Higher ARV

As we discuss different upgrade hacks, nearly all of them will fall into one of these four categories. Oftentimes the most common ones will cover more than one category, and most of them will cover at least the bottom three! I won't be able to cover every single upgrade hack possible—just some of the most common ones I use myself. This means it's essential you learn the concept so you can come up with some new ideas to use in your own projects when the opportunity arises.

Bathrooms

One of the most common and easy-to-implement upgrade hacks is using high-end, expensive tile when the surface area it will cover is small. This is most often found in bathroom floors or bathroom showers. Most of us are trained to look for the cheapest materials possible. This is because conventional wisdom states tenants will often be very rough on your property and spending money on nice things is wasteful because you will have to replace them again later.

This is definitely true when it comes to most things in real estate investing. Spending too much money on hardwood floors, granite countertops, or top-of-the-line cabinets and baseboards is usually a big mistake. The reason is twofold:

1. Those are items that can be easily destroyed.
2. Those are items that usually cover a large surface area—meaning you need to pay for a lot of them!

The reason this works in bathrooms is because tile is extremely durable (taking care of reason No. 1) and the surface areas of most bathrooms are on the smaller side (taking care of reason No. 2.). By using upgraded, hand-crafted, durable materials in a bathroom, we can increase the overall appearance and "wow" factor, without increasing our budget by much. Here's why:

Let's say you want to replace the disgusting, rotted linoleum in the master bathroom of the rental you just bought. This linoleum needs to be replaced, regardless of what you replace it with. The contractor gives you a bid based on the following information:

1. Demo: $150
2. Labor to replace flooring: $350
3. Materials (Option A) 18 square feet of tile at $3 a square foot: $54
4. Materials (Option B) 18 square feet of tile at $10 a square foot: $180

Now, as you can see, the different in the price of the tile itself is significant. Option B is more than three times as expensive as Option A (capital O). To the untrained mind, this would translate to the job costing three times as much if we use the nicer tile than if we use the cheaper tile. But not so fast!

Consider that items 1 and 2 are "fixed cost" items. These are expenses you will be paying regardless of what tile you choose, and their price is "fixed" in that it doesn't change based on the material. It takes the same amount of time to lay tile, regardless of its cost, and it takes the same amount of time to demo the flooring, regardless of the materials you choose. When we look at the total cost of the job, we find that the fixed costs represent a much larger chunk of the total budget than the material costs. This is why the upgrade hack starts to make sense!

Even though Option B tile is over three times as expensive as Option A tile, it still represents an over-project cost increase of only 18.5 percent. If we convert that into actual dollars, it's only $126 more to do the project with incredible materials and looking fantastic vs. the most basic and cheapest materials available. How can this be when Option B tile is 333 percent more expensive and nicer than Option A?

The reason is the fixed costs make up the majority of the cost for this project. You are going to be paying these costs regardless of the tile. Furthermore, you *have* to pay these costs because the flooring needs to be changed if you want to rent the place out at all! If you consider that your fixed costs ($500) are an expense you are going to be paying no matter what, the only decision you need to make is what material to choose.

If you were buying more than 18 square feet of tile, the difference in price would start to make a substantial difference in your budget. Buying 300 square feet of a material that is 333 percent more expensive than the cheaper alternative will add up BIG time. Due to the fact we are only buying a small amount of the material, we can get away with buying the nicer stuff for only $126 dollars more. Makes sense, right?

The difference in the appearance of the finished product you'll get from a bathroom remodeled with top-of-the-line materials is night and day compared to using the cheapest stuff possible, but the overall increase in price is very nominal. Because bathrooms are usually smaller spaces, they are frequently eligible for upgrade hack opportunities.

As a general rule, whenever you find the amount of material you need is a small amount, consider an upgrade hack as a possibility. This is especially true when you're using a durable material you likely won't need to replace anytime soon. In addition to floors in bathrooms, showers can be a great place to upgrade hack.

When you're replacing a shower, you'll typically have three options. A shower insert, "builder grade" sheets, or tile. When choosing which option will be best for you, you'll need to consider the area your rental is in, the ARVs of surrounding properties, and the rent discrepancy between the high and low rent prices. We'll talk more about why that matters later, but for now, I want to point out that your best upgrade hack opportunities will come when you're able to justify tiling a shower.

Much like the bathroom floor option, a shower has numbers that look similar. Showers have small surface areas and therefore are great candidates for using better materials. They also make a great impression when done well, and renters and buyers alike will enjoy the upgrade if you're intending to flip. Bathrooms are a big "bang for your buck" category when it comes to the impact they make on the value of a property.

If the area you're in supports upgrading your shower, consider doing a tile shower that feels modern if possible. Of course, this would only be the case if you need to do a new shower anyway. It wouldn't make sense to tear out a perfectly fine shower just to tile one. But if you have to replace it, you have a great upgrade hack opportunity. In the majority of houses I buy, the bathrooms are so outdated and in such terrible condition I would need to redo them just to have something I could even rent out.

Consider that the tile for a shower, like the bathroom floor, is also going to cover a small surface area. Since you won't be buying much material, consider getting something that is high-end to make an impression and also increase your ARV. Your demo cost and labor cost will be fixed, but material costs will vary and investing in these small spaces create the opportunity to increase the value of your property.

While using expensive tile for small areas can pay off, don't go overboard with the bathroom details if they won't add value. If you want to install a rainfall showerhead, consider the consequences: repairs for an item that isn't needed, or unnecessary spending for something in a low-end rental. Also, consider the work already being done in the rehab. The thing that makes adding a rainfall showerhead affordable is if you already have to rip out the existing shower and expose the plumbing. The rainfall showerhead itself can be bought for under $200. The additional plumbing and valve you need can be purchased and installed for under $200 as well. For less than $400, you can add a luxurious item like a rainfall showerhead, as long as you're tearing out the existing shower and exposing the plumbing in a way that makes it easy for your contractor to put in.

The last area I look to upgrade hack in a bathroom is the sink or vanity area. If you already need to replace it, consider spending a couple hundred dollars more and getting a vanity with a granite countertop and upgraded faucet. For a couple hundred bucks, you can get much more durable materials and a big wow factor—assuming those items needed replacing.

Kitchen

The kitchen is the next place I look to upgrade hack. This is because it is another area that is highly likely to need many renovations—or a total gut job—during a BRRRR remodel. Kitchens are the biggest "bang for your buck" area of a property. With this being the case, you are statistically more likely to be doing rehab work in your kitchen, leading to more opportunities for upgrade hacks.

One way to accomplish a quick and easy upgrade hack in the kitchen is to purchase stainless steel appliances instead of standard white appliances in situations where the appliances need to be replaced anyway. Appliances aren't cheap, and replacing perfectly fine and operational appliances with newer, nicer, fancier ones is usually a bad use of money in a rental property.

However, if the appliances need to be replaced anyway, the only extra money you're spending is the difference in price between standard and stainless steel. It typically costs a few hundred dollars more to replace your appliances with stainless steel versions.[2] Pretty sweet price to pay to get an updated kitchen!

Another way to hack your kitchen remodel is to use granite countertops instead of tile or laminate versions in situations where you need to replace them anyway. I've bought and seen homes before where the countertop is in such bad condition that it can literally be lifted off of the cabinets where it rests, and if someone leaned against it, it would shift. When this is the case, it often leads to water damage of the cabinetry underneath. As the wood cabinets rot, the countertop won't sit evenly on them anymore. This leads to cabinet repair/replacement and the need for a new countertop as well.

If you're already replacing the countertops, look at the price difference between granite and other options. In the last five years or so, I've seen a huge decrease in the price for granite slabs that are used in kitchens.

---

2 Van Thompson, "How Much Do Stainless Steel Appliances Cost?" The Nest. https://budgeting.thenest.com/much-stainless-steel-appliances-cost-30078.html

If your contractor has an employee or sub that can install the granite for a reasonable price, you just may have yourself a money-saving hack. Granite is much more durable than other options and difficult for tenants to wear down or break. The big thing to look out for here is the price of the labor to install them. If you can get that part squared away, you can accomplish this hack pretty easily.

If you're going to be replacing the countertops, you'll probably want to replace the backsplash as well (or add one if you don't have one). Look at pictures of kitchens with and without a backsplash—it makes a big difference. If you're trying to avoid spending big money on your backsplash, ask the person installing the countertops to use the extra countertop granite to make the backsplash with. You most likely won't have to purchase anything new, and the only extra cost will be the labor involved. If the employee was well priced for installing your granite, they'll likely be well-priced for installing the backsplash, too.

Miscellaneous Items

Dry rot is a form of fungus that damages wood (usually on the exterior of the house). When wood gets wet, this fungus can grow and start "eating" through the wood. Signs of dry rot are clear when the wood appears rotted to the eye, or soft and mushy to the touch. If left uncorrected, the fungus will eventually destroy the wood completely and lead to a costly replacement. If large parts of your property are affected by it, you may end up buying tons of lumber, then paying for paint and labor to have all your rotted wood replaced. Extremely expensive.

When you need to have something painted, ask the painter if they are capable of repairing dry rot. If they are, you have a great opportunity to save some money. Dry rot can be nipped in the bud if you are able to cut out the affected wood and either replace it with wood filler or smaller pieces of wood and connected together. If you don't catch it in time, the entirety of the wood will rot. If you do, you can fix it for a small fraction of the cost. Knowing that dry rot will continually take money from you the longer it exists, you can save yourself a lot of money by catching it in its infancy.

When landscaping, consider using items that won't likely ever need to be replaced. Pouring concrete is more expensive than putting down sod, but it's very difficult to mess up concrete. Sod can die pretty easily and your tenants aren't likely to take as good of care of it as you would.

Using mulch can be another great hack, particularly because it's so cheap. Mulch can be bought for a couple of dollars a bag and can be replaced with every vacancy for a very low amount of money. If you put in a yard that relies on a complicated sprinkler system, you are adding more things that can break and unnecessarily increasing your repair costs.

If you buy a property with carpet that needs to be replaced (this will happen often, trust me), consider replacing it with a very tough and durable laminate instead of more carpet. Carpet is the cheapest option, but it's also the least durable and easiest to be ruined. You are almost guaranteeing you'll be replacing it with every new tenant, or at least every other new tenant. While laminate is more expensive at first, it will save you lots of money in the long run. In addition to that, your house will likely appraise for more because of it! This gives you multiple benefits, which is the spirit of upgrade hacking.

Why Upgrade Hacking Fits Well with the BRRRR Model

The point of upgrade hacking is to find fixed costs (things you had to do anyway) and add value through creating work with your variable costs (using better materials, adding simple upgrades, etc.). Knowing this, I've discovered that upgrade hacking is most efficient when significant work already needed to be done. It's very hard to work this angle on "turnkey" properties (those that don't need any work other than to "turn the key" and open the door) because you have no fixed costs. If you're buying properties in good condition, there is no reason to upgrade hack.

Upgrade hacking works best on properties that need lots of work. The more you will be ripping out, reconfiguring, or replacing, the more opportunities you'll have to upgrade hack. This fits so well within the BRRRR model because BRRRR properties typically need significant work! We target run-down properties when we BRRRR because we want to add value before pulling our money out. Statistically speaking, we are way more likely to be doing big rehabs on BRRRR properties because that was our play to add value in the first place.

Remember, we want to be buying houses in such bad shape they likely won't even qualify for a loan. That means the houses will be in seriously bad shape. Of course, this won't be every deal, but it will be a lot of them! Knowing this is the case, we need to build a specific skill set that will enable us to be good in the areas that are the most significant. The two most important skills you can develop are finding deals and fixing up deals. Much like a professional athlete trains the most to improve skills that will help the team win (why pitchers are usually terrible at batting), we want to apply this same philosophy to our business.

So, if we know the BRRRR model gives us a mathematically higher likelihood of doing lots of rehab work, and we know the upgrade hacking model is more successful in projects with a lot of rehab work, it would make sense that the two strategies would fit hand in hand. There is a synergistic quality to pairing both strategies. Because I've done so many BRRRR projects, I've created the concept of upgrade hacking as a way to get more value out of my deals that make me a better investor in the process.

Remember earlier in the book when I mentioned the goal of BRRRR is to spend as little money as possible to purchase a property, then improve its ARV as much as possible? The difference between those two numbers is where our value is created, and the more value we create the more money we get back out of the deal. This is the whole purpose of BRRRR. Well, upgrade hacking is designed to make your property worth more without spending significantly more. It's a system created by looking for inefficiencies in your rehab and trying to root them out.

To me, upgrade hacking is the equivalent of what fast-food restaurants do with their combo meals (without being terrible for you, of course). If you were already planning on buying a burger and a soda, you can add on fries for an additional 50 cents if you do the combo. Normally, the fries would cost $3 on their own, and you'd never buy them. But if you are buying the burger and soda anyway, and are already committed to it, paying an extra 50 cents for fries isn't a bad use of money.

Of course, comparing fast food to real estate can be a bit of a stretch, but the concept is the same. If you're already paying the fixed costs for a project (labor), and the fixed costs make up the majority of your project's budget, why not spend an incremental amount more to get way more value? If the point of BRRRR is to push your ARV up as much as possible by spending as little as possible, it only makes sense to do this.

Black belt investors don't take the lazy road. They don't go with the cheapest option just because it's the cheapest option. They go with the *best* option, and they use their intelligence, experience, and creativity to decide what that option will be. This is our goal, and this is why we study real estate, so we can make the best choice and build our wealth the fastest!

Key Points

- A rockstar contractor is a must-have.
- Use leverage to amplify your results. Who on your team can help you with the things you need done?
- Make top priorities your top priority. Don't waste time on unimportant tasks.
- Memorize how talent acts and what it looks like.
- Find team members for your Core Four that also invest.
- Bring value in relationships first.
- Use itemized bids with contractors for an apples-to-apples comparison.
- Memorize and practice common rehab hacks.
- Use "investor-friendly contractors."
- Spend the bulk of your rehab budget on the kitchen and bathrooms when possible.

CHAPTER FIVE

Common Rehab Strategies

"Art is pattern informed by sensibility."

—HERBERT READ

As you continually purchase fixer-upper rental properties, you'll start to recognize patterns in your rehab that end up being repeated time and time again. The better you get at recognizing these patterns, the more successful your rehabs will become and the less stress you'll feel each time. This is the way our brains work, and it's the science behind why experience leads to success. The more we experience something, the more opportunities our brains have to recognize patterns and make adjustments to improve our performance.

As you continue to grow as an investor, you'll start to recognize these patterns as well. In this chapter, we are going to cover some of the more common rehab strategies to add value to your properties. My hope is that as you begin to notice the patterns in your rehabs, you'll take that same skill and apply it to the other parts of BRRRR. Learning to find these patterns of success at every level is how you'll become a black belt investor.

Adding Square Footage to Increase Your Property's Value
One of the very best ways to add value to your property is to make it more desirable—as you know. But one of the best ways to make your property

more valuable is to add square footage to a property that is smaller than ideal. This works especially well when your property has less square footage than the average surrounding properties. By adding more square feet, you make it easier for the appraiser to give more value to your property because you made it comparable to surrounding properties. You also make it more desirable to tenants looking to move to the area who know what the other houses look like, how big they are, and how much space their desired rent will get them.

If this is an option for you, consider looking for parts of the addition that are already in place. For example, it may cost $30,000 to build an entire new master bedroom. However, if you find a property that already has a concrete pad poured, has an overhang (roof extension), has electrical run to it (outdoor patio fan), or is very close to indoor plumbing, you can likely make this part of the square footage of your property for very little extra money.

Check with your contractor to find out what the rules are in your area first. Once you know them, ask them how much it would cost to make this addition part of the square footage of your property. Sometimes this involves running HVAC to the space, other times it means having both plumbing and electrical run. Whatever hoops you may have to jump through, if you can find a way to spend $5,000–$10,000 to add additional square feet, you can often improve your property's ARV an additional $10,000–$40,000. I actively look to do this on every single BRRRR property I buy, and it allows me to grow my wealth much, much faster.

Why does this work? It's because of the way appraisers value property. While it's not the same in every market, most of the time appraisers are taking the square footage of a property, multiplying it by the price per square foot of comparable properties, and then adjusting that number based on varying amenities. If I know an appraiser is going to start with two numbers (the price per square foot and the total square feet), wouldn't it make sense for me to do everything I can to pump both those numbers up?

I can only improve the price per square foot by making my property more similar to surrounding properties. This is typically done in the rehab process and is affected by the materials I choose. I can only improve the square footage of the home by adding square feet. Additionally, this only brings value if your property is less than or at least equal to the surrounding properties regarding its size. If you already have the biggest house in the area, making it bigger won't make it worth more. What we want to do is look for properties that are unusually small and make them bigger. This is where we get the most bang for our buck. Understanding how appraisers work makes this possible.

If we do this right, I find that the price to build new square footage is usually less than the added value that square footage provides. This is especially true if it's an upgrade hack and I can build onto the property without having to do it from scratch (already has a roof, foundation, etc.). If you talk with your contractor and find that the price to build is less than the value that square footage brings, look deeper into seeing if this is an option for you.

Adding Bedrooms and Bathrooms

Another way to add value to your property is increase the numbers of bedrooms or bathrooms it has. Homes built with less than three bedrooms won't meet the needs of a growing family the same way a home with three or four bedrooms can. Many older homes were built with two bedrooms and one bathroom. That was acceptable for the time in which they were built, but it makes the property worth much less than what it could be worth if some changes were made to make the property more suitable for a larger family.

If a house has less than three bedrooms, you can increase its value significantly (in most cases) by adding more bedrooms to it. While you can add value by adding bedrooms, keep in mind there is a point of diminishing returns. The biggest value jump is from two to three bedrooms, as there are more people looking for three-bedroom homes than two-bedroom homes. The next biggest is from three to four, and so on. While every market is different, the general rule applies that adding bedrooms to smaller homes will almost always increase their value.

A great upgrade hack is to take an area of the house that isn't providing much value and convert that into a bedroom. In most cases all you need to pay for is some drywall, a closet, and possibly some French doors. This is an extremely cheap way to add a large amount of value to a property.

An easy way to do this is to look for a two-bedroom home with over 1,100 square feet. If you find a home this size with only two bedrooms, there is a very good chance it has a space inside that could be converted to an additional bedroom without spending money to add on to the property.

You want to look for spaces like dining rooms, dens, offices, utility rooms, or living rooms that are not being used to their full potential. Once you find them, look to see if there is sufficient space to build a closet, put up drywall, and add a door. If there is, you just likely bumped up your ARV significantly for a few thousand dollars of work.

This works because of a concept in real estate called "functional obsolescence." Functional obsolescence is a term used to describe when a design feature of a property is so out-of-date or undesirable that it renders the property (or at least that section of the property) useless. Improving efficiencies are what we look to do to add value to properties. A common one is a two-bedroom home. If you can add a third bedroom, or a fourth bedroom to a three-bedroom home, you can make the property more desirable to a large number of families, making your property worth more in the process.

This same concept works for homes with one bathroom. Would you want to live in a one-bathroom property? That sounds horrible for anyone living with more than one person (although I know a lot of people do this!). Adding a second bathroom to a configuration like this can add quite a bit of value to the property and make it much easier to rent out. While we want to make a property worth as much as we can, we don't want to overspend to accomplish that.

Remember that when homes were built a long time ago, they were intended as "starter" homes for new families. As soon as a family had a need for a third bedroom they would move to another property and sell the one they were in. This would create an available house for a new family looking for a starter home and the cycle would continue.

The problem is families today are getting started before couples are buying houses. With today's generation valuing home ownership much less than they did before, many millennials aren't buying homes until they *already* have several children.[3] The same pattern is reflected in renting homes. Most people start with apartments and don't leave the apartment for a rental home until they need three bedrooms. This means you aren't going to find many tenants looking for two-bedroom properties, so there isn't much reason for you to own one.

---

3   Beth Braverman, "4 Reasons Millennials Still Aren't Buying Houses," *Forbes* (September 24, 2015). https://www.forbes.com/sites/bethbraverman/2015/09/24/4-reasons-millennials-still-arent-buying-houses/#53ea10102dcb
    Jessica Guerin, "More Young Families Opt to Rent Instead of Buy," *HousingWire* (July 16, 2018). https://www.housingwire.com/articles/46079-more-young-families-opt-to-rent-instead-of-buy

This why we look for opportunities to "hack" whenever possible. We do want to add value to our properties; we just don't want to pay top dollar to do so. Whenever I'm looking at new properties, the *first* thing I look for is where I can add square footage and where I can add a bedroom or a bathroom (assuming it needs this). Quite simply, this is the fastest way to skyrocket your property's ARV and receive the highest return on your money!

When you take a "starter" home and turn it into a "forever" home, you increase its value by a significant amount. This helps on your ARV and ultimately your refinance. It also means you'll get much more rent for the property and your tenants won't have to move out as often. (Having a tenant start off needing two bedrooms and then having one more child is virtually a guarantee they'll be moving out and into a bigger place.) From several angles, it makes the most sense to add a third bedroom or a second bathroom whenever possible.

Adding Value through Strategic Remodeling

When undertaking any kind of significant remodel, you'll want to make sure the areas you're spending your money on are the areas that will get you the best return. Going all out on crown molding in the family room or designing and installing a super fancy fireplace structure may be elegant, but it isn't likely to add much value to your property—both from an appraiser's standpoint or a renter's. Knowing where to put the bulk of your budget is an important part to rehabbing like a pro, and learning these common strategies should help you get there.

As a general rule, kitchens and bathrooms are the two areas where you are likely to get the most out of the money you invest in them, as mentioned before. Both appraisers and renters are going to give the most value to the kitchen and bathrooms—especially the master bathroom. Knowing this, we want to put the bulk of our effort, energy, and money into these two key areas as effectively as we can. If you can learn to remodel a kitchen and a bathroom, you are on your way to being able to handle an entire rehab.

I've already mentioned several upgrade hacks you can accomplish pretty easily in the kitchen. There are a few more ways you can learn to save money and add value on a rehab as well. For example, you can save on remodeling your kitchen by painting kitchen cabinets rather than replacing them. Many investors make the mistake of assuming they need to replace cabinets in every property they buy. This isn't true! I rarely ever replace them and in the majority of fixer-upper properties I buy, I paint them.

Paint makes a big, *big* difference in the appearance of your cabinets. Even though it's "just" paint, I can't state enough how much it can bring to life ugly, worn, or outdated cabinets. There are many different colors to choose from, and painting your cabinets gives you the ability to match them to the other upgrades you put in the kitchen. If you really want a killer finish, spend $60 and add new, clean, fresh-looking hardware to them. They are easy to install and inexpensive, adding value at little cost to you.

In most modern-day kitchens, people are opting for either very dark cabinets or white/light gray cabinets. I've found that it's one extreme or the other. You want to avoid the old brown oak style, and if you have those types already in there, stain them a darker color. Contractors usually aren't huge fans of painting cabinets as it's a time- and labor-intensive process, but if they give you a good price on the bid, I'd highly recommend the update.

Another area to consider in your kitchen is tiling the floor instead of putting laminate or linoleum. The kitchen floor is going to take a beating and will get worn or damaged faster than anywhere in the house, and a material like tile will be more durable and take the punishment. Also, the majority of kitchens you are buying in a fixer-upper property are not huge, luxurious, magazine-spread kitchens. They are smaller and more efficient. Much like the bathroom floor example we discussed, you can use a more expensive material without paying a ton more for it.

An easy way to accomplish this is to use the same tile for your kitchen that you used for your bathrooms. The contractors can pick it up in one trip, or you can have it delivered in one load. If you get a good price for it, you can just order enough to do both parts of the house. Once you find a tile you really like, you'll probably start ordering the same one for every job. This hack saves you time and effort in that you don't have to go looking for a new tile every time you work a rehab project. Experienced flippers and fixer-upper investors tend to use the same materials, over and over, on every project.

Many of the hacks that work in a kitchen will also work in a bathroom. Just like painting kitchen cabinets, you can paint bathroom cabinets as well. One of my favorite strategies is to ask your contractor how much it will be to paint the kitchen cabinets and negotiate them down to a price you're comfortable with. Once that's accomplished, tell them you'd like to throw the bathroom cabinets in as well for the same price per hour.

They can use the same paint, and the same subcontractor can do the work. Easy solution for everybody!

Though you can save money on—and add value to—bathroom remodels by tiling a shower, *don't* put in a glass shower door. The reason is pretty simple—glass shower doors are extremely expensive, easy to break, and easy to get moldy. They need to be cleaned frequently and your tenants often won't do this. Furthermore, they don't do much to improve the aesthetics of your bathroom, at least not for the amount of money you spend on one.

Another bathroom remodel strategy is to consider replacing your standard toilets with low-flow toilet and sink options in your rentals. This is an obvious choice when you are paying for the water in your rental. If you own a multiunit property and the building isn't individually metered, you will likely end up paying for the water, and a low-flow toilet or sink will save you money. Having a unit individually metered for electricity will often cost several thousand dollars, but in many cases that is an investment that will be recovered in year one! What I'm presenting here is that using low-flow options may be a good idea even if you aren't paying for the water.

I put low-flow toilets in all my rentals, and I let the property manager know to advertise my units with this information. For tenants who may really want your rental but are having a hard time justifying the rent you're asking for, let them know how much they're saving on the water bill. And if they're environmentally conscious, they'll see the value in the low-flow features. Remember, most people make monetary decisions based on their emotions and look to logic to rationalize or justify it. By rehabbing a rental to look great, you'll be making them want to live there. By adding in money-saving features like low-flow toilets, you help them justify the cost. This leads to less vacancy time and higher rent for you in the long run.

Landscaping Tricks

If you're buying fixer-upper properties at a discount, you can pretty much guarantee you'll be doing a good deal of landscaping in the process. If the owner of a home lets the building itself deteriorate to the point of a rehab overhaul, do you think they would have made the effort to take care of the yard? It would make sense to learn some landscaping tricks to save you money while getting your property in rentable condition!

When looking at the landscaping budget, I like to break the work down into two categories: cheap labor and skilled labor. I've found that on the majority of my projects I am either paying someone to do "grunt" work or paying someone to do skilled work that takes experience and training. The trick is to find a way to get cheap labor to do as much as possible and only use skilled labor when you absolutely must.

Cheap labor is best reserved for jobs that may be a lot of work, but don't require much skill to accomplish. This would be things like weed pulling, laying sod, laying mulch, hauling things off to the dump, breaking up concrete, planting flowers, etc. Cheap labor is one of your best friends as an investor, primarily because you shouldn't be doing work that isn't skilled! The skills you have as an investor (or even someone who has already read this far in the book) put you in an elite level of business acumen. If you're at that level, saving $10–$12 an hour to pull your own weeds isn't a good use of your time, skills, or resources.

Skilled labor is different. Skilled labor is more along the lines of someone who can pour concrete, build retaining walls, install gas lines, install sprinkler lines, etc. We want to avoid skilled labor as much as possible when investing in real estate because skilled labor is expensive. Oftentimes you are paying someone for a job that requires a license, extensive training, years of experience, or all three.

The trick to getting landscaping done for cheap is to use cheap labor to accomplish as much of the project as humanly possible, and use skilled labor to finish up what cheap labor couldn't do. By taking advantage of low wages for low-skill work, you get more bang for your buck. The truth is, if you're buying fixer-upper rental properties, you really shouldn't have a need for skilled labor much anyway. Finding a good, reliable handyman who can do yard work and landscaping to make your properties look presentable on a budget is a huge asset to have.

One of my favorite landscaping hacks is to hire cheap labor to rip out the existing problems (weeds, broken up concrete, rocks, etc.) and replace them with options that are easy enough for cheap labor to handle. I don't want to rip out weeds and replace them with pavers. I want to rip out weeds and replace them with a border of mulch along the fence line that cheap labor can handle! If I can avoid skilled labor in my project, I can keep my budget down to a minimum.

Another trick for backyards is to put a cheap chain link fence in if you have a narrow side yard that isn't being used for much. This creates a cheap "dog run" (if you allow your tenants to have pets) and gives you an entire feature you can advertise and boast about in your property listing without requiring you to spend a lot of money. By taking advantage of the existing narrow area that wasn't being used for much, you can get by with putting a cheap gate up and advertising your unit as having a dog run.

When it comes to front yard landscaping, you want to stick to two things: Make sure you don't put in any plants that die easily, and you want to pay cheap labor to keep the bushes, weeds, and front lawn trimmed. Don't make the mistake of buying expensive plants to put in the front yard of the property, because your tenants won't be likely to take care of them. Instead, find something inexpensive and durable you can plant there. A couple bucks for each plant is more than enough to get the look you want without affecting your bottom line.

Miscellaneous Common Rehab Ideas

Flooring is another item you will find yourself commonly replacing in rental properties. For experienced investors, replacing flooring is usually done on every "turn" (when one tenant moves out and another moves in). Flooring takes a huge beating. It's the only part of a property that is being touched at all times as you walk all over it. It's where everything gets dropped, spilled, and broken. By nature, flooring is going to be one of the items your property needs replaced more than almost anything else.

Knowing this to be the case, we want to avoid using materials for flooring that are soft, easily stained, easily damaged, or overly expensive. Sure, you can put in super nice laminate or marble to make a property look great, but your tenants are going to be pretty hard on it. If you were looking to buy a commuter car to handle massive wear and tear, would you buy a Ferrari? Probably not. You'd buy a Honda Civic or some other durable, efficient, and relatively inexpensive vehicle to get the job done. When it comes to choosing our flooring, we want to find the Civic of floors.

In general, you've got four common options: carpet, wood, laminate, or tile. Carpet is the cheapest but least durable—not ideal. Wood looks the best but is very easily stained, scratched, or destroyed—also not ideal. Laminate is a happy medium of durability, aesthetics, and not too inexpensive. Tile is the most expensive but also the most durable.

What I've found is that laminate tends to be the happy medium that works best. It's easy to install (meaning lower "fixed" labor costs), very durable (check with the sales associate to find which brands will be toughest!), easy to clean, and hides damage well. As a general rule, I try to put laminate floors in as much of the house as possible, other than areas likely to receive a high level of damage like kitchens and bathrooms.

Carpet can still be a good option, but you want to keep it to low traffic areas like bedrooms. Most people don't do much walking around in their bedroom. Instead they lay on a bed or sit at a desk. Carpet is vulnerable, but in a bedroom I may just have it cleaned if it's in good shape when I buy the property. Just note: a bedroom is the only place I'll leave carpet in place. If you leave it in any high traffic area, it's going to be worn out, frayed, or stained within a short amount of time.

Tile is my favorite option for an area likely to take a beating or be exposed to significant liquid spills. Most of these spills take place in the bathroom or kitchen, so these are areas I lay down tile. As I mentioned when talking about rehab hacks, sometimes it's smart to splurge for the upgraded, really nice tile when you only need it in small quantities. This is often the case with bathrooms and kitchens.

So, to sum it up, when reviewing flooring options your best bet is to shoot for:

1. Tile in bathrooms and kitchens
2. Laminate everywhere else
3. Carpet in bedrooms if it's already in good shape

A few things to keep in mind: If you leave carpet, you'll probably be replacing it later. If you choose laminate, you'll be using a lot of it, so find something on sale or cheap that is also durable. If you choose tile, only use the expensive options if it's for a small surface area and you don't need to spend much on it.

Ceiling fans are another great item you can put in a property to make it more desirable and not break the bank. The trick is to do this only if there is already a light hardwired into the ceiling. If there isn't, it can be very expensive to have an electrician run wiring to the required part of the ceiling in order to power the fan. If this is the case, it's probably not worth paying for. However, if there is already a light in the room, the majority of the work is done for you!

In these cases, all you have to do is pay for the fan and the hourly labor rate for the person who will be installing it. The installation should go pretty quickly as the majority of the work is done, and you'll have a new fan for not much more money. This can be a huge selling point if your target market has hot weather. I do this on all my properties because the climate is either hot, muggy, or both where I own. Tenants who know you've taken them into consideration and bought a fan for them are more likely to pay a little more and decide to move in a little quicker.

This same principle applies to another idea: installing air conditioning in homes that do not currently have it. Now, I know most of you may be thinking HVAC is incredibly expensive to install and isn't worth it. You may be right. What I'd like to propose is this: Ask yourself if tenants in the area you're buying would be willing to live in a property without HVAC, and if so, which kind of tenants would be willing to do so. In my experience, the only tenants who are willing to live in homes without air conditioning in the Florida heat are those who have no other option and would move out as soon as they found another unit that does have AC.

Understand it's not as simple as putting a new or used HVAC unit in the property and calling it a day. You'll also need to budget for how much it will cost to run all the ductwork and supporting infrastructure to move the heating and air to the home, and this could be expensive. Here's why I do this anyway: When appraisers value the home, there is a good chance its value increases significantly by having HVAC. This not only helps my ARV, but it also makes it more likely I will get a higher appraisal and therefore can borrow more of the money back from the bank than I spent on the HVAC unit and installation in the first place.

If an HVAC and installation costs me $7,000, but it improves my property's value by $10,000, I not only added $3,000 in equity, but I also borrowed back $7,500 of that $10,000 in equity (at a 75 percent LTV). This means I spent $7,000 to get back $7,500 ($500 more in my pocket) plus $3,000 in equity. While this will lower my cash flow (any time you borrow more money your cash flow goes down), it is still a win on many other fronts. In essence, your property paid for its own HVAC and made itself more valuable.

Making moves like this are what black belt investors do. This same principle can be applied to roofs. Many, if not most, of the properties I buy in the South need new roofs. The rain can be hard and constant, and if the previous owners were cash-strapped or unaware, the roofs can become damaged to the point where they are useless and need to be completely replaced. This becomes a significant expense, anywhere between $6,000–$15,000 to complete.

When a property needs a new roof, it usually leads to several results:

1. The property will no longer qualify for a loan, meaning the majority of investors cannot buy it.
2. The roof cannot be financed, meaning the majority of investors need to have enough cash on hand to buy the house, do the rehab, *and* replace the roof.
3. The investor cannot use their typical skilled handyman to do the work, as installing a new roof is skilled work.
4. The property will not be collecting rent for a longer period of time than normal since you can't rent out a house without a roof.
5. The work done will need permits, which complicates the process.

I've just spelled out five items that make a property needing a new roof more troublesome than investment property that doesn't. Usually, one item is enough to scare away most investors—this is five! While the novice, white belt investor sees this information and says, "Nope, I'm out. Too much hassle/headache," the black belt investor says, "Perfect. This is a great opportunity to solve a big problem." Remember, we make money on real estate investing by solving someone else's problem, whether it's personal, property, or market condition related. This is a big problem, and if you can solve it you'll receive a big reward.

I *love* buying properties and replacing the roofs! Here's why:

- I specialize in buying properties that won't qualify for conventional financing, and even target them specifically, so this is a hurdle I've already overcome.
- I use cash to finance every part of my deals, so needing enough cash to replace the roof doesn't scare me. I just budget it into the bid my contractor gives me.
- I use skilled handymen whenever possible, but they're not the only people I use. I have licensed contractors on my team as well. Issues like roofing, plumbing, foundation, structural, and electrical do not scare me because I have people in place to handle them before I get started.
- Because I keep healthy money in reserve and plan on taking on mostly big rehab projects anyway, this hurdle doesn't prevent me from jumping over it.
- Because my contractor handles the permit process, I don't need to waste my time, money, or energy trying to solve this problem. They will.

- In some areas, a new roof will lower the insurance premium and save me big money over the period of time I own the property.

Remember, I use a contractor to handle the entire rehab and I don't get involved myself. This means when a problem (like a new roof) arises, it is his company's problem to solve, not mine! I just need him to solve that problem within the constraints of my budget, and if he can, he gets the job and can make some money.

Because my contractor is also an investor, and works primarily with investors, this is not their first rodeo. Do you really think they've never had a client who needed a roof before? When I ask for estimates to replace the roof, my contractor usually brings me back two or three and recommends the company he thinks will be best. This takes the stress off of me and puts it on them.

Why does this work? Because I'm an investor. I don't come up with solutions. I buy properties. What I do is hire people to come up with solutions. I don't need to look at problems, worries, or "what ifs." What I need is to take whatever that problem is, convert it into a number, and plug that number into my deal to make sure it still works out. I need the contractor to solve the problem and give me the number. That's it. Seeing things this way enables me to move forward with confidence where other investors get scared and back out.

The more deals I move forward on, the more opportunity I have to succeed and grow my wealth. Learning to see opportunity where others see setbacks is what allows me to grow my wealth in any market, any area, or any property. In hot markets, you don't find good deals. You *make* good deals. Buying a property that needs a new roof gives you a unique opportunity to make a good deal where no one else could see how.

In addition to allowing me to buy properties others won't, there is another couple big reasons to replace a roof entirely during the rehab process. Appraisers know a roof is one of the biggest, most expensive items to replace on a property. Roofs are probably the biggest capital expenditure (capex) item you need to factor into any investment property you buy. Capital expenditures are "big ticket" items you need to budget to replace in your property. If the roof is near the end of its useful life (or completely at the end, as in this example), they will give your property a higher appraised value as they don't need to factor in the cost for you to replace the roof later. This means you may be spending more money, but you're also adding more value to the property. The more expensive a property is, the more value they'll likely give to a new roof.

This is great for us because not only have we improved the value of our property and taken care of a huge chunk of capex up front, but we've also done it *before* the property was financed! What does this mean? When we go to refinance it, we will be borrowing back 70–75 percent of the money we spent on the roof. So, if the roof costs $7,500 and made the property worth $7,500 more, we only had to leave $1,875 of the $7,500 we spent for the roof in the property. If the new roof made the property appraise for $10,000 more, we could be recovering $7,500, or 100 percent of the money we spent on the new roof in the first place.

This is why I love BRRRR. We can spend money to improve a property's value without worrying about losing it in the deal. Once we refinance, we get that money, or a good chunk of that money, back out of the deal to reinvest again. In this example, this helps us several ways:

1. We added value to our property by replacing the roof.
2. We eliminated future capex concerns/costs by addressing them up front.
3. We took care of the problem in the present, meaning there shouldn't be a foreseeable problem in the near future.
4. We likely lowered our insurance costs over the next several years by having a new roof.
5. We received all these benefits without having to dump extra cash in the deal, as the improved value the roof brought likely paid for the roof itself.
6. We bought a great deal and gained lots of equity by taking on a problem that scared our competition!

Not a bad return, right? As if that wasn't enough, let me tell you a story of how a bad roof cost me $5,000 on a property I didn't even own, and how it cost the owner of that property much more.

How I Lost $5,000 Because of a Bad Roof

About six months ago, I put seven properties under contract at the same time. During this period of time, my own real estate agent business was taking off. I had ten properties in escrow, several clients looking for new homes, was trying to hire assistants to help me keep up with the workload, and was getting ready to launch my first book. Of course, these are all great problems to have, because who wouldn't want all that awesome stuff going on at once? But, needless to say, my life was chaotic.

I'm not proud to admit it, but during this time I majorly screwed up. A house I put under contract slipped through the cracks somehow and I didn't order inspections before my inspection period expired. Now, I can't say I regret this, as it wouldn't be worth it to lose out on other opportunities to prevent what happened, but I can say I learned from it!

When the title company told me I needed to wire money to close, I reached out to my agent and asked what they were talking about. She informed me it was a house I had under contract and was legit. When I asked to see the inspection reports, we realized we didn't have any done. This left me with two options.

1. Close on the deal and hope the house was in good condition.
2. Spend money to order the reports and close if the house looked good or back out if it did not.

Of course, being the wise investor that I am, I opted for option two and ordered the inspection. The results were like a punch to the gut. What I thought was a small roof leak turned out to be a gaping hole, covered with tarp. It had been continually raining for three weeks and the entire inside of the property was completely soaked, rotted, and molding.

But that's not all! Not only was the floor of the family room (the area under the hole) ruined—that would only have been a couple thousand dollars to fix—but the water had been running down from the roof to inside the walls of the house, getting into the framing itself and rotting out the wooden frame that kept the house standing. The inspector was able to pull out chunks of drywall and realized the entire frame was rotted and needed to be replaced. In essence, the house needed to be torn down and rebuilt from the foundation, all because of a bad roof!

I tried to renegotiate with the seller and the listing agent wouldn't even entertain it. In the end, I lost my $5,000 deposit (which was totally my fault) but saved myself over $100,000 in loss to rebuild that house from the ground up. Not only did this roof cost me my deposit, but imagine what it did to the value of the home. The seller of that home had to eat that entire loss and now has a property worth virtually nothing.

The lesson from this story? Have systems in place so you don't forget when you put a property in contract. But more important, take roof problems seriously! A "small leak" can completely destroy an entire home. If you own a property that needs the roof replaced, get it done. This can cost you big money that you can't get back unless you refinance. If you've recently financed the home, you may be stuck paying out of your own reserves. If a roof needs replacement, do yourself a favor and get it done *before* you finance the property, so you can recover your investment and put it back into the next property instead.

I addressed this problem so it would never happen again by creating a spreadsheet in Google Drive with each step of due diligence I need conducted on every property. I then shared access to this spreadsheet with the agent helping me on the deal, as well as my assistant. It became my assistant's job to check the spreadsheet and make sure the Realtor was doing the items on the list, and confirm they were done within the time frame allowed. Now, I don't have to worry about this happening again, and I can keep buying properties with peace of mind.

Running Your Rehab

So far we've covered upgrade hacks as well as common rehab strategies I've used frequently on projects that have saved me money. Part of being a successful investor is making effective and fiscally prudent decisions with your rehab, but that's not all you need to learn. You also need to learn how to manage that project. Getting a great price on paper doesn't do you any good if the project isn't finished on time, goes over budget, or isn't completed as promised.

There are several different ways to run a rehab. Each method varies in the amount of work the investors wants to put into the job. Some investors want total control. These people basically assume the role of general contractor and hire subcontractors to perform the individual jobs that need to be done. This would be on the extreme side of the "hands on" spectrum. The investor is basically taking on a job and performing the work of one of the members of the Core Four.

At the extreme other end of the "hands on" spectrum is where I prefer to be. In this model, the investor does as little as possible and relies on other team members to accomplish the job according to the standards that have been set. In this model the investor creates systems and leverages other people (like members of the Core Four) to accomplish the tasks necessary to complete a rehab successfully. I call this the "business model."

It's when you're running your real estate investing more like a business and less like a job.

Each of us needs to determine where on this "hands on" spectrum we fit. For those who want more control over the process, less of the information in this book will be beneficial. For those who want to focus on higher dollar productive activities, the information in this book can be game-changing. In my opinion, an investor's best use of time is finding great talent to help them achieve their goals and find great deals. If you're performing the role of one of the Core Four (usually either managing your own properties or managing the rehabs), you can't be focusing on the activities that will grow your wealth the fastest.

If you're going to have someone else check to make sure work was done on your project correctly, you want to make sure they have some incentive to do a good job. The best way to accomplish this is to find someone whose interests align with yours. This is most likely going to be a member of your Core Four. Later in this chapter I'll explain how to choose which member to rely on for which project. For now we are going to discuss how to use them.

How to Use a Team Member to Check on the Progress of Your Rehab

Using a team member to check on the progress of another team member (the contractor) is a great way to build multiple layers of security into protecting your project. With this method, you can avoid putting unnecessary time into making multiple trips to the project site and only go when it works for you and your schedule. This method also opens up doors to buy rehab properties in markets that are too far away for you to visit—a great perk!

The trick to making this method work is to find someone whose interests align with yours when it comes to the rehab of the property. If you are rehabbing a property to rent out, I recommend you start with the property manager. There are several reasons why the property manager would take an interest in checking on the rehab of your property, the most important being they want to make sure the work is done right so they don't have to worry about redoing it when the future tenants complain!

If your relationship with your PM isn't established yet, consider paying them to check on the work your contractor is doing and making sure it's done right. Paying someone to check on work may seem unwise at first, but consider all the reasons this could help you.

- It saves you time by focusing on your work and building wealth.
- It improves your relationship with your PM and gets them more directly involved in your business.
- Your PM may have a more experienced eye than you.
- It lets your contractor know to stay on the straight and narrow as other people are monitoring them.

When you have members of your Core Four checking on other members, you add multiple layers of security to your investment business. Having another set of eyes looking over your deals and your projects is not a bad thing, and oftentimes can save your bacon when you missed something.

To check up on the work, have the PM take pictures and video of the work on their smartphone. This way, you have proof of the status of the project and can make sure things are being done as you intended. With the ease of smartphone use, you can gather information from team members quickly and accurately. In this day and age, most people can operate a smartphone camera. If not, it's easy to teach.

Another thing to keep in mind is you should never, ever, ever pay for an entire project up front. There are too many things that can go wrong, and the risk vs. reward just doesn't make sense. Paying up front opens you up to all kinds of potential risk. Your contractor could skip town, someone could steal the money from them, they could quit before the job is finished, etc. And what is the upside? You save a little time by not making a couple more deposits? Not worth it. Money should be wired in draws, every time.

My favorite method is to send the money in 25 percent draws, and ask them what work they will be doing with each draw. After they have finished the work with the money from the first draw, this is when I send someone to confirm the work was completed. I include the scope of work that should have been done so my team member knows what to look for, and I have them send me pictures and videos in return.

When I confirm the work was completed, I send the next draw. If this is a contractor I don't know well or haven't worked with before, I send another 25 percent. If it's someone I trust, I send 50 percent. The important thing is you *don't send all of it!* Part of my system is to reward the contractor with a bonus if they finish ahead of schedule and a penalty if they fall behind. How can I assess a penalty if I've already paid them the money? What incentive do they have to get my work done quickly and correctly if they've already been paid?

Imagine you are a waiter and you get your tip right away, before you've provided any service. Do you think you'll have the same drive to provide the best service possible like you'd have if you were trying to earn that tip? Probably not. Now, you may still have pride and based on sheer willpower you would do your best. But my point is, it's *hard* to do your best when you've already been paid. It's *easier* to do your best when you haven't been rewarded yet and still have to earn it. Ever wonder why professional athletes give their best effort every game in the last year of their contract? This is why. They are thinking about payday and it motivates them. We do our best when we are striving toward a goal, not when we are trying to maintain a high standard by willpower alone.

Brandon Turner's Story

As host of the *BiggerPockets Podcast*, Brandon has often told the story of the time he was ripped off by a contractor in Washington State. Brandon was looking for a contractor to do some work on a property for him and he found a contractor via Craigslist. He didn't vet him through any channels he trusted, and he didn't find him via a referral. In essence, Brandon was trusting this person to be a man of his word. Once they agreed on the work, Brandon sent the $5,000 to the contractor to buy the materials and do the work. When he called to check in on him, he stopped answering his phone. Later, it was confirmed that the contractor was gone and the work was not done.

So, Brandon had a lien placed against this individual he had paid who didn't do the work. This was a court judgment issued by a judge who heard the case and determined that Brandon was damaged in the relationship. The cool news is, a few years later this shady contractor sold his home. Because there was a lien issued against him, the title company withheld the money for the amount of the lien and Brandon got paid back! In the end, Brandon got his money and ended up with a cool story to share for all of us to learn from.

Stories like this are why I like to use people who have been referred to me by others I trust. I can't guarantee nothing will ever go wrong, but the odds are much, much higher in my favor when someone else has already vetted this Core Four member and has good experience with them.

Another way we can learn from this story is to consider buying the materials ourselves the first time we work with a contractor. This is a really simple tweak to put into the system and can save you money in the end. When you have the contractor write up the itemized bid, ask them to separate the materials from the labor. This way you see what you'll be paying for labor only. Then, ask the contractor to call the store where they'll be buying things from and put in their order.

Once the order has been placed, you will call and pay for the order over the phone. Then, either have the materials shipped to the property where the contractor will receive them, or have the contractor go pick up the items themselves. This way, you solve two potential problems.

1. You don't have to worry about the contractor overcharging you for materials.
2. You don't have to worry about the contractor stealing the money that would have been used for materials.

Doing things this way can also give you the opportunity to find materials on sale or build up your credit card points. I recommend doing this for the first few jobs with a new contractor until you get a better feel for their character and build up trust.

Key Points

- Add square footage to increase value.
- Add bedrooms and bathrooms to increase value.
- Use cheap labor, not skilled, when the opportunity presents itself.
- Use mulch to cover eyesores in a yard on a resale.
- Think long-term and durable when choosing flooring on a fixer-upper.
- Replace roofs before the refinance to recover a big chunk of your investment.
- Never pay a contractor for the entire job up front.
- Use a team member to check on the progress of your rehab.
- Pay for materials yourself the first time you use a contractor to be sure you aren't overpaying.

PART FOUR

The Rental Process

CHAPTER SIX

Understanding Rent Prices

"Money is a terrible master but an excellent servant."

—P. T. BARNUM

Once you've bought and successfully rehabbed your property, the worst is over! Now all you need to do is find a tenant for it, refinance it, and buy the next one! Intelligent investors don't buy a property "hoping" it will cash-flow. They have run these numbers long before they closed on the property—and probably before they even wrote an offer. This gives them a really good chance of knowing what they are in for before it's too late to back out.

Calculating cash flow is pretty easy. We went over that in the beginning of the book. In this chapter, we are going to discuss how to estimate what your rents are likely to be, what we can do to increase them, and how to determine if they are likely to continue to rise. For the vast majority of investment property you will ever purchase, the *only* form of income you will receive will be your rents. This means that getting your rent numbers right, and buying in areas likely to see an increase in rent, is paramount to the performance of your property and your success as an investor.

There are numerous variables that affect the rent you receive for a property, both now and in the future. Learning how to read these variables, and anticipate them when possible, will lead to a huge compound effect on your wealth. If you choose the right area to invest in, and rents continue to increase every year, you're virtually guaranteed to make money in real estate investing. If you choose the wrong area, and things go badly, it can be incredibly difficult to avoid losing money.

Remember, rents are the only form of income your property can generate. This isn't a business where you can change to a new product if the current one isn't selling. We are putting all the marbles on the rent supporting the property. It's vital to make sure we understand how to do this correctly. In order to be as efficient as possible, I've broken the process down into two parts—preliminary rent estimates and more accurate rent estimates.

Finding Preliminary Rent Estimates

When you're first analyzing a property, it's often not sensible to dig in and put in serious due diligence to find an exact rent number. At this stage, the process for finding rents is very similar to that of finding the ARV when you're looking at comps. We don't need something exact, we just need to find something that lets us know if we are even in the ballpark.

In my experience, the more accurate the information you receive is, the more time it takes to find it. This is why real estate investing due diligence is typically done in chunks, as opposed to all the work up front, on every deal. Consider an old gold prospector. Did he put his nose in the dirt and look for flashes of gold in the middle of the entire river? That would have taken forever! Instead, miners developed a process for sifting gold. They took big chunks of earth, shook it up through a filter, eliminated the big stuff, and then dug deeper into the materials that sifted through.

This is the same way we want to approach real estate investing. We start with very big numbers of properties, tons of options. We then use "rules of thumb" (like the 1 percent rule I mentioned at the beginning of the book) to filter most of those properties out. Of the ones remaining, we dig deeper, putting them through another filter (making sure they are able to be purchased below market value). Of those ones that are left, we do a preliminary rent estimate to see if they would cash-flow. For those that do, we consider making an offer. If that offer is accepted, we look deeper into the rent numbers to get as accurate of a picture as we possibly can.

This method is meant to save you time and help you filter through more deals. To get started, we need good systems or tools to help us determine what the rent is likely to be. The best tools are easy to use, quick, and accurate enough to trust for at least a preliminary number. Once you've figured out your system for establishing preliminary rents, you'll find you can analyze a property really quickly and move on to either digging in deeper or throwing it into the garbage heap!

Rentometer.com

Much like a peanut butter and jelly sandwich, www.Rentometer.com is brilliant due to its simplicity. This is one of my favorite websites on the entire internet, by far. Rentometer.com uses an algorithm that considers rental properties near the subject property and plugs their rent amounts into a secret formula. This formula then spits out the numbers we need for our preliminary rent analysis.

When Rentometer.com gives you your result, it shows you four categories related to surrounding rents.

1. The average rent of surrounding units.
2. The median rent of surrounding units.
3. The rent spread 80 percent of the units will fall into.
4. The rent spread 60 percent of the units will fall into.

I typically just use the average rent, as the other numbers aren't as concerning to me—especially during this preliminary stage. At this point, I want the average rent to be at or near 1 percent of the sales price of the property, and I want to see the average rent is close to the median rent. If there is a huge discrepancy between the average and the median rent, that could be indicative of potential problems. If this is the case, you'll need to dig deeper into this property. Is it right on the fringe of a split between a good neighborhood and a bad one? Is it really close to a large apartment complex where rents are much lower and some of that complex's problems could come spilling into your property's front yard?

In general, you want data to be consistent. When we find inconsistencies, we need to dig deeper to understand why. Rentometer.com has another feature that makes this simple to do, and it's one of the reasons I love this site. Not only does it display the average rents, but it also shows you *which properties around yours are renting for which price!* It's helpful to know what the average rent is, but it's imperative to be able to see the addresses of the properties and their specific rents!

In order to use this feature, simply find the map directly below the numbers we just discussed and hover your cursor over the symbols on the map representing various properties. You'll notice these symbols are vertical lines coded in different colors. Red lines represent properties with significantly higher rent than yours, yellow lines are properties with a rent similar to yours, and green lines are for properties with a rent lower than yours. Because the properties are displayed on a map, you can see exactly where they lie and what part of town they are in.

My favorite technique is to hover over another property and copy the web address that shows up when I click on the symbol. I then paste this address into www.Zillow.com, www.Trulia.com, or www.Realtor.com and look at the condition and pictures of the property itself. If the property is similar in size and condition to mine, I know I have a reliable comparable to base my potential rent on! If the property is bigger or nicer than mine, I know my rent will likely be slightly lower. If my property is bigger, nicer, or in a better area, I know my rent will likely be higher!

This is one of the fastest, easiest, and most reliable ways I've ever found to analyze the expected rent of a potential property I'm interested in. The whole process takes a matter of minutes, and even though this is only a preliminary step, I've found that it is just as accurate as the more detailed steps I take. Keep this website in your arsenal and it will help you analyze deals much faster, especially when you compare it with the next tool.

BiggerPockets.com Calculators

BiggerPockets has a feature you can find at www.BiggerPockets.com/calc that takes all the work of analyzing a deal and does it for you. Most of the work we need to do as investors involves finding the right numbers to plug into a formula. With the BiggerPockets calculators, you don't need to actually do the math! Just find the numbers, plug them in, and the analysis is done for you.

BiggerPockets has several different calculators you can use depending on the type of project you're doing. They have calculators for flipping, wholesaling, cash flow, and yes—even BRRRR. These calculators are designed to prompt you to enter information such as the expected rent, vacancy, repairs, closing costs, etc. The whole analysis can be run for you in seconds and gives you vital information like your expected cash flow, ROI, etc.

Having a tool like this at your disposal helps you in several ways. It not only takes away any issues you had with analyzing property because of a dislike for math, but it also makes a full and complete analysis of a property easy and *fast*. It also allows you to leverage off a lot of this work to someone else. It doesn't take much skill to plug numbers into something and click a button to get an analysis.

Let's say you have found a property you want to buy for $120,000 that rents for $1,000 a month. You enter all the relevant information into the BiggerPockets calculator and find this property would provide you with an ROI of 7 percent. This won't work for you, as you want at least 10 percent. Seeing immediately this won't work, you go back to the data entry portion of the calculator and change the purchase price from $120,000 to $100,000. You run a new analysis.

The new analysis shows at this new price the ROI would be 11 percent. Bingo! You now know you can offer $100,000 to buy this property and the deal will work for you. You tell your agent to write the offer, and the seller counters at $105,000. Now that you know you're close, it would make sense to dive into the deeper analysis of the deal and do a more thorough check of the rent and rehab numbers to make sure they work. If they do, you accept the counter or counter yourself.

This is how real estate is bought. It's not a decision made once and then a lot of "hoping" that everything works out. It's a series of small decisions, made over and over, with each one revealing more information about the deal and you deciding if you like what you see. Knowing we'll be making numerous small decisions throughout a transaction, it doesn't make sense to try to do all the work for every decision at the very beginning! Breaking down this due diligence into several phases will make real estate investing more enjoyable and will make you more efficient with your time and work. Tools like www.Rentometer.com and the BiggerPockets calculators will help streamline the process for you.

Finding More Accurate Rental Estimates

Once we've conducted our preliminary rent estimate analysis, we need to decide whether we'll be moving forward. This is oftentimes simply a matter of making an offer and seeing if it's accepted or not. If the offer is accepted, or if for some other reason you decide you want to move forward more aggressively on a property, you're going to want to do a much more accurate and time-intensive analysis of the property.

The purpose of a preliminary rental estimate is to see if the property is worth pursuing. The point of a more accurate rental estimate is to determine what you can expect regarding the rent of a property if you end up purchasing it. Having accurate rent numbers is important because it helps us determine our ROI. You need to have an accurate assessment of your ROI so you can compare properties to each other and know which one is likely to bring you the best return.

There are several ways to determine a more accurate idea of what to expect for rent. Below are some of the methods I've used most often that have led to accurate results without too much time invested.

Asking Other Investors in the Area

If you want to know what to expect, ask someone who's gone before you. This is good advice for real estate and good advice for anything else as well. Asking others who have already done what you're doing is a great way to skip a lot of the mistakes you'd inevitably make while shortening your "learning curve." If you know another investor in the area where you're looking to buy, this is a great time to reach out and talk to them.

Start by asking what kinds of properties the investor owns. You don't want to be asking a multifamily or commercial apartment investor about single-family houses, or vice versa. If they own properties similar to what you want to buy, ask them which area they own in and make sure it is similar to where you're looking. If both of these questions yield positive answers, you've found a potential resource.

The first question I ask is for the addresses of the homes they own and the amount they are getting for rent. If they aren't comfortable giving you the full address (or you aren't comfortable asking), ask for the street name—most of the time people are fine sharing that. Once you have these numbers, do a cross reference on Rentometer.com and see if the rent they get is in line with market rents for the area. You may find rents have increased and Rentometer.com is not reflective of this yet.

If you find the rent prices they receive are close to what Rentometer. com says, your work may be done. You can trust Rentometer.com and move forward to the purchase with a good idea of what your rents will be. If this isn't enough for you, and you want even more due diligence to conduct, check out the next method.

Asking Property Managers

Asking property managers is, in my opinion, the hands-down best way to get accurate numbers for your potential rental property. The reason is simple. If they are good at their job, they work with renters every day looking for a rental property. This means they know what amenities tenants want, what they are willing to pay for them, which part of town they want to be in, etc. Property managers have the information you need when trying to make your decision on where to buy or what to expect in rent.

The reason I don't go to them right away is because I don't want to burn my relationship with them by asking too many questions and taking up too much of their time and then not buying the property. Just like any other business relationship, it needs to be a two-way street. Too many newbie investors make this mistake and burn a relationship with a potential serious business partner by asking for too much and not providing anything in return. I don't want this to happen to me, so I don't get PMs involved until I'm serious about moving forward.

The system I have in place for getting information from my property managers is simple. I send them an email asking three questions I want answered. (If I've worked with the same PM for any significant period of time all I have to do is send them the address and they know to answer these three questions for me.) The questions are:

1. What rent can I expect for this property?
2. What do you think a rough idea of this property's ARV is?
3. Is this a neighborhood you want to manage in or not?

The reason I ask question No. 1 is pretty obvious. I ask question two because I'm looking to verify that the numbers my Realtor, wholesaler, or other party gave me are accurate. It is *always* a good idea to get a second opinion, as long as that opinion is educated and relevant.

Do you remember how I mentioned I prefer members of my Core Four to be investors themselves? This is one of the reasons why. If my property manager is also an investor, they are much more likely to know the value of the property—not just the market rents. If I have one more set of experienced eyeballs looking over my deal, I will feel comfortable to pull the trigger and close or back out because the numbers didn't add up.

I ask the third question because the first two don't tell the whole story. Investors often get into trouble because analyzing properties on paper can often lead to a false sense of security. If we are clever, we can make numbers say whatever we want them to say, and that isn't always a good thing. When analyzing a property, it's not just the rent we should consider. It's *all* the data. Rent is great, but if the property is in an area not conducive to real estate investing, the rent numbers are never going to look in real life like what they appear to be on paper. There are lots of issues that can lead to your cash flow evaporating that won't show up on a typical online calculator or spreadsheet.

Consider how badly even one eviction can hurt your cash flow. Or a tenant who trashes a house, requiring thousands of dollars invested to restore it. Consider that not every tenant will pay their rent on time, or at all, and that sometimes tenants let entire families or groups of people move into your property in a way that violates your lease big time. Yes, the law will be on your side when this happens—but the government doesn't reimburse you for lost rent, expenses, or legal fees. Anytime this happens, the responsibility falls on you and your wallet to fix it.

I tell my PMs to check and make sure the properties I send them are located in areas they don't mind managing. Here's a tip for you: If you're buying properties in rough neighborhoods, your property manager likely won't want to manage them, either. By making it clear it's okay if they tell you this up front, you are much more likely to get an honest and transparent assessment of the neighborhood than if they feel pressured to tell you what you want to hear. This communication is crucial to you and your due diligence process.

By checking with a property manager on both the expected rent, the value of the home, and the condition of the neighborhood, you are getting some very valuable and professional information to help you make the best decision possible. Before I buy anything, I run it by my PMs first to make sure they are on board and aren't seeing anything I'm missing. At the very least, you should be having this conversation to make sure they validate all the other due diligence you've done so far!

Asking Agents to Provide Rental Comps from the MLS

Many investors don't know they can ask real estate agents to search the MLS for rental comparables. This isn't well known because in many areas real estate agents don't also manage rental properties so they don't specialize in this service. While I don't use agents to manage my properties (meaning I don't use people whose primary purpose is selling homes to manage mine), I *do* use agents from time to time to verify or validate information being provided to me by another party.

Consider this: Your property manager tells you they expect the rent to be around $1,000 a month. You know from checking Rentometer.com that you were thinking $1,200 sounded more accurate. You ask a real estate agent to check the surrounding comparable rentals and tell you what they are renting for. They come back and tell you most are somewhere between $1,200 and $1,400.

This information would suggest that either something is very wrong with or different about the property you're thinking about buying, or your property manager is bad at their job at best and downright dishonest at worst. When you have this tool in your tool belt, you can feel a lot more confident that you aren't being taken advantage of and aren't relying on the wrong person's advice to collect the data you need to make an informed decision.

How to Determine if Rents Are Likely to Increase

As most of us understand from Economics 101, the price of an item is determined by two things: supply and demand. Real estate is no exception! Understanding the market and how rent prices are affected by it is mandatory if you want to be a black belt real estate investor.

Just as ROI is determined by two numbers (yearly cash flow and the investment basis), home values are also determined by two factors (supply and demand). Learning what affects each of them in a given market will help you make the most intelligent decision regarding what to buy, how much of it to buy, and where. The good news is you don't have to be an economist to be able to understand market factors! Let me explain.

Demand for areas is dependent on how many people want to move there. Supply for an area is determined by how many properties are available for people to move into. Pretty simple, right? I'm going to give you an overview of how to determine the demand for an area as well as how to determine if there is insufficient supply. Understanding these factors helps protect your investment from a decline in value as does choosing areas that are likely to appreciate at a rate faster than the national average.

Determining Demand Based on Supply

Demand is simply the measurement for how badly somebody wants something. In 1996, a toy was released that quickly became infamous for its ridiculous demand.[4] Tickle Me Elmo became *the* toy of the year. Due to its short supply, prices skyrocketed as people fought to get their hands on one. Some people were selling them online for very high prices (sometimes several thousand dollars!) after buying them at the store for $30.[5]

This is an extreme example, but it highlights how demand works. When a lot of people want something, they will pay more for it. If supply is also low, they will pay exponentially more for it. If you look at most of the big runs in real estate value, they were the result of housing demand surpassing supply. If you look at the areas where prices have appreciated the fastest, they are the areas where people want to live the most.

Factors that Determine Where to Live

Employment Opportunities

Employment is becoming more of a factor when it comes to affecting where people live than ever before. Sure, people choose their home based on their family needs, but most of us choose our location based on work opportunities.[6] Think about your own self. When you last moved, why was it? Odds are you chose your house based on its proximity to your job. Once you knew the area you wanted to live in, you then started looking at other factors like how much house your money could get you, nearby school district scores, etc.

There are many things that affect housing values and rental prices, but none more important than employment. Our jobs are a huge part of our life. We spent more time there than just about anywhere else. Consider also that the health of the employment sector can have a huge effect on your home's value. When wages in an area rise, home prices tend to as well. When jobs leave, or wages fall, it can have the adverse effect. In almost every part of the country, real estate prices continually rise over time. The few exceptions to this rule are in areas where the job market

---

4 Jake Rossen, "Oral History: Tickle Me Elmo Turns 21," Mental Floss (November 16, 2017). http://mentalfloss.com/article/83563/oral-history-tickle-me-elmo-turns-20

5 Jonathan Silverstein, "Tickle Me Elmos Selling for $5,000," *ABC News* (October 19, 2006). https://abcnews.go.com/Technology/story?id=2583572&page=1

6 Troy Onink, "The New Geography of Jobs: Where You Live Matters More than Ever," *Forbes* (May 22, 2012). https://www.forbes.com/sites/troyonink/2012/05/22/the-new-geography-of-jobs-where-you-live-matters-more-than-ever/#7260f59038f1

fell into distress.

Consider Detroit, Michigan, when the auto industry fell apart. As more demand (that word again . . .) grew for foreign automakers, fewer cars were built in Detroit. This led to factories closing down, and with that, jobs disappearing. Large parts of Detroit became barren wastelands where the city was willing to literally give houses away for free to anyone that would pay the property taxes.[7] How does any area become that destitute? Jobs. Lack of jobs will destroy any economy and with it, home values.

Jobs are the lifeblood of an economy. Employers are the heart that pump blood to the people who live somewhere. Without that blood, the body dies. Housing is tied directly to jobs in a way that can't be erased until technology reaches a point where we can all work from home. I avoid investing in any area dependent on just one job market. Markets known for only having one industry like oil fields, fishing, automobile manufacturing, etc. are all very vulnerable to a huge collapse in demand if something disrupts that, and a loss of demand will result in a lowering of value.

Desirability

The next reason people choose where to live is the desirability of an area. This is why we often hear people talk about school districts, crime, and "walkability scores." Things like proximity to parks, shopping, and nearby freeways all become a factor. Once you know where you will be working and settle on the city you want to live in, you'll usually start looking into secondary factors. If you have kids, school scores will be a determining factor. If you're religious, you'll want to know about churches. If you're elderly, the quality of the hospitals. If you like to be outdoors, you'll look for parks or walking trails.

When choosing an area to invest in, you need to be looking at it with these same eyes. Are you buying somewhere that has a well-developed infrastructure? Did the city planning council make sure sufficient shopping and commercial areas were included in an area? Are there enough freeway on- and off-ramps to ensure a short commute? Buyers look at all these things, and so do tenants! If the city did a good job planning the development, demand is likely to grow over time.

---

7 Beth Dalbey, "5 Houses You Can Pick Up For As Little As $1," Detroit Patch (May 25, 2017). https://patch.com/michigan/detroit/5-houses-you-can-pick-little-1

Affordability

Another huge factor people consider when moving is affordability. How much house can someone get for an area's median salary? If you live in a city where the median salary is $50,000 yearly, talk to a lender and find out how much the average person earning that salary can borrow. Once you have that number (let's say for this example it's $250,000), go online and look at what the average house looks like that's listed at $250,000. If the houses look updated and impressive, there isn't much incentive for someone to move any farther away.

If the houses *don't* look updated or impressive, assume that buyers/tenants will start looking elsewhere. Look around the city and find which neighborhoods have really nice houses and at what price point they are. If you find a pocket where houses listed for $200,000 have beautiful upgrades, bigger yards, more space, etc., you just may have found the next market to appreciate. Understanding how buyers think is crucial to understanding how to determine market value.

Understand that buyers drive markets. It is the demand to live in an area, and then in a specific property, that drives the price of the homes up or down. Tenants behave similarly to buyers, and rent prices behave similarly to home prices (though not exact). If home values are rising in an area due to strong demand, rents will usually follow suit. Finding these areas before other investors do gives you an advantage with building your wealth.

Up-and-Coming Areas

Many people choose an area because of its reputation. If an area is considered "up-and-coming," people will flock to it just to check it out. Think about markets like San Francisco. Young college graduates are willing to pay half their salary to live in a closet so they can experience all San Francisco has to offer. Madison, Wisconsin, is currently growing rapidly as young bright minds move there to experience the city's growth. So is Austin, Texas. Why is this?

When a city or area has a reputation as a growing, hip place, people start looking for work there. Whereas generally people look for a job and then take the job they want in a city, some people will look for the city and then take any job they feel comfortable doing while there. As more people move in, more property taxes are collected and the city can reinvest in its infrastructure. This leads to a growing, thriving area where demand increases faster than supply. Finding areas like this to invest in *before* prices run up can be a strong wealth builder.

If you're going to use this strategy, be careful you don't wait and get in too late. If you hear a lot of people talking about how prices in an area have already risen, you may be too late to the party. The trick is to hear an area has a buzz and check to see if prices have risen yet. If they haven't, this may be an area to look into buying, renting, and selling a few years later.

Climate

Another reason people choose an area is for the weather. Think about retirees. Don't you always hear they are moving to Florida or Arizona? Why these two states? They both have two things in common—weather and affordability. As a general rule, areas with more pleasant weather will be more attractive than those without.

I've also found that in addition to demand rising in these areas, pleasant weather is also a benefit when it comes to maintaining your property. If it's not constantly raining or snowing on your roof, the roof will last longer. If you don't have to worry about shoveling snow in front of your apartment, you'll have one less expense. If you can avoid freezing pipes during a vacancy or replacing boilers and furnaces constantly, your capex will be significantly lower and your NOI (net operating income—the profit your property generates) should be stronger.

These are all factors that affect the demand of an area. Learning to find them and weigh them out before deciding will help you make better choices and see better returns. Remember, the key is to look at the market through the eyes of home buyers. Knowing what they look for will give you an advantage in your business!

Determining Supply

On the other side of the coin from demand is supply. Supply in real estate is easier to regulate and control than demand. Whereas demand is a complex formula based on many of the variables I mentioned previously, supply is much simpler. When there are too many homes in an area, prices will drop. When there aren't enough homes, prices will increase. Because there is always someone looking to make money in real estate, there will always be opportunities to develop and build properties when there is insufficient supply to keep pace with demand.

So how do we determine the supply in a given area? Well, there are several factors to look at, and some will work better for certain areas than they will for others. I recommend using several of these strategies, so you can get a clear, overall picture of the health of an area before deciding to put your time, energy, and capital into investing there.

DOM

First, ask a Realtor for the average DOM (days on market) it takes houses to sell there. As a Realtor myself, I can tell you this is an underrated way to gather intel on the pulse of a market, which investors don't look at often enough. Because most of us are investing for cash flow and passive income, we too often get sucked into the numbers on a spreadsheet and ignore other factors like DOM. Take my advice and learn to look at the whole picture so you can become a black belt investor.

In a normal market, an average DOM is somewhere between 30 and 60 days. This is the period of time from when a property is listed to pending and into escrow. I define "normal market" as a market with a healthy amount of demand vs. supply. At the time of the writing of this book, my market in the San Francisco Bay Area has an average DOM of less than 14 days for most homes. I often sell them in less than three!

When this becomes a pattern, it can start to feel like the "new normal" and it becomes easy to see why many investors or home buyers assume this will always be the case. Homes are selling so fast right now because hardly any new homes are being built. The supply has remained consistent while new jobs have come into the area, increasing demand. This lack of supply has led to a red-hot housing market, and low DOM is the metric that exemplifies that.

If I'm going to look into buying in a market, a low DOM is an indication there could be a lack of supply. This can be a good thing for house prices, but might be a bad sign for buying. Low DOM is a sign you are likely to be facing more competition and need to write offers above asking price or with more lenient terms. One thing I can definitely tell you is if you are seeing signs that indicate a lack of sufficient supply, but you still have a high DOM, something isn't adding up and you should be digging deeper to find out why.

Property Manager "Turn Times"

Another technique is to ask a property manager for the average vacancy period between tenants for their other landlords—often called a "turn." It's not necessarily important we get the exact number of days, but we do want to know if it's a short period or a really long one. A good rule of thumb is: more than 30 days isn't a great market to buy a rental. If you're finding properties are only vacant for a week or two, this can be a very encouraging sign.

If I found properties were being rented out in seven to ten days from the time they were advertised, I would know it's not important I fix them up substantially. A bare bones rehab job would do the trick as far as getting the unit occupied. And if the ARV doesn't support a higher price point, I might severely limit my rehab budget. On the flip side, if properties were taking more than 30 days to find a tenant, I would consider a larger rehab to attract more people.

Craigslist

Then, it's a great idea to get on Craigslist.org and email a landlord with a unit for rent. Ask them how many applications they've received for their rental unit/property. Ask them how long they have had the unit advertised for, and how long they expect it will be before it rents. As a general rule, if the landlord is dismissive of you and doesn't seem too engaged, they are probably getting lots of attention for the vacant unit. If they are extremely responsive and excited to hear from you, it might mean you are the first or one of the first people to inquire and they don't feel optimistic about getting many more inquiries.

This can be a good way to gauge what a rental market is like when you are considering buying somewhere, and if you find the properties are renting out right away, it's a good bet your rents will be increasing by a healthy amount each year. Do this with several different Craigslist posts to get an overall picture of a rental market and target areas where you feel there is a lack of supply.

Permit Watch

In addition to this, you can call the city planning division and ask them how many permits they are planning to assign home builders. No new construction can take place in a city unless the city issues a permit for it to begin. These permits are like "permission slips" that allow home builders to build a property—for a fee, of course. Many cities limit the amount of permits they issue for new construction to avoid too much supply hitting the market at once and having properties sit vacant for too long.

If you call the city and find out that they issue a limited number of permits that isn't keeping pace with supply, this is an indication you are more likely to see home values, and with them rent values, continue to increase year over year. If the city appears to be handing out permits like candy on Halloween, this is a sign you may want to avoid this market and focus on somewhere else with a more restricted supply chain.

Property Manager Yearly Rent Increases

Next, ask a property manager how much their average rents are climbing with each lease renewal. If the rent isn't increasing much from year to year, that's a surefire sign that tenants have other options and will move if the rent goes up too much. What landlord won't raise their rent as much as they can when it won't hurt them to do so? (Before you object: Most of the landlords who "don't raise the rent because the tenant is so great" are managing their own properties, not using a PM.)

Of every technique I've listed so far, this one is my favorite. If rents are increasing by a healthy amount (5–10 percent or higher in most areas), this is a very good sign. In fact, if rents are increasing by this much, it's almost guaranteed there is a lack of supply. Here's why:

Tenants will never want to pay more than they absolutely must to live in a property. While some people do choose to rent, the vast majority of tenants are renting because they have to. For those that are renting a property, there will never come a time when they cheerfully and happily pay more than they need to. Most tenants will take the cheaper option, wherever it is, as long as it's a similar property. If rents are increasing every year, it's not because tenants are unaware they could pay less somewhere else. It's because there is *no other option that is cheaper.* If there are no cheaper options, that's a strong sign there is a lack of supply, which is a good sign for your business.

Downtown Construction

Another huge indicator of a lack of supply is when you see big construction equipment in the skyline when driving through the downtown of an area—if you have one. If you're looking into investing in a city with a downtown area, you want to know if the lack of supply you think you're seeing is specific to the downtown area, the suburbs, or both. If you see a lot of new home construction going on in the suburbs, but not a lot of downtown construction, you should ask why. It could be that a nearby city is thriving and people are commuting from your city to that one.

It could also be that the average population of the city is getting older and the young professionals are leaving the downtown area to buy bigger homes and raise families. This might actually be a bad sign and could be an indication that the supply isn't the problem, but the type of property is. If that's the case, you wouldn't want to be investing in a multifamily property downtown when the majority of the population is moving away from that area.

If you see lots of construction taking place in a downtown area, it's almost always a strong sign there is a lack of supply. New construction is expensive—there's no way around it. It's usually cheaper to buy something used and fix it up than to build brand-new. If companies are shelling out big dollars to pay for materials, permits, salaries, and equipment rental, it's usually because there is no other option. The existing inventory is lacking and they are forced to pay top dollar to build new properties—a sign of a lack of supply.

Real Estate Agent Intel

You should ask top-producing real estate agents in the area how many new homes are being built. New home builds are an easy way to know there is limited supply, as most new home builders are very careful they don't overbuild and only build when there is very strong demand with insufficient supply. If you find there are several new home builders all building in an area, that is *usually* good news, but we don't want to assume.

When I find this to be the case, I call the home builder and I ask their sales team how many homes they are building a month and how fast they are selling. In some small cases, I've found the builder got a great deal on the land, or the city is incentivizing them to build, and the lack of supply isn't necessarily the reason why they are building. One conversation with a sales agent of a new home builder can answer a lot of these questions and help you understand how to interpret the information. You should also be aware of what surrounding homes offer in terms of amenities.

Research Your Competition

The first question we want to ask before moving forward is "What amenities do other properties have near mine?" The principle is the same as fixing your property up to look like surrounding homes when you're flipping it. We want to make sure other rental properties don't have amenities we are missing, otherwise we might miss out on tenants.

To start this off, I get my property manager involved in the rehab of my units. I want to show them what I'm planning on doing and what materials I'm planning on using so they can let me know if I'm doing too much, or not doing enough. PMs actively rent properties out every day, so they know what my competition is doing much better than I do. It's faster and better to ask them than to try to go learn it all for myself.

Once I know what materials or finishes nearby properties have, I then ask the PM what features tenants are typically requesting the most. Do they want space in the side yard for extra storage? Are they looking for an outdoor patio? Do they mind carpet or are they specifically asking to see homes with only laminate or tile? How important are stainless steel appliances? If I know what tenants want, I can reverse engineer my rehab to make sure these are the materials I use in my rehab.

Using Better Materials

Keep in mind that if we are to BRRRR the property, we can usually get away with a nicer rehab and still recoup more of our capital. This gives us the luxury of using better materials than the traditional model would but not losing too much capital. When we end up with a nicer remodel than our competition, it helps us in several ways.

For one, it cuts down on vacancy rates. As I've mentioned before, tenants behave similarly to buyers. This means they go online and look at pictures of homes before going to see them. If your property looks better in the pictures because you used better materials, this can cut down on your vacancy rate significantly. This is especially important when vacancy periods or turn times are higher than 30 days. If you can cut down on 30 days of vacancy, that can save you anywhere from $500 to $1,500 in most cases! If you can do this for three turns in a row, that's big money and can pay for some of these upgrades on its own!

Buying in the "Path of Progress"

The "path of progress" is a term used to describe the direction of growth. If you look at the way cities and markets expand, there is a pattern to it. When you recognize the pattern, you can anticipate what's likely to happen in the future. When you can do that, you can make moves that put yourself in the position to capitalize on future growth, increased rents, and appreciating values. Learning the pieces that make up this pattern is one of the elements you need to master if you want to become a black belt investor.

Buying in the path of progress allows you to pay less when you buy, wait, then see appreciation. It is one of the tricks for "buy low, sell high." Most of the BRRRR process is about *forced* appreciation. This is appreciation we create through buying right, wise renovations, and a shrewd understanding of numbers. While forced appreciation is usually a safer bet because you control it, you'd have to be a fool to just ignore market appreciation as well. Market appreciation should always be looked at like icing on the cake. Your BRRRR process is the actual cake.

But if you already have a cake, why not go for icing too? If you can buy a home in the path of progress *and* BRRRR it, why wouldn't you? The idea is simple. You look for the direction you believe housing values are likely to rise, you buy there, and you wait. Just like supply and demand, the path of progress is determined by buyers. If you want to understand real estate, start by understanding the psychology of buyers.

Below are some of the way you can recognize when an area is about to turn for the better. When you see these signs, you'll know the path of progress has made its way to you. Learning to recognize these signs will help you to determine the path of progress. Finding these areas before the rest of the market does is a great hack to get more icing on your cake!

Buyer Bob's Story

Because real estate is so lending based, you must learn to start with what a buyer or a tenant will be paying per month and work backward from there. Let's start with Bob. Bob recently got a new job at a city waste facility in the heart of Smallville. He's paid an average salary for someone working in Smallville. Bob is excited to finally buy a home and gets pre-approved with a lender. The lender determines that based on Bob's debt to income ratio, Bob can afford to pay $1,500 per month. This means Bob can buy a house for, say, $200,000.

Did Bob know he wanted to pay $200,000? Nope, the lender told him that's what he could pay, so that set Bob's expectation. Bob finds a real estate agent and asks to see homes listed at $200,000 and under. The agent sets Bob up on a drip campaign that notifies Bob when new listings in this price range hit the market. Bob checks his email daily and asks to see homes he likes. When he finds one he likes, Bob makes an offer, gets accepted, closes escrow, and becomes a homeowner. Congrats, Bob!

This is how the vast majority of buyers in America buy homes. But, what would have happened if Bob didn't see anything he liked for $200,000 or less? Well, Bob would have had a few options.

1. Save up more money, get a promotion, and get approved for the house he really wants.
2. Rent an apartment or live with a family member or friend.
3. Adjust his expectations and buy something he does not like as much to live in for now, and start saving to buy his dream home later.
4. Start looking farther away to find an area where nicer houses cost less, and keep looking until he finds houses he will like for $200,000 in his target area.

Which of these options do you think the average American is most likely to choose? Sure, there are a few people with the self-discipline to delay gratification and save money to buy a house they love. There are even fewer willing to buy something they don't like to invest for the future. But the vast majority of Americans will move farther away from their ideal location to find a house they love. Remember, a lot of people make decisions based on emotion, and the home we buy affects our emotional state. Don't underestimate this just because you're an investor and tend to look at numbers more. Most people don't.

So, what is Buyer Bob most likely to do? He's going to ask his agent to include cities farther away until he finds one where he can get the homes he likes for $200,000. If the city isn't unreasonably far from his work, he'll buy there and find a way to adjust his life around the home purchase. He may trade in his Chevy Camaro for a used Honda Civic, cut down on eating out, and start working a little overtime, but he'll make the adjustments he needs to get the house he wanted.

If we understand this is how most buyers think and act, it becomes very logical that we should try to anticipate where they will be moving. Buyer Bob's journey detailed the path of progress for Smallville. Central Smallville was too expensive for the average blue-collar worker, so these workers started moving away until they found the area they could afford to be in.

The direction these buyers moved in is the path of progress. Looking back, it's easy to see why an area appreciated in value. Bob's story is an example of how this works. Values spread when the central location reaches a point where it becomes unaffordable for the majority of buyers. This then pushes the buyers slowly outward, in a circle, toward neighboring cities or areas. This "circle" expands outward unless it hits some form of barrier, in which case the buyers are redirected.

A Case Study of San Francisco

At the time of writing this book, the city of San Francisco is experiencing a growth surge like I have never seen. Property values are absolutely exploding to unrealistic levels.[8] In 2018 alone, the median home price has risen by $205,000.[9] With this, rents have climbed so high that people making six figures a year have to share one-bedroom apartments just to afford to live! If you bought a property in San Francisco a year or two ago, you'd probably already have made six figures in equity. The growth has been staggering. San Francisco is an extreme example of what can happen to an area's property values in a few short years. This tsunami of demand causes values to explode when the supply is limited. Learning from San Francisco can help us notice when it starts happening in other areas so we can be prepared to act.

As San Francisco became insanely expensive, buyers and tenants were pushed outward into the greater Bay Area. This led to home prices rising steadily farther and farther away. As these homes become too ex-

---

8   Troy Onink, "The New Geography of Jobs: Where You Live Matters More than Ever," *Forbes* (May 22, 2012). https://www.forbes.com/sites/troyonink/2012/05/22/the-new-geography-of-jobs-where-you-live-matters-more-than-ever/#7260f59038f1

9   Adam Brinklow, "SSan Francisco's Median House Price Climbs to $1.61 Million," Curbed San Francisco (April 5, 2018). https://sf.curbed.com/2018/4/5/17201888/san-francisco-median-home-house-price-average-2018

pensive for the average worker to afford, they were pushed farther and farther away. San Francisco became the epicenter of a massive rise in home and rent prices creating an affordability crisis in the Bay Area. If you saw this coming, and bought early, you made lots and lots of money. The path of progress was logical and predictable, therefore repeatable. Learn to recognize when you see similar signs in the area you invest, then take action accordingly!

Geographic and Economic Barriers

As San Francisco became too expensive, buyers could not head south because that led them right to Silicon Valley, where the tech industry is headquartered. Big, successful mega companies like Apple and Google have their headquarters there, and home prices were already higher than San Francisco's! Because going south wasn't an option, buyers couldn't move that direction and the path of progress did not follow that route.

West was not an option because of a geographic barrier, namely, the ocean. That left east and north as the only available ways for the path of progress to take. If we start looking north, that leads us into Marin County. This is an area with very expensive homes owned by typically wealthy people. This is also the direction of Napa Valley, where some of the best winemakers in the world get their grapes. This was not a feasible direction for the path of progress because it was already too expensive, much like heading south.

This led to many homebuyers moving northeast into Sonoma County and east into Alameda, Contra Costa, and San Joaquin counties. Sonoma County saw a boom in demand as buyers flooded the area. Even though the commute was an hour or more in some places, buyers were still willing to make the drive because wages were so high in San Francisco (see the next segment, "Economic Growth," for more info on that). As houses started selling over asking price with multiple offers, comparable sales continued to rise, allowing appraisers to give home sales higher values.

This led to increased rents as more and more people chose to sell their rentals and cash in on the higher values. With fewer available properties to rent and rising rents, landlords came out way ahead. After enough of this, home builders moved into the area and started building tons of homes. At this point, many home builders are moving into this area to meet the rising demand and lack of supply. If you bought before any of this happened, you found your property growing in value quickly.

The path of progress also found its way east, most notably to the city of Oakland. Oakland is the first market buyers would come to heading east from San Francisco. It's also a city nationally recognized for being one of the most dangerous, crime-riddled cities in the country. In spite of this fact, Oakland property values increased at a crazy rate as more and more buyers moved in there.

Why? Even though most buyers in a normal market would want nothing to do with Oakland, many found a way to make it work once they realized they simply could not afford to live in San Francisco and didn't want a lengthy commute. This led to a "gentrification" of the area as more executive-level businesspeople moved in. Currently, the entire city is experiencing a revitalization in some parts and home prices are higher than they've ever been. This has all been as a result of the path of progress moving this way first.

As the path of progress spilled over Oakland, the surrounding cities all went up in value, too. Cities known for being dangerous or high-crime had more and more buyers moving in because they didn't have any other options. Cities considered to be "too far away" rose in value as buyers had no option but to commute. The local transit system, BART, was extended to help commuters take the train from Contra Costa County into downtown San Francisco. Entire market centers changed to support the path of progress.

One friend of mine, Derek, bought a rental property at an auction in one of these "crime-riddled" cities and made it a rental. Derek recognized the path of progress was making its way into this city and also knew about the public transit that was being extended there. Even though Derek went through several evictions and lengthy repairs from tenant damage, he *still* made tens of thousands of dollars when he sold the property a few years later. This is a prime example of how buying in the path of progress can lead to big results even when everything else is going wrong.

Economic Growth

Economic growth is what drives the path of progress to happen in most cases. As jobs move into an area, people follow. If more people move into an area than there are units to house them, prices will slowly rise. If the jobs that move in offer much higher wages than existed before, prices can rise at a much faster rate. If the home buyers make high wages and can qualify for more money than the house costs, they will make an offer over asking price to be the winning bidder. When homes start selling way over asking price, housing values start rising fast.

This happened in San Francisco because of the tech industry. Many technology start-ups and successful tech companies moved into the area because of its desirable location and amenities. These companies (many of them funded by venture capitalists dumping loads of money into un-proven start-ups) were able to pay wages much higher than the area was used to seeing for employees much less experienced and skilled than the traditional San Francisco employee.

This led to many college grads making over six figures at their first job. Because they all needed to move to San Francisco for work, rental units were snatched up and there wasn't much room left for everyone else. This drove up rent prices, and with that, increased NOI for invest-ment properties. With that, new construction started to take place in the city as more buildings were erected and higher rent was charged. Remember that growing demand and lack of supply is the same moment when you start to see construction equipment downtown? This is every-where in San Francisco. Look to the skyline and you're guaranteed to see a crane somewhere.

Nice Restaurants

When the path of progress has made its way to an area (but before values have already peaked), there are several warning signs things are starting to turn. One of the first warning signs an area is beginning to turn is when what used to be dive bars, liquor stores, and cheap restaurants are starting to turn into upscale establishments with upgraded decor and impressive menus. Restaurants don't turn before an area turns. Business owners do serious due diligence before they make the decision to open a new location and invest that much capital.

If fancy restaurants (or at least not dives) start opening up, it's a very strong indication things are starting to improve. In San Francisco, many of the old diners that hadn't been upgraded in decades were bought by newer establishments and immediately flipped. Talking to locals and asking about what's new and being talked about is a great way to find out if there are new restaurants being opened—a good chance a neigh-borhood is turning.

The "Can You Believe That House Sold for That Much?" Talk

When an area is beginning to turn, this is one of the first things you will hear everyone saying. For those who have lived in the area for a long time, a baseline expectation regarding home values is set in their minds. When something has been a way for a long time, we assume it "should" be that way, and when change is proposed or made known, it catches us off guard and feels "wrong." We see this whenever a new boss starts at a company. Many of the employees will say things like, "That's not the way we used to do it." Usually, nobody is asking how things used to be done, so the only reason for someone to say that is to express their surprise with the current changes.

We see this take place in real estate when people seem shocked that prices are rising. It is a clear indication that buyers and their agents know prices are rising but this information hasn't made it to the general public yet. If the general public doesn't know, you still have a shot to start scooping up properties before it's too late! If people are commenting with shock that properties are rising in value, there is a really good chance the path of progress is knocking at the door.

Key Points

- Find preliminary rent estimates on Rentometer.com.
- Use BiggerPockets calculators to run numbers.
- Get more accurate rental estimates from property managers.
- Look for an area with growing employment opportunities.
- Know the DOM (days on market) of the area you're investing in. The shorter the DOM, the hotter the market.
- Use Craigslist.org for rental comparables.
- Look for signs of construction downtown.
- Buy in the path of progress.
- Look for barriers to entry. Geographic and economic barriers are big.

CHAPTER SEVEN
Tenant Tips

"All wealth comes from adding value, from producing more, better, cheaper, faster, and easier than someone else."

—BRIAN TRACY

Part of being a successful investor is finding the right tenants. If you consider that buying a property is really nothing more than buying a small business that produces income, it becomes very apparent the only income an investment property will generate is the rent. Since there is no way to earn additional income other than waiting for rent to increase with time, keeping our expenses in check becomes crucial to our success!

Without a doubt, the two biggest expenses that hurt your bottom line when it comes to real estate investing are repairs and vacancy. One month of vacancy can wipe out a year's worth of rent increases from a new listing agreement. One tenant destroying a property can wipe out several years of cash flow! With this being said, choosing your tenants wisely can make you quite a bit of money. Several factors go into choosing tenants wisely and it's important you understand them before buying a property.

How to Find, and Keep, Great Tenants

If you want to find the best tenant, consider the process of choosing the best buyer for your home when you're selling it. As a Realtor, I've learned the No. 1 factor that determines what a house sells for isn't the money that's been spent upgrading it or what the seller believes it's worth. By far, the one and only metric that affects the price a home sells for is how many people want it.

Every single thing I do to market a home, every decision I make, is geared toward drawing multiple offers. Once we receive multiple offers, the ball is in my court. I have the ability to drive the price higher. I have the ability to counter the buyers to improve their terms. I have the ability to pit buyers against each other and capitalize on their emotional state of wanting the home more than it makes sense to. When I get multiple offers, I put my clients in the driver's seat.

Listing a home for rent is very similar to listing a home for sale. The more potential interest you can gather, the more you can tweak the terms of the lease and the rent amount in your favor. Knowing this, I've learned there are certain things I can do to improve my odds of finding the best tenants, and finding multiple tenants who want my property. The following are some of the techniques I've used to do just that.

Buy Near Hospitals

As we discussed earlier, the economic engine of a market is a huge driver toward the success of that market. Buying near a hospital is one of the single most critically important things you can do to ensure you always have a steady stream of reliable, well employed, professional tenants willing to rent your property. Renting to tenants like this isn't a guarantee you won't have problems, but it does put the odds significantly in your favor.

Hospitals hire highly educated employees for most of the positions they need to fill. Doctors, nurses, anesthesiologists, bookkeepers, insurance workers, floor managers—they all require varying levels of education and professionalism. This is good for the quality of tenant looking to rent near a hospital. Additionally, not only do hospitals tend to hire highly educated employees, they also hire part-time, traveling employees to fill many of their positions.

Why does this matter to you as a landlord? Traveling employees taking part-time positions in hospitals who know they will be leaving in a matter of months or years aren't very likely to buy a property to live in when they know they'll be leaving the area soon. So what are they going to do when it comes to looking for somewhere to live? They are going to rent. Where is the first place they are going to look? As close to the hospital as they can get!

Many successful investors have raved about the success they've had buying near hospitals. If you ever have the opportunity to scoop something up near one, I highly recommend you look into it. One technique I like is to have my real estate agent set up a search for an area that is geographically half a mile around each hospital in town. I then have the agent add my other criteria into the equation such as number of bedrooms, bathrooms, and price. Whenever a property hits the market that meets these criteria in this area, I get an email notification alerting me so I can consider making an offer.

Buy in Areas Where Pride of Ownership Is Apparent

Pride of ownership is hard to define, but I know it when I see it. The idea to this technique is to look to buy properties in areas where the other tenants/owners are taking good care of their property, because your tenants will be more likely to do the same. In police work, we have a concept known as the Broken Window Theory. It is based on a study that showed if a run-down part of town was allowed to stay run-down, the people who lived there would have an easier time keeping it that way.

The theory was introduced in 1982 by social scientists James Q. Wilson and George L. Kelling. It gained traction in 1993 when the new New York mayor, Rudy Giuliani, made it a priority for the New York Police Department to implement. In the article "Broken Windows," published in March 1982 in the *Atlantic Monthly*,[10] Wilson and Kelling stated: "Consider a building with a few broken windows. If the windows are not repaired, the tendency is for vandals to break a few more windows. Eventually, they may even break into the building, and if it's unoccupied, perhaps become squatters or light fires inside. Or consider a pavement. Some litter accumulates. Soon, more litter accumulates. Eventually, people even start leaving bags of refuse from take-out restaurants there or even break into cars."

The authors of the study concluded when someone lives in an area where things are taken care of, they tend to stay that way. When someone saw a building with a broken window, they were more likely to think it was okay to pick up a brick and throw it, breaking another window. When this happened repeatedly, all the windows ended up broken, and people were more likely to litter, commit vandalism, etc. Small crimes, when left

---

10 George L. Kelling and James Q. Wilson, "Broken Windows: The Police and Neighborhood Safety," *The Atlantic* (March 1982). https://www.theatlantic.com/magazine/archive/1982/03/broken-windows/304465/

unchecked, led to bigger crimes—including increases in violent crimes like robbery, rape, and murder.

The theory was used as a police tactic to cut down on small crimes (infractions) in order to try to prevent more serious crimes, leading to an improvement in the police statistical numbers for New York City. It goes to show the psychology of the human mind and how it relates to its surroundings. Most of us will be on our best behavior when surrounded by others who are, or when the standard is set higher. When in an environment with low expectations and others behaving poorly, most people will lower their standard to that of the group.

This is highlighted in "mob mentality," where people do things in a riot they would never do alone. If we know this is how people behave, it makes sense to make the most of this information when developing our investment strategy. If you buy a property in an area where the majority of your neighbors let their lawns overgrow, your tenants are much more likely to do the same. If the majority of homeowners leave their trash in the front yard or keep broken-down vehicles on the property, your tenants will as well.

This is why we buy in areas known for pride of ownership. It doesn't need to be a class "A" property; it just needs to be in an area with a high standard maintained by the majority of those who live there. If the neighbors are applying social pressure (albeit often subconsciously) to maintain the standard of the neighborhood, your tenants are more likely to adopt that same mind-set. This means good things for your property and the way your tenants will maintain it.

Additionally, consider that the best tenants will not feel comfortable living in a property where the neighborhood is full of broken windows and vandalism. If there is low pride of ownership, the best tenants are going to feel uncomfortable and look to pass. Finding a neighborhood with fewer broken windows gives you a higher chance of success when it comes to keeping your repair costs lower and the quality of your tenant higher!

And once you find tenants who show pride in ownership, you should reward them. You may be asking why you should have to spend money to "reward" someone for something they should be doing anyway. That's a fair question! My challenge to you is, ask yourself if it's fair to expect everyone else to think the same way you do. Let's take a step back and look at this situation from a broader perspective and see if that provides a little more clarity.

Those of you reading this book have already shown several things that separate you from the majority of investors:

1. You invested money into your education by buying this book.
2. You invested time into your future by setting aside time to read it.
3. You want to own investment property, which requires some work to be done and oftentimes doesn't provide an immediate reward.
4. You are willing to spend your money on an investment, not just on yourself or gratifying your immediate needs.
5. You understand it takes something to get something.

To those of us who live our lives this way, this all seems like common sense. To those who may live their lives differently, these are all foreign concepts. Many humans have never been exposed to this kind of thinking and don't see the world through this viewpoint. This is relevant because more often than not, these are the kinds of people who are renting our properties. Let's examine some of the reasons people rent instead of buy:

1. Renting makes more sense than buying for those who have a temporary job or some other reason that requires them to move often.
2. Renting is usually cheaper than buying short term, but much more costly long term.
3. Buying requires the ability to get a loan, which requires a healthy debt to income ratio.
4. Getting a loan also requires a healthy credit score.
5. Getting a loan requires a down payment in most cases, and renting allows one to save up for this down payment.

With the exception of the first example, the other reasons people rent tend to center around the fact that buying a home requires a higher standard of finance management than renting one does. Sure, renting a home may be cheaper than buying one, but 10, 20, or 30 years later, do you really believe it still will be? Rents tend to go up every year. Mortgage payments do not. Tenants and landlords do not think the same, so you, as a landlord, need to tailor your strategy for success around your tenants. If you want your tenants to pay on time, you must reward them for doing so, and punish them for not doing so, and then be consistent about that. If you want your tenants to maintain the landscaping, keep the house clean and in good condition, and not get you fined by the city for code violations, you need to treat them to do just that. When you notice the tenant is keeping great care of the lawn, reward them! One easy way is to wait for the lease renewal, and if the property is kept in good condition, tell the property manager to talk with the tenant and only raise their rent by $50 a month instead of the usual $100.

Buy Near Great Schools

As mentioned earlier, properties near the best schools tend to appreciate the most. This leads to higher-priced homes attracting wealthier families, which oftentimes leads to more well-behaved children attending those schools, increasing the school scores even more. This "virtual cycle" can ensure property values don't drop as much during a recession and will increase more during a good economy. We want to take advantage of this.

To understand this principle, we again have to acknowledge this isn't always the case, but more often than not is the way it works. People who value their children's education want to live near the best schools, and will pay a premium to live there. If they are willing to pay more to live near the best schools, they will usually personally invest much more heavily in their child's lives. Buying near great schools is likely to get you home appreciation, but it's also likely to get you a better tenant. Buying near top-scoring schools is a way to stack the odds in your favor toward finding a higher-quality tenant.

Higher-quality tenants save and make you money in many ways! These are the people who are more likely to be able to afford the rising rent. They are also less likely to trash your property or allow things like water drips to go unreported. They will either fix it or notify you immediately. This leads to less likelihood of mold, dry rot, or other forms of water damage. These properties are also in higher demand, so your vacancy rates will be lower as well.

Lower Vacancy

With vacancy being one of the biggest enemies of your bottom line, you want to look for ways to reduce its negative impact on your profitability. The good news is, there are several things you can do to help your cause in that way, and none of them are too difficult or complicated to pull off! Most of these strategies are all things that work if you go into the situation knowing what your plan will be from the start, and make efforts to set yourself up for success before buying the property.

In certain situations, demand is so high you can advertise a unit for rent with a maximum price and people will still be lined up to rent it. In others, this isn't the case, so we have to be a little more resourceful. To understand how to maximize this tactic, we are going to take a look into human psychology and learn the mind-set of buyers/tenants and what drives their decision-making process so we can develop our strategy around them.

Let's focus on two powerful human character flaws: our greed and our laziness! The vast majority of tenants or buyers want to pay as little as possible for whatever property they buy/rent, but they are usually too lazy (or need to move under a fast timeline) in order to look deeply enough into the entire process to understand exactly how they can save money.

This is why we lower the rent from the start. We want someone in that property ASAP. It rarely makes sense to have a unit vacant for even one week more than it needs to be. The extra rent we may be collecting is usually very small compared to the rent we could lose during an extra month's vacancy. Let's take a look at a hypothetical example.

Shortsighted Steve bought a duplex to rent out as an investment property. Steve ran his numbers and saw he could rent the unit out for anywhere between $1,000 and $1,100 a month. Steve's PM told him the units were typically renting out in 30–90 days after being advertised. Steve was smart enough to buy in an area with a healthy economy and more and more jobs moving in. Additionally, wages were rising in this area and it was known for its top-rated schools.

Steve did everything right! Then, when it came time to rent out the property, his shortsighted nature came back to bite him. Steve insisted on advertising the property for rent at $1,100 a month. He knew at the end of the year that would net him an additional $1,200 minus property management fees. Steve wanted every penny!

As you can guess, Steve's unit sat empty for longer than it needed to. Rather than finding a tenant after 30 days or so, it took Steve 90. Steve ended up finding a tenant to pay the full $1,100, but the rest of the tenants who viewed Steve's property didn't see why they should pay $1,100 a month when there were plenty of options available at $1,000. The tenants instead went with the cheapest option available.

Steve won the battle but lost the war. Had he advertised the unit for $1,000 or even $950 a month, he could have landed a tenant in 30 days or sooner. Because he insisted on a higher rent, he collected an extra

$1,200 at the end of the year (over what he would have collected at $1,000 a month) but he incurred $2,000 in lost revenue (two months of $1,000 a month) had he just advertised the units for less to find a tenant ASAP. Steve's shortsighted perspective cost him $800.

Now, you may be wondering if this is *really* the best option. After all, that extra $1,200 a year will add up over several years, right? If you give it enough time, this strategy would make more sense. The beauty of this strategy is we aren't done! There is a whole other element to this strategy we haven't covered yet. That being, after the first year, we raise the rent back to what maximum rent for the area would be and watch as most of the tenants would rather pay than move.

Why does this work? The vast majority of people will not want to move out of their home, pay a moving company to move their stuff (or bother their friends), turn off the power, garbage, electric, cable, etc. in their name, then move it all over to a new property, or pull their kids out of their great school, all to save $100 a month. This, of course, does not apply to college rentals (or other yearly-rental situations) where students move in and out of apartments each year during school.

This is why we start by advertising a unit at a cheaper price, get someone in right away, then make up for that lost rent in year one over the next 30, 40, or 50 years we own that property. Once our tenants are established in their new home, they aren't going to want to leave unless something very compelling pushes them out and we can take advantage of that fact to bring rent back to market level as soon as it's time to renew their lease.

Another way to decrease your vacancy period is very simple: Be good at your job of being a landlord! When something breaks, fix it quickly. When your attention is needed, give it promptly. Don't let you as the owner be the reason your tenant decides to move out and find a different property because you acted like a slumlord. Handle things correctly on your end and your tenants will be less likely to leave.

Now, it's clearly my position that for most of us, we should be using property management to handle our rentals. If this is the case for you, you don't need to be good at your job of landlording, but you do need to *hire* someone who is good! Finding a great, responsive, and wise property manager will shorten your vacancy periods because your tenants will have less reason to go through the inconvenience of a move in areas where most people don't move each year.

Another perk of hiring a property manager is you don't have to be the bad guy; they do. Oftentimes my tenants make frivolous requests for things not covered in the lease. And they usually are requests the tenant could easily handle themselves. Things like asking me to replace the lawn mower when theirs breaks because the lease states the lawn must be mowed, or asking me to replace air filters or light bulbs, or to repair things *they* broke. I know the right answer is to say no, but do I really want to be the jerk who says it? This is why you want a PM. Let them be the jerk! Actually, it's easy for them to say no, because they get to blame you—the anonymous owner! "I'm sorry Mr. Smith, but unfortunately the landlord has denied your request to replace the window you broke playing catch in the house with your son. It looks like you'll have to pay for that yourself." See how much easier it is for them when they can blame us? See how much easier it is for us when we can have them be the bad guy?

Another great hack you can use to lower your vacancy involves something as simple as the date you write in your lease. In most parts of the country, the majority of leases are set for one year, and then become month-to-month after that. During that year's time, rents usually rise. If a tenant stops paying rent during the time period of the lease, they can be sued. Once the lease is up, the tenant can give their notice and move out of your unit without owing you anything.

This becomes a problem when the tenant decides to leave during a time of year when nobody else is looking to rent or buy property. Typically, this is the case during the winter months. If you find you have a vacant unit during this time, you may be lowering the rent dramatically or finding your unit sits unoccupied for much longer than normal. This increased vacancy can kill your bottom line, all when it doesn't need to be that way at all.

If you have a tenant move in during the winter, don't assume you need a 12-month lease that will also expire during the winter. Consider a 15–16 month lease for the first run, and time it to expire in the spring when other people are all looking to buy or sell. This way, when you get a winter vacancy, you're primed to have a house to sell or a rental to advertise when everyone else is already looking! This one simple move can decrease your vacancy by thousands of dollars over time.

The vast majority of tenants are not going to care if the lease is for 15–16 months instead of 12 because it's less common for people to move into a new unit expecting to only live there for a year if they really like the location and the property. If anything, they are buying themselves a few more months of last year's rent before the new rent hike comes in! If you do this right, you only have to do it for the first year, then your lease will be set to expire at the perfect time of year, every time, every year.

Self-Management vs. Professional Management

With all this talk about using a property manager, how do we know if it's the right choice for us? Hiring a property manager sounds more convenient, but it's also more expensive. Managing a property ourselves can save us money, but is it really worth all the headache? Before you can decide if you should manage your own property, or if someone else should, let's examine some of the pros and cons to each. By matching up the benefits to each method, it's much easier to decide which is right for you.

Pros to Self-Management

First off, there are two *major* pros to self-management that compel the overwhelming majority of those who practice this method to do so. They are:

1. No one will care about your property as much as you do.
2. Like every other service, property management costs money.

With both reasons being important, I still believe number one is the more important reason to self-manage, should you go that route. Your taking care of and treating your property with a high level of effort is by far the best reason to commit to self-management of a property.

Property managers, like everyone else, are a mixed bag. Some are good, most are not, and a handful are exceptional. Odds are, no matter who you use, they won't care as much as you do, and that's something you need to accept right away. If you can't accept it, self-management may be the only option that will keep you sane. A property manager's job is to keep your unit occupied, in reasonably good shape, and money flowing into your bank account. They'll likely do the bare minimum, simply because it's not their property.

Many investors drive by their properties routinely and notice things like newspapers piling up in the driveway, the shrubbery overgrown, or the lawn not being cut. For some people, this drives them crazy and robs them of their peace of mind. For these kind of people, self-management may be necessary just to stay sane! When I rent my property out to someone else, I relinquish control of maintaining my personal standards because I can't impose those on someone else. All I can legally impose are the details contained in the lease.

The biggest pro to self-management is the fact you get more control over the property. You get more control over the lease you have the tenant sign. If you see something you don't like, you can have it corrected. Also, you're more likely to see things you don't like if you're paying more attention. Property managers will walk the property according to the amount of times you pay them to. If you self-manage, you don't have to worry about spending a dime to walk the property, which means you're likely to go to your property and make sure it's up to your standards.

Many people don't realize it, but property management often charges for more than just collecting the rent. Property management can charge you for walking the property, advertising the property for rent, collecting rent, managing a rehab, managing repairs, and renewing the lease (even if the same tenant remains). When you manage your own property, you do all this work, but you also avoid having to pay for it. For those with more time and less money, this can often be a better strategy for managing your rental.

Cons to Self-Management

The biggest con to self-management is the amount of time and energy it takes to do so. This, frankly, can ruin real estate investing for many different types of personalities. In my opinion, property management is the worst part of real estate investing. It is demanding, gives the least amount of satisfaction, and provides none of the "thrill of the hunt" that makes investing exciting. Finding a great deal can feel like making a great play. If real estate investing was football, finding and closing on a deal is equivalent to a wide receiver catching a touchdown pass. If we stick with this analogy, property management is like the offensive line. Underappreciated, no glory, no fun, and only gets blamed when things go wrong.

For some people, this isn't a problem. Taking care of the daily tasks and keeping the wheels rolling is something they enjoy! Much like the offensive line, they keep things moving and make up the backbone of the team. If this is you, and you actually enjoy this stuff, managing your own properties (at least in the beginning stages) may make sense. But if this *isn't* you, I would consider more than just money before jumping in.

In my opinion, most people who choose to manage a property don't do it because they believe they'll be good at it. They do it because they want to save money. Not always a good move! Managing a property, much like other jobs, is an acquired skill. It takes a certain kind of mind-set, temperance, disposition, and ability to communicate that makes this possible. Before attempting to learn this trade, ask yourself if it's really the best use of your time. Is the money you save doing this yourself more than you could make doing something else like finding a new deal, managing a rehab, or working overtime at your current job?

Don't assume you're saving money by doing a job yourself. Sometimes it costs you money in the long run by robbing you of time, energy, and effort you could have put somewhere else. Any time we choose to do one thing, we choose not to do something else. This could be time spent with kids, time reading the next business book that could change your life, time in the gym, or simply time recharging so you can do everything else more effectively. Understand the value of your time before you decide to manage your own properties. The cons to this aspect of real estate are significant!

Pros to Property Management

There are many pros to property management, but the best reason might surprise you. In my opinion, the biggest pro to using property management isn't the money you save, it's the experience you leverage by using someone else who is better at this and has done this longer than you. This is where you learn how to become a better investor, see things through different eyes, and improve your own systems through being exposed to those of others!

A good property manager has to be efficient. They don't make much money for what they do, so if they want to turn a profit, they need to have high volume. In order to handle this increased workload, they have no choice but to develop killer systems to save time and save money.

If you get close enough to them, you can learn from the way they have set up these systems and start implementing them in your own business. Property managers often need to find cheap handymen. If you find the one they are using, you may just be able to use them on your other properties as well.

Another pro to property management is the fact you can learn a lot about an area through asking their opinion of it. You may be managing one or two houses. Most property managers are handling many more than that. They know which areas draw their best tenants. They know what amenities tenants in an area want. They know how long units are staying vacant, where people are moving to, and which areas are seeing rent go up the fastest. When you use a property management company, you are gaining access to all this intel as you gather it from them! Property managers also understand the law much better than most investors do—after all, it's their job. Now to be clear, I'm not referring to a real estate agent who manages property on the side. I'm talking about a business, or a company, that deals solely with managing rental property.

The final big pro to using property management is you get to benefit from their experience. Property managers screen tenants for a living. They are much better at recognizing a good one than you would be just starting out. They can start, execute, and finish an eviction much faster than you, as they are more experienced in doing them and have more resources to throw at them than most of us. We have to take time from finding a deal or working our full-time job to manage the eviction, but for a property manager this *is* their full-time job. Property managers also know how to get tenants to pay on time, or can advise you on matters like not taking partial rent from a tenant you plan to evict. Many a newbie investor has made a mistake like this. Don't let that be you! You can benefit from their knowledge and experience by hiring a good property manager.

Cons to Property Management

The biggest con to using property management is it's so hard to find a good one. In fact, finding even a decent one can seem hard. It takes a lot of time, as well as some trial and error, to find a property manager that will work for you and meet your needs. This up-front investment is one of the biggest cons to property management.

Another big con is the money you have to spend. As we've already covered, their services aren't free and you have to pay them to do the jobs you don't want to do. Many investors see a better ROI by avoiding paying for property management and don't want to give that up. Others buy a property without budgeting for property management fees and end up in a situation where they literally can't pay for one without losing money every month. Property management eating into the bottom line is another big reason people don't get them.

The last con is the fact that property managers will usually tell you what you want to hear up front, and it's not until later that you find you're not happy with their services. At that point, it can be costly to get out of your agreement and you may find yourself stuck with this property manager. Having to go through an experience like this can really sour you on using property management and can make the entire process more frustrating than it already is.

How to Find a Great Property Manager

So how do we find a great property manager that isn't a dud? If finding a good one is so important, it stands to reason we should make this a priority in our business, right? Your property manager will become the only link between you and your property. They will be caring for it, managing it, and helping it thrive. If you get a good one, not only will they manage your property well, but they will also help you grow your business.

Just like every other part of your business, finding great talent starts with getting referrals. Great referrals come from great people, and can help successfully grow your business. When you boil it down, there are traditionally two ways to hire someone.

1. You sift through strangers, found through random means, and trust your gut.
2. You interview strangers, found through trusted sources, and trust a combination of your gut and the information provided to you by people you trust.

Which would you rather do? I know for me, it's option 2. I prefer having someone referred to me because it either came from someone I've worked with—and trusted—or from a rockstar who I know would demand a high level of execution. And it's not like I have to fly blind, because I will still be able to interview the referral myself. I'll also be informed if the property manager has any weaknesses and can decide for myself if I'd help them improve, or should move on to another candidate. The important thing is that I'll know ahead of time, not when it's too late. You'll save time and money when you hire trusted referrals rather than a stranger whose claims you can't back up.

These are all strong reasons why I believe the first place we should look for help is from the people we already know who are crushing it in their line of work. For example, Grant Cardone is nationally recognized as a big-time investor, who buys big-time properties, and is running an effective business. If he's using a property manager for one of his buildings, what are the odds that person sucks at their job? Not very high. I don't know Grant, but I know his level of success and I doubt he's very likely to allow sub-par performance from someone managing one of his properties.

Who do you know that is already crushing it in a space that you can ask for a referral from? If the only people you know have no reason to help you out, what can you do to incentivize them to help you? Finding out what others need and meeting those needs is a great way to get them interested in doing the same for you. Learning how to meet others' needs is a powerful business skill to develop. Why not start now to accomplish this important task of finding a great PM?

Another great place to look for a referral is BiggerPockets.com. Many of the regular contributors on BiggerPockets have content you can read through to see if they know what they are talking about or not. Bigger-Pockets makes it simple to search through the site and find content each member has provided.

In addition to finding members who can provide referrals, you can also find property managers themselves on the site. Remember, for every problem you have investing in real estate, there is a person whose job it is to fix that problem. These people are looking for you. They are looking to find business for themselves, and you are their client! Finding solid, reputable property managers on BiggerPockets is a matter of searching for them in the navigation bar, finding a few who seem intelligent, then researching their name to see what other investors have to say about them.

One way to verify if your PM has a good reputation is to ask them what other BiggerPockets members they are managing property for. Once they give you the names, simply send a colleague request to that member and start a dialogue asking them what they like and don't like about this particular property manager. Most investors love to talk about real estate investing and will tell you everything you could want to know about the property manager. If the majority of the time is spent venting about what they don't like, that's not a good sign. If you ask several investors and they all provide you with the same negative feedback, that's not a good sign, either.

Your goal is to interview several different investors who use the same property manager and look for patterns in the feedback. If one investor says the PM is slow getting back to them, it may be because that investor is particularly annoying and the PM is avoiding them in order to stay productive. If the majority of the investors are all saying the same thing, you have found a pattern and should recognize that. Patterns reflect what you can expect. If the majority of the feedback you receive is positive or negative, that's what you can expect to experience yourself.

The final way I look for great property managers is by asking members of my Core Four which property manager they or their clients are using. Remember, I try to only work with Core Four members who invest themselves. This means they are more likely to have a property manager I can trust! If they work with many different other investors, odds are they are seeing the same property management company being used for the majority of their clients. This would represent a pattern and would be a positive indication I should be digging deeper into that company and finding more out regarding why they are so popular!

How to Interview Your Property Manager

A good reputation is a strong starting point, but it's only the beginning of your due diligence. Once you find a PM with a good reputation, it's time to interview them to find out if the two of you would be a good fit. As with any good relationship, it's important to remember the interview is composed of two parts:

1. Determining if the PM is a good fit for your needs and expectations.
2. Determining if you are a good fit for your property manager's needs and expectations.

You may find it surprising that the second part exists. Many people forget that even though they are "hiring" the property manager, they are still entering into a business relationship, and relationships are always two-way streets. If you find yourself not holding up your end of the bargain, you are also likely to find the communication souring between the two of you as the relationship deteriorates. If this happens, everybody loses.

When I interview a property manager, I am looking to accomplish four things:

1. Find out about them as a person.
2. Find out about their experience and skill as a property manager.
3. Find out if they invest in real estate themselves.
4. Gather a list of resources for me to verify them with.

Because my first priority is to learn about them as a person, I usually start the conversation there. By asking them personal questions about their life and work, I can get a better feel for who they are, what their values are, and sometimes even gather information regarding their character. It's important at this stage to ask open-ended questions and let them talk as much as possible without interrupting. I've found if I'm not careful, I'll guide the person I'm interviewing to answer in the way I'm looking for—and this isn't helpful. By limiting my participation in the early stages of the interview, I'm more likely to see who this person is at their core.

If the property manager has a hard time answering simple questions like this, it doesn't mean they can't do the job, but it would be concerning to me. Part of what makes a PM good is their persuasive ability to get tenants to pay or adjust a tenant's unrealistic expectations. For most tenants who are short on money on any particular month, they will have the money to pay rent, but will choose to pay other bills instead. A good property manager can use their skills to get the tenant to pay their rent before paying other bills—and keep them from being evicted in the process.

Below are some of the open-ended questions I use to start off a conversation with a PM.

- What got you started in the business?
- What do you find to be the most challenging part of this business, and why?
- What do you find to be the most rewarding part of the business, and why?
- What are some attributes of your favorite clients?
- How do you handle difficult clients?
- Which type of properties do you like to manage, and why?
- Which areas in town are you familiar with and manage?
- What are your plans for the future?
- What do you do for fun?
- If you were immediately gifted with five insanely talented employees, what are the parts of the job you would never want to give away because you enjoy it so much, and why?

Asking questions like this forces the person I'm interviewing to share more of who they are and what they believe their strengths are. It also lets me know what I can expect from them and how they like to operate. By asking questions about their ideal client, they share with me the blueprint for how I can "win" with them. By asking questions about their nightmare clients, I learn what I need to avoid. The trick is, most people will answer what makes a dream or nightmare client by responding with what they enjoy most or least about the job. If a nightmare client is someone who never listens to them, I know they have a high level of confidence about their opinion. If their dream client is someone who emails instead of calls, I know their system is set up to support that level of communication better than a phone call.

Again, the key is to get them talking without interrupting or guiding them. Asking open-ended questions prevents them from answering with "yes" or "no," and also prevents them from telling you what they think you want to hear. If I find the PM is extremely unskilled at carrying on a conversation and establishing rapport, I would ask who does the communicating with the tenants. If they give me someone else's name, I would end the interview by asking for that person's contact info. If they tell me it's them who communicates with the tenants (and they are not great at conversing) I wouldn't consider hiring them since a strong ability to communicate is too important an element of doing a project manager's job.

When I'm listening to their answers, I'm looking for a particular pattern to reveal itself. I want to see a trend of several character traits that are going to make me feel more comfortable entrusting them with my properties. These trends include:

- Blunt honesty
- Pickiness with who they take on as clients
- Specificity regarding how they handle problems or which of their employees handle problems
- Details regarding the systems they have in place
- A proactive, rather than a reactive, approach
- A specific market knowledge about real estate
- A flexibility to learn better ways or get better at their job
- The fact they own and invest in real estate themselves
- The ability to understand the language of real estate investors (cap rates, ROI, cash flow, capex, etc.)
- A strong understanding of current rental rates
- A strong understanding of the economic environment

Makes sense, right? By asking the right questions and carefully analyzing their answers, you can get a good idea for if the property manager really is the rockstar you were told they were, or if they are ruthlessly good at tricking people into believing they are! The questions I ask are too specific to real estate and too detailed for them to lie their way through—giving me a higher level of confidence they know what they are talking about.

If you don't like the answers the property manager has given you, politely end the interview and excuse yourself from the conversation. If you *do* like the answers they've provided you, congratulations—you are halfway done! The next part consists of clearly communicating your needs, your expectations, and what you can bring to the relationship. If what you bring matches what they want, you just might have found yourself a match!

I always like to present myself in the same way. I explain where I'm from and how I got started, go on to talk about what my needs are right now, then finish by detailing what my future plans are. While talking, I pay careful attention to their facial expressions. Many people have a difficult time keeping a "poker face" while listening to someone else talk. A flash of their eyes widening lets you know you just said something that impressed them, and a furrowing of the brow lets you know you touched on a nerve and said something they don't like or don't agree with. The way they respond when I talk lets me know if my goals and values align with theirs, and that's what I'm looking for.

My story would go something like this:

"Well, I'm a police officer who started working lots of overtime and using the money to buy rentals. Because it took so much time and effort to save the money to buy these properties, *I obviously value them very highly*. They are representative of hours and hours, years really, of lost sleep, damaged relationships, and unhealthy living. I gave it all up to get the money to buy them, *so the way they perform is really important to me*!

"Now I'm looking to buy *one to two properties a month*. If you do a good job with the properties I give you, *I see no reason why I couldn't bring them all to you*. What's most important to me is you are *brutally honest*. Anyone can manage a property halfway decently and collect rent. I need more than that. I need advice on *which markets to invest in, which parts of town to stay away from, what kind of rehab work I should be doing, and who the best agents, lenders, and rehabbers to work with are.*

"In the future, I plan on buying *three to five properties a month*. I'd like to own 75 to 100 units in the next ten years, and *I'd prefer to use the same property manager for all of them*. What's important to me is that my PM is handling all the issues I can't, and *making sure my portfolio is profitable enough for it to make sense for me to keep buying*. I need repair costs to be low and for rents to be *raised every year consistent with the market average*."

As you can see, I have emphasized certain parts of the conversation. This doesn't mean I'm pronouncing these words differently, it means these are parts of the conversation where I have just said something I deem to be significant and I'm looking closely at the facial expression of the PM to see if they agree or disagree with my feelings. These "tells" are what I rely on more than the actual answers they give me. It's easy to fake a reply when you have time to think about what you're going to say; it's very difficult and takes a high level of focus and determination to fake facial expressions!

These are all tricks I learned working as a cop, by the way. When suspects would lie, there was almost always a way you could tell by their response—and it had very little to do with the actual information they were providing. A change in the tone of voice, a look of "oh, shoot" given away by raised eyebrows, a hesitancy to speak after they just opened their mouth to reply. All these things gave away the true feelings of the suspect and were much more accurate than how clever they were with their words.

When you get to an italicized part of the conversation, pay careful attention. In the first paragraph I say, *"I obviously value them very highly."* This is me explaining I'm going to have a high standard for the property manager. If they are in agreement with the value I place on my properties, I'd expect to see a subtle head nod or them inching forward to get closer to me as a way to display their interest in something I've just said. If they look taken aback, fearful, or give a smug smile, they are giving away the fact they think I take my portfolio too seriously or that it's unrealistic to expect them to care as much as I do.

In the third paragraph I say, *"I prefer to use the same property manager for all of them."* At this point, I'm expecting a look similar to a dog when dinner is about to be served. I want them to look hungry! Any property manager worth their salt would be sensing this means big opportunities, and they don't want to screw it up. If I don't see a positive response, I'd be worried. I may even find they interrupt me at this point to let me know how good they are and how they won't let me down. This would be a good thing! I want to see they are excited and really want to impress me. If they look apathetic, I would be concerned because it shows they are not particularly driven to succeed. If they aren't driven to succeed for themselves, why would they be for me and my portfolio?

In the final paragraph I say how *"making sure my portfolio is profitable enough for it to make sense for me to keep buying."* At this point, I'm expecting to see a long, slow nod, indicating they understand the picture I have been painting and are eager for the ability to show me what they can do. I've painted a very ambitious picture for them regarding my future goals, and I've done this on purpose. If they have a "deer in the headlights" look, it's more than likely because they know they don't have the systems, people, or infrastructure to handle what I want to do. If they have the look of eagerness paired with understanding, it likely means they believe they are just the person to help me achieve my goals.

Now, I haven't explained what to look for at every turning point of the conversation, but I think I've explained enough for you to understand what you should be noticing. Practice talking and articulating your thoughts without being so focused on yourself that you miss catching how others are reacting as you talk. You'll be amazed at how much information people give away with no idea they are doing it!

The last thing I want to take from a conversation with a PM is a list of other investors they work with. Now, of course, they are likely to only refer me to the people who love them the most. I get that. But I don't let that deter me. It's not their job to provide me with referrals that will provide me with bad feedback, it's my job to dig deep on these referrals and find out what it's really like to work with this PM! If I can get a list of names, a sense of confidence that this PM can handle what I want, and a strong feeling from them that they want to work with me, I'm usually ready to consider hiring them for the job.

How to Establish Systems with Your Property Manager

Once you've decided you want to start working with a PM, it's important to note I *don't* think it's a good idea to give them your entire portfolio right away. If you have a portfolio, I'd recommend giving them one property to manage. If you don't have a portfolio yet and this would be your first property, I would recommend buying your first place and letting them manage it, then finding a different property manager to manage the second. As a rule, I have a minimum of two property managers in every market I invest in. This serves several purposes, the most important being if there is a change of leadership in one (someone quits, sells the company, dies, etc.) I have a backup plan in place to take over my portfolio. The other big reason is if a property manager starts to do less than a stellar job, I'm not forced to stay with them and be frustrated.

And why do property managers sometimes do less than stellar jobs? It typically comes down to two reasons.

1. Lack of effort or care.
2. Lack of systems.

Lack of effort is something I can't fix. If my PM is showing a lack of effort or concern for my properties, I can't do anything about that but find someone new. Lack of systems, however, is something I can help them with. Creating systems to manage my own business is something I'm always looking to accomplish. After all, that's an entire section of this book! It's important when we first start working with a property manager that we develop systems with them to get the desired results.

All good systems start with communication. The property manager needs to know what I expect, and my expectations need to be reasonable. It is one thing to say I expect a phone call every week to tell me nothing happened, or a weekly walkthrough of my property. It is another thing to expect a property manager to actually do that—without paying them, that is. Property managers run on slim margins, and for those who don't understand that, they can get a little unreasonable with some of their requests. Communicating your needs to the PM is important, but so is listening to them if they tell you it's not going to happen, or you'll be charged extra for that.

Once you've communicated your expectations, the PM is likely to let you know the systems they currently have in place to meet your needs. Unless you are their first client, they likely already have at least a few systems to help run their business. Common systems I see are online portals that allow investors to check to see what rent came in that month, monthly automatic email statements, a policy that dictates the terms of things like lease renewals, and rules set in place for when the PM will make a repair or replacement.

Knowing what systems the PM already has in place will help you understand what to expect from them, as well as what you cannot yet expect from them. It is the things you cannot yet expect, because they do not have a system in place, that you need to start addressing with the PM. This communication is crucial. I find that the majority of relationships that go sour are from expectations not being met. The most common cause of unmet expectations is poor communication of those expectations in the first place.

Lack of communication takes place for several reasons. Sometimes one party is too shy, other times they get too busy. Sometimes one believes it is "common sense" and they shouldn't have to say anything about it. Other times we know in our hearts the expectation is unreasonable so we just avoid mentioning it. In some cases, we are so afraid of conflict or not being liked that we won't say how we feel or what we want or need. Regardless of the reason, if we don't communicate our expectations, we have no one but ourselves to blame when things go badly because of it.

One big topic I want to make sure I cover with the property manager is who they will send to do work when something goes wrong. Most PMs have a system in place for sending someone to do work when a tenant requests it, but many of them don't verify that the work is actually the landlord's responsibility. It is much easier to just pay someone to make the problem go away, using the landlord's money, as long as the landlord isn't noticing it. This is one of the problems with authorizing a PM to make repairs under a certain amount without your approval. You can't know if the repairs are something you should be paying for.

To cover this problem, I'll request the PM create a system of notifying me or my representative when a tenant makes a claim. I ask for a picture of the damage to be provided, as well as a description of how the tenant believed it happened and how they discovered it. After this, I ask the PM to send me an email with their recommendation on who should pay for it, and why. If the PM recommends I pay for it, I ask them what in the lease or in landlord case law justifies this opinion. Most PMs know if they can't provide this, it's better not to even ask me. In those cases, they tell the tenant they should pay for it before the request even makes it to me. Creating this system keeps me from paying for things I shouldn't just because it's easier for the PM to resolve the problem that way.

If an issue arises, and it's determined to be my responsibility to fix, the PM can either send a handyman they have on the payroll, or call someone I prefer using. This is something I want to square away early on, because many PMs use management agreements that specify they have the right to send their own person. In most cases, I want to find a handyman of my own choosing, not theirs. I prefer this because I trust my own handyman more, they are usually cheaper, and I can get info from them regarding the condition of the property and how the tenants are taking care of it when they show up to make the repairs. I'm not likely to get this from the property manager's recommendation.

Another system I like to create with my PM is to have them set a reminder to notify me two months before a tenant's contract is set to expire. I want to know two months ahead of time so I can start doing research to find what current market rents are and give the tenant the opportunity to renew their lease before it goes month-to-month. This also gives me the opportunity to consider selling the property if that's an option, but most importantly, it makes sure the PM doesn't forget the lease is month-to-month and go to the tenant with a rent increase letter!

I also go over with my PM how I want to receive my money. Some PMs want to send you a check in the mail, as it can be easier for them, but this does *not* work for me. Having to run to the bank to deposit checks is one reason why I don't want checks mailed to me. I prefer to receive mine via direct deposit or mobile deposit, and it's important to communicate this to the PM *before* signing an agreement with them. This is when you have your leverage! If you want your money deposited a certain way, you have a much better chance of getting them to agree to an exception when they are still trying to win your business than you do after they have already won it.

Creating systems you and your PM are both comfortable with is a crucial part of ensuring your rental property business runs smoothly. Be sure you read the entire management agreement before signing it, as oftentimes you are going to be charged for things you assumed were included in the monthly percentage you're paying for. Lease renewals, handyman callouts, and walkthroughs are all things property managers used to do for free but now charge for. Reading their agreement and negotiating what you want changed is something you should do early on in the relationship if you want things to go well!

Key Points

- Have your PM notify you two months prior to your property's lease ending.
- Buy near hospitals.
- Buy near good schools.
- Know the pros and cons to self-management vs. professional management.
- Learn how to find and interview property managers.

PART FIVE

The Refinance Process

CHAPTER EIGHT
Choosing Your Lender

"Twenty years from now you will be more disappointed by the things that you didn't do than by the ones you did do."

—MARK TWAIN

A crucial part of ensuring the BRRRR process works for you is to know you can actually pull money out before you start the process. It can be crippling to your success if you invest all your capital in acquisition and rehab of a property, only to find out at the end of the project that you can't qualify for a loan and can't refinance the deal. Talk about watching your ROI plummet! The wise investor makes sure they are pre-approved for a loan before writing offers, and this will pay off for you at the end. Finding a lender to give you good terms and approve you to borrow money is a huge part of pulling off BRRRR correctly.

Why is it important to find a lender before you start? Can't you just find one sometime during the process? Well, maybe. You might. It could definitely happen. Or maybe it won't. The fact is, the less you know about lending standards, practices, and the business, the less confident you should feel about getting a loan in a last-minute fashion. The truth is for all but the most experienced investors, the lending process remains a great mystery. Most people have no idea what bankers are looking at, how they think, or why they think that way.

But most people don't have this book to help them out, and you do! I'm going to help you get into the mind of a lender, understand why they ask the questions they do, and how you can stack the odds in your favor when it comes to obtaining financing. Remember, in the beginning of the book we talked about the ways to increase ROI, and the easiest method was to reduce the amount of capital you leave in a deal. You can't do this without pulling capital out, so obtaining financing becomes really important.

Getting the Loan, and Asking the Right Questions

As a Realtor who works with buyers, the first thing I always do is to get them pre-approved. A pre-approval letter is a verification from a lender that they have taken a look at your finances and believe they can give you a loan for a specific amount. Lenders collect things like tax returns, W2 statements, pay stubs, and credit scores in order to issue a pre-approval. Pre-approvals are crucial when writing offers to purchase a home when you'll be using a loan because it lets the sellers know you are serious and actually able to obtain financing to close the deal. Many buyers are reluctant to obtain this pre-approval and want to start looking at homes right away. This is a bad idea. Looking at homes may be the fun part, but obtaining the financing is the important part. We should always start with what's most important.

As an investor, if you can't get pre-approved for a loan, that should tell you right away you are not ready to BRRRR a property yet. If this is the case, you should look at flipping or partnering with someone else who can get the financing. But most of us have no idea if we'll be eligible for financing until we talk to the lender. The good news is that if we are not eligible for financing, most lenders can let us know exactly why and what we can do to fix it. In this case, knowledge is power, and having someone show you the path you'll need to walk to achieve your goal may be all you need to get there.

In most cases, you are going to reach out to a lender and ask for a pre-approval letter. The lender will ask you a few qualifying questions over the phone, and then send you a loan application to fill out. They will usually also send you a list of items you need to acquire for them (taxes, pay stubs, etc.). My advice to you is to open a file in your email and save all the electronic copies of the forms you'll be sending them. In many cases, one lender will turn you down and you'll need to reach out to another. When this happens, you'll already have all the necessary files saved in this folder and it can be as simple as forwarding them to the new lender's email address.

If you're anything like me, you have a horrible time remembering usernames, passwords, and confirmation codes required to sign into the various websites where you'll be collecting this information the lender needs. Putting it all in an email and saving it in this same folder can save you a lot of headache in the future when you need to log in to your company's HR website or your H&R Block account to get required paperwork. Do yourself a favor and make it easier on yourself.

If everything goes well, your lender will send you a pre-approval letter stating what you are able to borrow. There are several things you need to make sure you cover with your lender so you don't end up in big trouble. Some of the big ones are:

- How much you are able to borrow (pre-approval amount)
- What the current interest rates are for investment property
- How long the "seasoning" period is before you can borrow money against the property (how long you need to own it)
- What your LTV (loan to value) will be
- What your closing costs will be
- How much it will cost to buy down the rate
- What is your "cash out" refinance rate
- Does the lender work with out-of-state investors

Now let's break down each category for a deeper understanding of these questions.

Pre-Approval Amount

The pre-approval amount is the actual amount of money a lender is willing to let you borrow. Lenders base this amount on the level of income you bring in compared to the debt you hold. This metric is referred to as the "debt to income ratio." Lenders will look into how much money you bring in vs. what debt you are responsible for paying and will come up with a monthly payment they believe you can afford.

Once they calculate the amount of money you can safely borrow, they will issue you a pre-approval letter stating this amount. This letter is provided to the seller of a home when you write an offer so the seller can know you are serious and are likely to be approved for the loan you are requesting. Now keep in mind, this is what the lender feels you can afford to pay. It doesn't mean it's what you actually should borrow. It's your responsibility to understand your own finances and know what amount you are comfortable paying.

I recommend getting at least two quotes from different lenders. Trust me, not all lenders are created equal, and being pre-approved by two lenders can help you for several reasons. Here are a few of the big reasons why you should get two pre-approvals:

- Lenders have rates that fluctuate. The lower lender today might be the higher one six months later.
- Not all lenders have the same closing costs. Some can be substantially higher than others'.
- As I've stated above, not all lenders are created equal. Some have the skill and ability to solve problems, while others (like online lenders with great rates) will cave as soon as one thing goes wrong. If your loan falls apart, you don't want to start the entire pre-approval process over from scratch. You want to be able to jump right in with the backup lender—especially if you're using the loan to buy the property and have a limited escrow period.
- If a lender knows you are comparing them to someone else, they are more likely to give you a better rate or closing costs.

Current Rate

The rate the lender provides you with is based on that day's rates for the loan you are requesting. Be aware that this can change because interest rates fluctuate. Several factors affect mortgage interest rates, including:

- Demand of money
- Supply of money
- The prime rate determined by the Federal Reserve System
- The stock market's health
- Treasury bill rates

What does this mean for you? It means don't expect the rate you're quoted to be the same rate you get on your loan. If rates go up, so will yours. If rates go down, well, make sure your lender is giving you the current rate and not the higher one they quoted you. If you want a better rate, ask the lender what you need to do to get it. Sometimes paying down a small credit card, or improving a credit score by a few points, can make a really big difference on your interest rate.

Remember, if you're dealing with a portfolio lender or commercial lender, you can't expect the same rates as residential/standard loans. Most portfolio lenders will also have adjustable rate mortgages (ARMs) that will track up and down with benchmark rates like the prime rate or *Wall Street Journal* rates.

Seasoning Period

The seasoning period refers to the period of time after you buy a property but before you can take a loan on it. Many lenders don't want to finance something right after an investor buys it. This is because they want to make sure the property is stable, rented, and wasn't a "fire sale" situation. This is one of the methods lenders use to protect their investment.

Asking a lender for the length of their seasoning period is crucial. You *don't* want to get involved in a project assuming you can take a loan on it two months after it's completed, just to find out later it has a six-month seasoning period and you can't access your money until then. Different lenders have different seasoning periods, and different types of loans do as well. Portfolio lenders tend to have more flexibility with these periods while conventional lenders often do not. Ask this question up front to save yourself some time.

In general, a shorter seasoning period is better for you, as it will increase the velocity of your money. If the lender quotes you a longer period, ask them if there's anything you can do to shorten it. Sometimes these periods are flexible based on the circumstances of the loan. In some cases, lenders just want to know the property is occupied by a tenant who is stable, and they assume it will take six months to get there. If you finish your rehab quickly and have a tenant in place, ask your lender if they can shorten the seasoning period for you.

Loan to Value

Your loan to value (LTV) percentage is a huge thing to find out right away because it has such a big impact on your ROI. The best lenders will have programs with a 75–80 percent LTV. Some of the mediocre ones will do 70 percent, and anything less than that is typically considered not ideal for investors.

The higher LTV you can get, the more of your money you can get back out of a deal. This leads to higher ROIs and more money to invest later. This *is* the whole point of the BRRRR strategy, right? We want to start with the end in mind. Since this is the case, ask your lender right away what kind of LTV they are offering and only move forward with those who provide one that works for your goals.

Some lenders have flexible LTVs, while others don't. Some lenders will offer you a higher LTV at a higher rate. Some lenders will even let you borrow the rehab cost along with the loan. Make sure you ask questions to dig deeper into why they are showing you a certain LTV, and if there are other options they aren't telling you about. Don't assume they are telling you everything, and don't even assume the lender you're talking to *knows* everything.

In my experience, small businesses don't always do a good job training their employees. Most of the time the leadership comes up with loan programs, rate sheets, and lending options that are not disseminated effectively, and the employee you're speaking with isn't aware of what the bank can do. Make it your responsibility to ask them exactly what you want to know and if they aren't sure, ask them to find out!

Closing Costs

Closing costs are the fees associated with getting a loan. Let me tell you, they can be much higher than you expect. In my area of Northern California, we routinely see clients pay $7,000 to $10,000 in lender closing costs alone. This doesn't include title, escrow, taxes, or Realtor fees, showing that closing costs on their own can be expensive.

"Closing costs" is really a generic term used to encompass a whole lot of different fees. You want to ask for specifics when inquiring about this. In a transaction, closing costs will typically refer to lender closing costs, title closing costs, escrow closing costs, as well as taxes and fees. You want to ask the lender specifically about *lender* closing costs.

Lender closing costs tend to be broken up into names like origination fees, underwriting fees, points, application fees, credit report costs, etc. Different lenders charge different fees for each type. Some lenders will try to bury their fees among all the other title/escrow/tax related fees and tell you to expect "2 percent" of the purchase price in closing costs. You don't want this—ask for specifics.

Many lenders are trained to quote you one specific closing cost—say, for example, the origination fee. Don't get fooled by this. Ask for a "net sheet," or a list of *all* the closing costs you'll be paying, and compare these costs between lenders. Many investors will haggle over $1,000 on the purchase price but pay $2,500 more for one lender than they would for the next. Don't be that person—ask for this information up front.

Rate Buy Down (Paying Points)

In some cases, lenders will offer you the option to "buy down" your interest rate. This is basically an opportunity for you to pay more in closing costs so you can get a better interest rate. Sometimes this is a good idea, sometimes it's not.

My advice is to ask how much you'll have to spend to buy down the rate (in dollars), then look to see how long it will take for you to recoup that money in loan savings. For instance, if you can spend $3,000 to buy down your rate to a point where it will save you $100 a month, it would take you 30 months to recoup your up-front expense of $3,000 ($3,000 / $100 = $30). If you plan on owning the property for more than 30 months, and don't need that $3,000 for anything else, it might be a good idea to buy down that rate.

Cash Out Refinance Rates

Many new investors are surprised when they find out the interest rates on "cash out" refinances are higher than purchase refinances. Trust me, I've never understood this one either. Basically, lending institutions have decided that when someone is pulling cash out of a property (when the loan amount is higher than the current mortgage balance), the loan is riskier for the lender and therefore needs a higher interest rate to offset that risk.

For us, as BRRRR investors, this isn't good. Since we are likely taking out a loan on a property that has no debt on it, or a small amount of hard money debt on it, virtually all our refinances will be cash out refinances. So be sure to ask your lender what their rate is for cash out refinances as they may be assuming you are getting pre-approved to purchase a house, not refinance one you've already purchased.

Out-of-State Investors

If you're looking to finance a property out-of-state, make sure you let the lender know this right away. Many lenders won't lend on properties when the owner lives out-of-state as they are worried the owner is more likely to lose the property. Lots of misconceptions still exist about out-of-state investing and many still believe it is riskier than it is.

Oftentimes you'll find yourself going to credit unions to find loan products that will work for an investor. Credit unions (CUs) have rules about who can be members, and the location where the member lives is a big one. I've had cases where I thought I was approved for a loan, only to find out the CU said no to the loan at the last minute when they heard I didn't live in their county. Learn from my mistakes and ask this question early on in the process.

Portfolio Lenders

Ask right away if the lender is a portfolio lender or if they plan on selling your loan after it's originated. If a lender is a portfolio lender, you can adjust your expectations up front that you won't be getting the low interest rates and terms that GSE (government sponsored entity) loans usually have.

You'll also realize this is a lender that would be a great asset to your business in the future. Portfolio lenders can make loans when other people can't, especially to real estate investors, so be nice to these people. You want to build a relationship with portfolio lenders because as you grow your business, you'll use them over and over again. Because portfolio lenders are such a crucial element to the success of real estate investors, I've included a section on how to establish an incredible relationship with them.

Relationship Building Advice with Portfolio Lenders

So how do you bring value to a relationship? That is a two-part process:
1. Understand the point of the relationship. What are you trying to get from it?
2. Understand the other person's position. What do you have that will benefit them?

Now before you jump in and tell me you should never get into a relationship wanting something from it, and you should only do what's good for other people without thinking about yourself, let me challenge that logic.

If you really want to be honest with yourself, everything we do we get something out of. You should do a good job at work, even if your boss isn't watching right? But how long would you be working really hard at your job if they stopped paying you? If we are honest, even the most benevolent act we commit still makes us feel good when we do it. We get something out of everything we do.

Wise people know they should bring value to every relationship. And honest people demand it of themselves. Black belt investors are very good at bringing value and are shrewd about who they bring that value to. Our time is limited; so is our energy. Making sure you get a good ROI with your time and energy is crucial to success. This means choosing the right people to invest in, just like choosing the right properties.

If we know portfolio lenders can be a big help to our business, it stands to reason we should be developing relationships with the right ones. How do we do this? We ask ourselves step two of the two-part value bringing process:

"Understand the other person's position. What do you have that will benefit them?"

If we want to bring value to a portfolio lender, just like anyone else, we need to understand what their job is, what is valuable to them, and how we can provide that. If you find the right one, and do a good job bringing value, you can establish a relationship that will last for a long time.

Sending Referrals

Portfolio lenders work for banks. Banks make money by bringing in deposits at a low interest rate, then providing loans with that money at higher interest rates. Lenders make money by making loans. If a lender isn't making loans, they aren't making money.

This makes you, as a borrower, a "lead" to them. A lead in business is basically any contact or opportunity that could result in the desired goal of the person collecting that lead. For us as investors, a great potential deal is a "lead." When we hear, "Hey, my neighbor is in money trouble and needs to sell his house fast. Here's his number," that number is a lead. Well, you as a borrower are a lead to a lender. Leads have value.

Now, of course, not every lead becomes a deal. That neighbor might not have any equity in his house, or might not be that motivated after all. Borrower leads work the same way. You as a lead might not have a good enough credit score, debt-to-income ratio, or money in reserve to qualify for a loan. The key is, serious business people are *always* looking for leads. I know this because I am one, and I work with many. Whether it's a new client for my real estate business, or a new house to buy, or a new great contractor, I'm always looking for new leads.

Sending your lender other people who are looking to buy properties is a way of providing them with value. Leads are valuable, and you providing leads is a way of providing value. It's a form of currency you can use to buy yourself into a deeper relationship with them. Providing a lender with leads of other investors or primary residence homeowners is a tactic to get yourself into their good graces and show them you are an asset.

The best thing you can ask them is what kind of leads they are looking for. Not every lender is looking for the same type of lead. Some lending institutions go through periods where they feel they are too exposed to residential real estate investment property and want to move more to the commercial side. Others prefer to work more with primary residence loans than with investment loans.

Whatever the case, you need to ask these lenders exactly what kind of loans they are looking to provide, then tailor your search. Ask them to provide you with a sheet or some kind of marketing material you can spread around. Learn about their products so when someone asks you about them you sound informed and educated. Showing these lenders you're working to make them money will motivate them to help you do the same.

Bank Deposit/Loan Cycles

Just like not all banks are looking to give out the same kinds of loans all the time, they are also not looking to give loans out during certain periods of their deposit cycle. If you want to help someone, you need to learn as much as possible about their industry, job, and responsibilities. Learning to help lenders means learning about banking cycles.

When a bank or lending institution decides it wants to make loans, it charges a certain interest rate for the right to borrow their money. The difference in the interest the bank charges you and the interest they pay their customers to keep money at the bank is the profit they'll make. When a bank is looking to provide loans, you can usually tell from their marketing. Walking into a bank that wants to make loans is usually an experience where you're being hit by sign after sign advertising their "low interest rates."

When banks are overfunded, their marketing is geared to pull in those who need to borrow money. Banks need to loan this money out, as they will slowly be losing money with all the interest they are paying to the customers who deposited funds if they don't. Conversely, if banks are advertising their "high interest rates on deposits," they are usually in a fund-raising stage, meaning they are low on money to lend out and want more to deposit.

How does this help you to know? If you are approaching a bank looking for a loan when they are low on money to lend out, the odds of you getting the loan are much lower. So should you just wait until they have more money to lend? Maybe. That is certainly an option. But what if you don't want to wait? Is that really all you can do, other than find a different lender?

One thing that's worked for me in the past is to offer to keep money on deposit with the institution if I'm turned down for a loan. This may seem odd to you, but it can work wonders. The following is a script I use if a lender tells me they can't do my loan, but can't quote any specific reason why I'm not eligible:

Hello Mr. Smith,

I just wanted to thank you for your time earlier with reviewing my application and getting back to me so promptly. I understand you don't always get compensated with results like these and I appreciate you treating me like a valued customer nonetheless.

I also wanted to propose an alternative scenario. I understand your institution has determined it's not in their best interest to provide a loan I requested at this time. I wanted to know if it would make any difference to you and your bank if I put a sizeable deposit of $_____ in a savings account before funding the loan.

My hope is for you to see I want a mutually beneficial relationship with you and your institution, and I understand and am willing to go the extra mile to establish that. Would you mind running this by the other parties involved in the decision and seeing if we could work something out under this new scenario?

I hope to be banking with you all for a long period of time and I'd love to know more about how to create a win-win situation for everyone.

Thanks again for your time,

(Your name)

I have used this script several times, and it's worked for me before. Banks aren't used to customers caring about their position or looking for ways to pitch in. I can almost guarantee emails like this will catch them off guard, as most people who are told no tend to walk off in a huff rather than look for a win-win solution. Credit unions are typically smaller institutions that are relationally based. They *want* to develop relationships with customers they can trust to pay back their loans. This is a large part of what their business model is based on.

Offering to keep money on deposit with your lender is a way of starting off the relationship on the right foot and showing you care about their success just as much as you want them to care about yours. If you're applying for a loan at an institution that is relationship based, this is likely to go a long way with them. You are speaking their "love language" in so many words.

While this is one way to develop relationships, that isn't the only reason this method works. There is a logical component to it as well. When a bank is considering offering you a loan, they have to consider the "opportunity cost" of giving you the money—just like you have to consider it when choosing to buy one property over another. If a lender gives you a loan, they will make money on the closing costs. If the lender is low on funds, they will have the problem of not being able to lend this money to someone else. If that someone else is a high roller, valuable client, or person who has an expectation their loan will be filled, this can put the institution in a tough spot.

You solve this problem by offering to put money on deposit with them. In addition to strengthening the relationship, it gives them capital to lend to someone else. When they are considering several different borrowers all applying for loans, yours will stand out since you're willing to put money on deposit with them. It makes your loan much more difficult to turn down and offers less risk for the bank.

This is an underutilized and valuable strategy not enough people are talking about because it doesn't apply to a large number of investors and it involves a level of sophistication when it comes to understanding lending cycles not everyone has. There isn't a ton of content on building relationships with lenders, but it's a valuable tool to have in your tool belt if you're serious about building a big portfolio. If you want to start hearing "yes" instead of "no," I would suggest considering working this into your strategy.

How Many Loans Can I Have with Your Institution?

Each lending institution is different and has different rules for how many loans they will allow any individual borrower to hold with them. This is designed to protect the institution from overexposure to one person and mitigate risk in case that one individual passes away, loses their job, files for bankruptcy, etc. It is one safeguard they use to avoid having "too many eggs in one basket."

This is not the same as the rule that any individual borrower cannot have more than ten financed properties. That rule is specific to Fannie Mae/Freddie Mac loans. It's important to check with the lender you're considering working with before getting into business with them. This is especially true if you're just getting into a new market.

For instance, you may be applying for loans at five different banks. This process involves feeling them out, looking into their products, and seeing how responsive their customer service and systems are. During this process, it would be wise to ask if they have a limit on the number of loans any one person can have with them. If the first bank says there is no limit, the second bank says there is a limit of ten, and the third, fourth, and fifth all say there is a limit of three, would it make sense to even consider three, four, and five?

Once you get rolling with your investing, you're going to want to know you have a well you can continue to return to when you have a lending need. It's not very efficient to get a system going with one lender, then have to stop and build an entire new one after your third property is purchased. Finding out up front which bank will let you get the most loans is a resourceful method that will pay off in the long run.

What Is Your Institution's Appetite for Residential Loans?

For those unfamiliar with how banks operate, one loan operates the same as another loan. For those lending out the money, however, this is not the case. Banks don't consider all loans to be equal. Different banks make different returns and take on different risk based on the types of loans they provide. Some loans make money for the lender because of closing costs; others have very low closing costs but higher interest rates. Some loans are risky and therefore more expensive while others are very low risk for the bank and make them less of a return.

Each bank is making different decisions on how they will lend and who they will lend to as leadership sets parameters for the lending division. It is leadership's job to determine where they believe the economy or local market to be heading and make the loans likely to benefit the most. Understanding the leadership position on this gives you a big advantage when it comes to knowing which institutions to put the most time into.

Banks tend to take the kinds of loans they are giving out and classify them according to the collateral securing the loan. This is why they are referred to as "car loans," "HELOCs" (home equity line of credit), "business loans," "rental property loans," "commercial loans," etc. The name of the loan usually refers to the asset the bank gets to take as collateral if the loan doesn't close. Banks will look at which of these types of loans are getting the best return vs. the amount of risk they pose, and make lending decisions based on their assessment.

These assessments often get shared with the lenders during company meetings. Each bank meets at different times and with different frequency. Once you've established the appropriate rapport with the lender you think you'll be working with, it's a good idea to ask them what type of appetite the bank currently has for the types of loans you're interested in. Odds are, you'll be looking for residential investment property. If the bank feels they are overexposed in that area, or doesn't like the fundamentals of that particular market, you may find yourself barking up the wrong tree.

If you can find out from your lender when the bank's leadership will be meeting, you can ask them to make a request during the meeting to find out what types of loans the leadership committee is looking for. If they want to limit their exposure to investment properties, this isn't the right time to be working hard on a relationship with that institution. You want to find a bank that *wants* to give out more residential loans, or better yet, has special programs in place to keep the costs and fees low on these products!

Taking a few extra steps to learn more about the lender you plan to work with can go far for you and your business. You have to be careful not to pry too much in the initial stages of getting to know them, but once you do it can be beneficial to know what kinds of loans they want to give and how you can ultimately help the lender reach their sales goals. Providing value in this way is one way to incentivize them to want to do the same for you, and that's how valuable business relationships are built!

Key Points

- Find the lender first.
- Get pre-approved.
- Know your lender's seasoning period.
- Ask about closing costs.
- Send referrals to anyone you want to win over.
- Find banks at the part in their lending cycle where they have money they need to lend out.
- Know your lending institution's appetite for residential loans.

CHAPTER NINE
The Value in Financing

"It is much easier to put existing resources to better use than to develop resources where they do not exist."

—GEORGE SOROS

Loan to Value vs. Loan to Cost

Loan to value (LTV) and loan to cost (LTC) are two terms used in the lending industry to describe the amount of money a lender will let you borrow relative to the value of the collateral. Put in more practical terms, the LTV is the amount of money they will let you borrow against the value of the property, and the LTC is the amount of money they will let you borrow against the total amount you invested in a property. Here is a quick example to demonstrate.

Loan to Value

You BRRRR a property that is appraised for $120,000. The bank will let you borrow 75 percent LTV. This means they will let you borrow $90,000 ($120,000 x .75 = $90,000) as they are letting you borrow against the appraised value of the property.

Loan to Cost

You BRRRR a property and spend $90,000 total between the acquisition and the rehab. The property appraises for $120,000. The bank will let you borrow 75 percent LTC. This means they will let you borrow $67,500 ($90,000 x .75 = $67,500) as they are letting you borrow against the total amount of money you put into the deal.

As I'm sure you can see, there is a big, big difference between the end results of $90,000 and $67,500. When you consider that the BRRRR model is most effective when repeated over and over, the impact of the difference is compounded even more. This difference of $22,500 is a significant amount of capital and it's the reason why we try our best to look for lenders that will lend against the value of a property, not the cost. When reaching out to find the lender you want to pre-approve you, *make sure you ask right away if they lend against the value or the cost*. If they tell you they lend against the cost, they had better have a really high percentage (like 95 percent!). In essence, they are telling you there is a zero percent chance you will be able to pull out more than you've invested, or even all that you've invested. For this reason, I avoid banks that will only let me borrow LTC.

The reason I avoid LTC is because my strategy involves adding as much value as I possibly can to a project before pulling money out. As I've mentioned, my goal is to add lots of equity to a deal before I refinance it. Equity grows wealth quickly. At this state in my investing career, I want to grow, and grow fast.

But what if that's not where *you* are? What about if you're looking to buy properties and refinance them, but you aren't trying to maximize the value before doing so? There are many reasons why this might make sense. Pushing your property to its limit before refinancing is a lot of work. It's also a lot of stress. There is a lot more communication with contractors. A lot more thought and research that goes into the deal. A lot more variables where things can go wrong. For some investors, this just isn't worth the headache.

In instances where you're not trying to increase the value a great deal before refinancing, using the LTC won't be that different from LTV. You may ask why someone would use the BRRRR strategy in instances where they aren't adding big value to the property. That's a good question, and it's true that BRRRR is much less effective in these cases. However, some people purchase properties with cash simply because they can get a better deal that way. Cash offers are more appealing to sellers, and it's one way that buyers can get themselves a better deal even if they don't plan on a massive rehab.

There is something to be said for buying a property, having a smooth rehab, then refinancing when you're finished. If capital isn't an issue for you, then using a LTC model won't necessarily have such an adverse impact on your bottom line. The main reason for using a LTV model is to recover more of the money you put in, so if this isn't a concern of yours, LTC can work just fine.

Different Types of Loan Products

When looking into financing a home, you may have heard different loan names get thrown around. For most of us not involved in the lending industry, it's easy to get confused by this. Throw in the fact that nobody likes looking ignorant and odds are you aren't likely to ask anybody what these names even mean.

FHA, VA, conventional, jumbo, etc. If you've ever wondered what the differences are between all these loans, I'll teach you what they mean and how to know which option is best for you. Keep in mind as you read this, the vast majority of loans are made for borrowers looking to finance their primary residence. With this being the case, only a handful of most loans are options for those buying or financing investment property.

Conventional

A conventional loan is basically the "generic" home loan. Conventional loans offered by lenders are typically insured by Fannie Mae/Freddie Mac—meaning the government is insuring part of your loan so lenders are more willing to give them out. When a lender originates a loan, the vast majority of them then sell this loan to someone else on the secondary market. If the loan is government insured, it is much easier to find a lender who will buy the loan from the originator.

Conventional loans are what the majority of real estate investors will start off using. Although you can find conventional loans for as little as 3, 5, or 10 percent down, these are products only offered to those buying a house as their primary residence. If you're looking to purchase a rental property, you'll need to put a minimum of 20 percent down, and sometimes 25 percent.

Keep in mind most lenders classify conventional loans into three categories: primary residence, vacation/second home, and investment property. Investment properties are considered the riskiest and therefore have the highest interest rates of all three. Vacation homes are slightly better rates than investment properties, and primary residences come with the best rates and terms of all three.

FHA

FHA stands for Federal Housing Administration. This is a department of the federal government that is involved in providing fair housing for all Americans, as well as other duties. An FHA insured loan is a U.S. Federal Housing Administration mortgage insurance–backed mortgage loan, which is provided by an FHA-approved lender. FHA insured loans are a type of federal assistance and have historically allowed lower-income Americans to borrow money for the purchase of a home that they would not otherwise be able to afford.

As I'm sure you've already guessed, FHA loans are only for primary residence homeowners. They typically provide for much lower down payments and lower credit scores but come with other caveats. FHA loans currently have mortgage insurance (MIP) that exist for the lifetime of the loan. This means if you take out a FHA loan, you'll have to refinance completely to get rid of the mortgage insurance; otherwise you'll be paying it for the life of the loan.

VA

VA loans are insured by the Department of Veterans Affairs. They are offered for service members of our nation's military. VA loans provide great value for those eligible to use them. VA loans allow for zero percent down, letting the borrower borrow 100 percent of the property's value. They also come with no mortgage insurance, a big savings over time.

The downside of VA loans is they are notorious for being more difficult than conventional loans to close. Experienced listing agents know that VA loans have stricter guidelines than conventional loans. Additionally, VA loans have a reputation for ending up with low appraisals. If a property doesn't appraise at value, there is a high likelihood it will fall out of escrow or the buyer will demand the seller to lower the price (especially if the buyer is expecting to put zero percent down). For this reason, many listings agents look to avoid VA loans unless they have no other option.

Jumbo

A jumbo loan is a term used by lenders to describe a "high balance" loan. Each housing market (usually divided by county) has a "limit" placed on it. Any borrower looking to borrow more money than the limit in place is considered higher risk, and with that comes less favorable terms. High balance loan limits differ by area and can sometimes be substantially more or less than neighboring areas.

This is rarely an issue for investors as we are typically investing in "C" class areas (areas where the average home is at the median home price or below). Most investors don't make money buying at the top of a market, so jumbo loans don't come up much for us. Be aware that if you ever want to buy a property that requires a jumbo loan, you'll likely be paying a higher interest rate, more lender fees, and may need a higher interest rate to qualify.

Portfolio

Portfolio loans are made by a lender who doesn't plan on selling them on the secondary market, hence keeping them in their own "portfolio." These loans are typically offered by credit unions and savings and loan institutions as perks for their members. If you want to finance more than ten properties, you'll want to learn how these loans work. Currently, you can't have a conventional loan on more than ten financed properties.

Because they aren't sold on the secondary market, the terms of a portfolio loan are not as favorable as those that are. These loans are not insured by the government and that makes them riskier to the lender. If you're looking into a portfolio loan, be prepared to see adjustable rate mortgages and higher interest rates than you're used to. Most portfolio lenders I see are offering a 5/1 ARM. This means the loan will be made at a set interest rate for five years, then can adjust every year after that by a certain amount specified in the loan documents. Developing relationships with institutions that will give portfolio loans is a crucial part of growing your portfolio over ten properties.

Hard Money

Hard money loans are those made by a private lender that are secured by a "hard" asset. Because these loans are not guaranteed by the federal government and not intended to be for long periods of time, they typically have very high interest rates and fees. Hard money lenders are primarily used by house flippers, or investors looking for a "bridge loan" to get them into a property and then later refinance into a more stable loan. Hard money loans are often used to purchase property that would not qualify for conventional financing.

Because hard money loans tend to be so much riskier than normal loans (they are used for risky deals like flips and rehab projects), the cost of these loans is very high. Lenders need to protect their investment, and they understand if the borrower defaults, they are likely taking back a property in terrible disrepair that cannot be easily sold. It's not uncommon in my areas to see hard money loans given at terms of 14 percent interest and four points (a point is 1 percent of the amount of the loan, so four points would be 4 percent of the loan amount. Not cheap).

Owner Financing

Owner financing is when the owner of a property agrees to be the bank and hold a mortgage note against their property. This is often used for real estate investors who can't qualify for any more loans but still want to buy more property. In the case of owner financing, the borrower will usually offer the seller some form of down payment, and then the seller will finance the remaining balance of the purchase price.

In these cases, the borrower will make payments to the seller based on the loan agreement. The owner holds a mortgage note secured by the property itself, and can foreclose on the borrower (or perform what is basically an eviction in states with land contracts) if the borrower fails to make the agreed-upon payment. Owner financing is a creative solution for those who can't qualify for conventional or portfolio loans but still want to buy properties.

Private Financing

Private financing is when one individual lends money to another. In the case of real estate investing, this is usually done for the purposes of buying or financing investment property. Private financing can be short-term (as in the case of flips) or long-term (as in the case with mortgage notes). In most cases, private financing is a better alternative than hard money. The best investors have large pools of private financing to draw from and do so successfully to continue their investing endeavors long after they have committed all their own capital to real estate investing.

HELOC

HELOC stands for home equity line of credit. HELOCs are loans given against the equity in a property. They are "second place" mortgages that are usually cheap and incredible opportunities to get money to invest with at a low rate. HELOCs function just like credit cards but with very low interest rates. Credit cards carry high interest rates because the debt is unsecured, meaning there is no collateral. This makes these loans much riskier for the lender. A HELOC is secured by a property, making it much less risky and therefore much cheaper for the borrower.

HELOCs function like a line of credit. You only pay for money you have borrowed against the line, and when you pay that money back, you don't owe anymore. Lines tend to stay open for a 10 to 15 year period. After this "draw period" is over, you have to either pay the balance in full or, in some cases, the balance converts to a traditional amortized loan in which you will make payments of principal and interest. The size of the line of credit is based on the amount of equity in your property.

80/10/10

An 80/10/10 loan isn't really a loan, but more a way of structuring two loans together, usually for the purpose of avoiding mortgage insurance for borrowers who don't have 20 percent to put down. Mortgage insurance is usually required by borrowers who don't have 20 percent to put down on their property (80 percent LTV) because this makes the loan riskier. For those without 20 percent equity, lenders force borrowers to pay for mortgage insurance to protect the lender in the case of default.

An 80/10/10 loan is a way of combining two loans together to avoid this. It's basically stating the property will be funded by:

1. A first loan at 80 percent of the property's value
2. A second loan at 10 percent of the property's value
3. A 10 percent down payment

For borrowers who have a 10 percent down payment, they can avoid mortgage insurance by taking out a second mortgage against the property for 10 percent of the property's value. This second mortgage covers the extra 10 percent the borrower did not have and allows the first mortgage (the one that would have required mortgage insurance) to only be for 80 percent of the value. This second mortgage is usually a HELOC and HELOCs don't require mortgage insurance.

Which Types of Loans Work for Investors?

As I've stated above, investors can't use FHA or VA loans, at least not for the purchase of a property. If you want to use these loans for investment property, you have to be clever about how you go about it. Remember, loan guidelines are related to the purchase of a property. They aren't necessarily made to govern the use of a property after its purchase. If you'd like more advice on how to use one of these loans to help you get started investing in real estate, speak with a lender or legal counsel. I do know that I've seen investors buy properties with a VA or FHA loan and later rent them out when they moved into a different property, and I'm not aware of any laws or regulations prohibiting this.

Using low down payment loans to buy what will eventually be an investment property is very similar to the way the BRRRR method works—without needing the cash up front. You are significantly lowering the amount of money you're putting into a deal. That is the key to increasing your ROI.

Another way to accomplish this would be to use hard money or private financing to buy a property. Once purchased, you can either use more hard/private money to finance the rehab work, or you can use your own cash. Once the rehab is completed and the value has been raised, you refinance into a conventional or portfolio loan and voilà! You get the lion's share of your money back and increase your ROI substantially.

A final, and *epic* way to take advantage of FHA or VA financing when it comes to investment property, is to "house hack." House hacking is a term first coined by Brandon Turner. It refers to finding creative ways to get someone else to pay your mortgage. This can be accomplished in many ways, but there are two that are easier and more common than all the others. They are:

Get roommates: A very underrated way to buy an investment property and own it for free is to use an FHA or VA loan (or a 3–5 percent down conventional loan) to buy a property, then rent the rooms out to others who pay you to use them. If you do this right, you can often get your entire mortgage paid, or even more! Having others make the payments while you build equity and eventually cash flow is a simple and effective way to get started in real estate investing. It also allows you to take advantage of the best loans at your disposal relatively easily.

Buy a small multifamily: As I mentioned earlier, two- to four-unit properties are still considered single-family loans to lenders. What does this mean to you? It means you can use a loan to buy one of these homes as your primary residence, put very little money down, and still end up with an investment property that provides you with a significant ROI.

Buying a two-, three-, or four-unit property allows you to rent out the units you aren't living in and use that rent money to reduce the amount you owe toward your own mortgage. If you combine this with the first method (get roommates), you can increase your cash flow even more. Imagine buying a fourplex, renting out three of the units, then renting out a bedroom or two in the unit you live in. That's a lot of cash flow for little money down!

The Story of Insightful Ivan

Insightful Ivan was aptly named. From the time he was a young boy, Ivan was always able to find the silver lining in a storm cloud. When other young children would complain about the snacks their mothers packed in their lunch that they didn't like, Ivan learned to trade these snacks to other kids and get something better. When other children complained about the basketball referees calling too many fouls, Ivan learned to adjust his game to the referees' style and got an advantage over the other players. Ivan was shrewd, wise, insightful, and willing to work. His motto was always "do more with less."

Ivan began listening to podcasts like *BiggerPockets* at age 19. He instantly became hooked listening to the co-hosts share ways they had built their wealth coming from humble beginnings. This was exactly the type of content Ivan was drawn to. He didn't take handouts, so it was up to Ivan to make it in the world if that's what he wanted to do. Ivan became determined to do everything he could and everything that was within his realm of possibility to make that happen.

One day while listening to the podcast, Ivan heard the story of an investor who had built major equity for himself by "house hacking." As Ivan listened more intently, his face lit up as bright as the light bulb he felt appearing above his head. Of course! All this time Ivan had been thinking he needed to save 20 percent to put down on a house. This is what everyone had always said! Oh, how wrong he had been.

Ivan listened as the guest explained how he bought a fourplex for $300,000 with a 5 percent conventional loan. Each unit had two bedrooms, two bathrooms, and 900 square feet. The units were individually metered for electricity and water. The investor then rented out three of the units for $750 each. Ivan listened in amazement as the investor explained the numbers.

Mortgage of $285,000 (95% of purchase price) at 5% interest = $1,529.94

Property Tax of 1.25% of Purchase Price = $312.50

Insurance = $60

Mortgage Insurance = $200

Sewer/Garbage/Landscaping = $150

Total = $2,252.44

The investor then explained how he had previously been paying $750 a month to rent the apartment he had been living in. After buying the fourplex, the investor rented out one of the two bedrooms in the unit he lived in to a buddy from work for $450 a month. This brought the investor's total income to:

Unit 1 = $750

Unit 2 = $750

Unit 3 = $750

Bedroom for Unit 4 = $450

Total = $2,700

The investor was careful to explain he was managing the property himself and doing all the repairs himself. Ivan realized this wouldn't work for him, as he was not handy, so he'd have to budget for outside help. Just as Ivan was beginning to think this could work for him, the investor shared the ROI on the property he was living in:

Income = $2,700

Expenses = $2,252.44

Cash Flow = $447.56

Total Invested = ($15,000 down + $6,000 closing costs) $21,000

Yearly Cash Flow = ($447.56 x 12) $5,370.72

ROI = ($5,370.72 / $21,000) 25.57%

Ivan was blown away! How on earth was someone achieving a return of over 25 percent *and* living somewhere for free? This house hacking thing seemed too good to be true. As he turned over the possibilities in his mind, Ivan realized something the investor had not shared. Not only was the investor making 25 percent, but he was also avoiding the rent of $750 he had been paying before. Ivan pulled out his calculator and did some quick math. If he added the rent the investor was no longer paying ($750) to the income already being collected ($2,700), the new amount was actually $3,450. This was a more accurate depiction of how much the property was generating for the investor, as he was now living there and saving an extra $750 he had previously been spending.

Ivan checked out the new numbers.

New Income = $3,450

Expenses = $2,252.44

Cash Flow = $1,197.56

Total Invested = ($15,000 down + $6,000 closing costs) $21,000

Yearly Cash Flow = ($1197.56 x 12) $14,370.72

ROI = ($14,370.72 / $21,000) 68.4%

Ivan was astonished. If he factored in the rent the investor was now saving, the ROI skyrocketed to 68 percent. This was *not* including principal pay down, the equity in the deal at the time of purchase, or the tax savings owning real estate can bring. This investor had saved up $21,000, and was now earning the equivalent of nearly 70 percent on that money while owning an asset likely to appreciate (with rents also likely to appreciate) over time.

Insightful Ivan knew exactly what he needed to do. The next day he sold his Camaro and bought a used Civic. Ivan looked at his budget and found ways to cut unnecessary expenses like cable, eating out, and buying new clothes. Ivan knew what he wanted to do, and he put a plan together to achieve it. Now that Ivan knew what kind of fouls the financial referees were calling, he was darn sure he would learn to play this new kind of game, and he'd build massive wealth doing so.

To Leverage or Not to Leverage? That Is the Question

At its core, the BRRRR method does two things great:
1. It recovers capital
2. It increases ROI

By recovering more of your capital, you reduce your investment basis in a property and that increases your ROI. (That's how the investor in the above example achieved such stellar returns.) You also recover the ability to buy more properties and earn a higher return on those properties as well. If neither of these factors is important to you, the traditional model will work just fine.

So how do you know if you should be trying to recover capital and use the BRRRR method? My guess is, if you've read this far into the book already, you are hungry to grow your wealth and you want to find ways to do that faster, wiser, and more efficiently. To BRRRR well is to do everything with insight and plan for what you want. BRRRR investors don't leave things up to chance; they go after what they want.

So why am I such a huge fan of leverage? While I will always believe in the power of leverage to achieve more, I find it to be uniquely suited to capitalize on leverage when it comes to real estate investing. Whether it's leveraging time, money, resources, knowledge, or more, many investors have already found ways to incorporate other people or resources into their business to help them scale faster. Below are some reasons I think investors should be considering more leverage.

Other People's Money

If you're going to be a serious investor, you had better get used to both the phrase and the concept of OPM. OPM, or "other people's money," is used to describe the concept of building your wealth off of—you guessed it—other people's money. Now, to be fair, OPM has received a lot of negative press because shady people used this concept not as a way to grow everyone's wealth, but as a way to defer risk to someone else. For the purposes of my advice and this discussion, I am never referring to deferring risk as a benefit of OPM. If you wouldn't do it with your own money, you *should not* be doing it with someone else's.

Now, the *right* way of using OPM is that it benefits both parties. You see, real estate investing requires three things to be successfully done:
1. Money/Capital
2. Knowledge
3. Hustle/Work

The bad news is you can't make it happen without all three. The good news is, you don't need to do all three yourself! Finding someone else to supply one or two of the three allows you to do several things that will increase your own success:
1. Allows you to focus on sharpening your own skills
2. Allows you avoid the things you're not great at
3. Allows you to increase the volume of deals you're doing
4. Allows you to specialize in one thing, avoiding the "jack of all trades, master of none" trap
5. Allows you to take on projects that would otherwise seem impossible to do alone

Seeing as how the No. 1 item I've listed is "Money/Capital," it becomes pretty obvious why if you want to go far, you'll need to do it with OPM.

When done correctly, OPM helps your business, immensely. But it also helps those you are borrowing from as well. For many people out there, they have the "Money/Capital," but they don't have the knowledge, hustle/work, or both. For these people, real estate investing simply isn't a legitimate opportunity. If they want to make money in real estate, they have no choice but to partner with someone else who has the other two required abilities.

If you play your cards right, this can be you. Being the person who has the knowledge and hustle can open doors for you to use OPM to make deals happen. This becomes even easier when you have some experience to add to the mix. Experience isn't required to make money, but it sure makes the whole process easier to do. Once you've done a few deals yourself, several things will happen. You start to make your requests known more boldly, see problems arising before they do, and have learned from any mistakes made. This plays a major role in helping others to have enough confidence in you to trust you with their money. If you want to do big things, you'll need to leverage OPM at some point to do it.

Low Interest Rates

In 2018, interest rates are at historically low levels.[11] When you step back and really think about it, it's borderline stupid that lenders are willing to let us borrow hundreds of thousands of dollars for 30 years at rates below 5 percent.[12] Would you do that? I sure wouldn't.

The federal government has adopted a monetary policy that is designed to keep interest rates ridiculously low in order to stimulate the economy. What does this mean for us? Money is cheap. This helps us in several ways. The biggest two are:

1. Banks are making loans at extremely low interest rates.
2. You can use OPM for rates much lower than ever before.

The fact that banks are giving away mortgages at rates this low shouldn't be taken for granted.[13] In October 1981, interest rates reached 18.45 percent. The Yahoo Finance article goes on to state:

"Imagine paying over 18% interest on a 30-year fixed mortgage. It's almost unthinkable. But that was the reality for home buyers in October

---

11 "Federal Funds Rate—62 Year Historical Chart," Macrotrends (2015). https://www.macrotrends.net/2015/fed-funds-rate-historical-chart

12 Tim Lucas, "October 2018 Mortgage Rates Forecast (FHA, VA, USDA, Conventional)," The Mortgage Reports (September 28, 2018). https://themortgagereports.com/32667/mortgage-rates-forecast-fha-va-usda-conventional

13 Zelkadis Elvi, "Why Mortgage Rates Once Reached a Sky-high 18.5%," Yahoo! Finance (November 22, 2013). https://finance.yahoo.com/blogs/just-explain-it/why-mortgage-rates-matter-152241574.html

1981[14]—a year when the average rate was almost 17%."

Can you imagine? I remember clients complaining when rates increased to 4 percent. How would they have responded if it climbed to 18 percent? It's easy to get lulled into a false sense of confidence that interest rates "should" be this low. Don't let that happen to you! We are in a period of time with *incredibly* low interest rates. If you can lock in a cash-flowing property for 30 years at this rate, you should be doing it. We may never see opportunities like this again.

As far as using OPM, the same principle applies. When someone is willing to let you borrow their money, it's usually because they want a better return than they can get in the bank or the stock market. This is reasonable. Right now, interest rates are so low that banks are paying basically zero, and the stock market is flooded with concerns it's overpriced. All this combines to make this a historically easy time to raise money. Also, you don't have to pay as much for it.

If the federal government is keeping rates low, this takes a toll on those trying to live off their savings and the interest they provide. If they want to avoid digging into their principal, they need to get a better rate of return than zero to 1 percent. This is where you come in. By paying more than they're currently receiving, but less than you'd normally have to, you can create a win-win scenario in which everyone makes money and you are incentivized to continue growing your business and making money for everyone.

Long Amortization Periods

But wait, there's more! Not only are interest rates very low, but the period of time lenders are willing to let you borrow money is extraordinarily high. Now I know this might seem odd for me to say, especially if you're used to seeing 30-year mortgage periods. Let me just call your attention to something you might not realize—very few countries, if any, offer this besides the United States.

In our country, we take huge steps to incentivize home ownership. Many of us take these steps for granted. Remember how we talked earlier about Fannie Mae/Freddie Mac? Those are government sponsored entities (GSE) created to make it easier and safer for banks to give loans.

---

14 "30-Year Fixed-Rate Mortgages Since 1971," Freddie Mac. http://www.freddiemac.com/pmms/pmms30.html

The government doesn't have to do this, and it helps keep loans available to those who would never be able to get one without them!

Additionally, the government also keeps the prime rate low (artificially) so interest rates can be kept low! This isn't natural. It's only possible because our government created policy to do so. Most other countries don't offer this. Want to know what else we offer that most countries don't? Thirty-year loans. This is something American investors should be taking advantage of. If someone is willing to let you borrow hundreds of thousands of dollars, knowing you may have *zero* experience using it (managing a rental), and they are willing to let you borrow it for *30 years*, at insanely low interest rates, why on earth would you not take advantage of this and borrow as much as you can to buy healthy, performing, cash-flowing properties? We take so much for granted because it's "always been that way." Don't make this mistake. The power of leverage may not always be this readily available.

Real Estate Is Low Risk

First things first: don't be deceived. Every investment involves risk. Every. Single. One. Even putting your money in a bank involves some element of risk. That's why the federal government provides insurance against loss. (Have you ever noticed that "FDIC insured" seal you see in banks?) While every investment involves some form of risk, some are much riskier than others.

Think of it like a spectrum. At one end of a spectrum is a high return. At the other end is a low return. At the same end of the spectrum for high returns, we find other, less desirable traits. High risk, high work, high headache, high time, etc. On the low return side of the spectrum we find the opposite. Low risk, low work, low time, low headache, etc. If you want better returns, you have to be willing to accept all the negativity that comes with that.

Why do I love real estate? Because real estate, in my opinion, provides the highest returns for the lower number of negative traits. Sure, real estate is risky. Every investment is. There is no investment that doesn't have risk somewhere on that spectrum. But when you compare all the ways you can make money in real estate vs. losing money, real estate comes out way ahead. On the same token, when you compare all the ways you can control your outcome in real estate vs. other investments, real estate wins every time.

Why am I talking about risk during a leverage portion of the book? Because the less risk you have, the more leverage you can take on before you start to worry. If you're involved in a high-risk investment play, say, shorting stocks, you would have to be much more careful about borrowing someone else's money to do it. Because it's so risky, you would also have to pay a much higher interest rate for it to be worth their while. At a certain point, you're paying so much for OPM that your profit isn't worth the time or risk you're taking yourself.

Real estate is different—especially when you've got some experience. Because this is such a relatively low-risk investment, it becomes much easier to feel comfortable using OPM, as well as selling your lenders on why they should lend to you. If someone came to me with an idea to start a small business from scratch, I would be very hesitant to lend to them. If they came to me with an idea to buy a multifamily property and could clearly show me the numbers of cash flow, I would be much more likely to consider it.

Inflation Hedge

When we call something an "inflation hedge," we are usually referring to an investment that will protect your money in the case of inflation. Inflation is a term used to describe when prices rise and money becomes less valuable than it used to be. Inflation can cause a lot of harm when you have money sitting in the bank that isn't growing. If inflation is at 3 percent for the year, and you're earning 1 percent on your money, you're really losing 2 percent of all your money's value, every year. When inflation rises quickly, you can start losing 8 percent, 10 percent, 12 percent, or more, very fast.

Investments that act as an inflation hedge are those that appreciate quickly along with inflation. Think of your investment as an item you plant in the dirt. That item stands and hopefully grows with time. Rising inflation is like a rising tide. If your investment doesn't grow faster than the tide rises, the water will eventually overcome it and it will lose value. Investments that act as inflation hedges rise *with* the tide, like a buoy.

Real estate is one of these types of investments. As inflation increases, property values and rent values increase along with it. This buoy, or floating relationship with inflation, makes real estate a very appealing investment to own in times of high inflation. Now what does this have to do with leverage? A lot! When you owe money to someone, it's beneficial when inflation hits. The value of the money you owe becomes less and less as inflation increases, while the value of the asset you bought with that money becomes more and more!

Consider you borrow $100,000 to buy a property worth $115,000. The property is stable and cash-flowing. Suddenly, inflation hits. Each year your property gains 10 percent in value and the rents increase by 10 percent as well. Within a couple years your property is worth much more, and is cash-flowing much more, *but the money you're making on it is worth less.* This is how inflation works. That tide is rising and bringing the cost of everything else up with it!

Now, consider who the real loser is in this situation—it's the person who let you borrow that $100,000. Unless it was an adjustable rate mortgage, they are in trouble. The terms of your note say you only have to make the agreed-upon payment every month. Each year, that payment becomes less and less valuable as that money becomes worth less and less. This is great for you. You won twice! The first win was when your property and rent appreciated. The second was when the value of the money you paid back depreciated.

It's not likely we are going to ever see the dollar deflate. I don't have a crystal ball, but it's never happened before, at least not long-term. You can't take advantage of the nature of inflation if you don't own any investments that act as an inflation hedge. My bet is to own as much cash-flowing real estate as I possibly can, throw my buoys out into the ocean, and wait for that tide to start rising—and carrying me with it!

Don't Just Work for Money

The final reason why you should be leveraging properties is the fact that your money should be working for *you.* If you're not taking advantage of leverage, you're not making your money work very hard, and trust me, your money will take full advantage of that. Leveraged money is hardworking money.

Why is this? Because the lower your ROI, the less work your money is doing. The less leverage you're using, the lower the ROI. You worked hard to make, earn, save, and borrow that money. Why let it off the hook? I've mentioned lots of reasons why you should be leveraging your money right now. Can you think of any reasons you shouldn't?

The only reason against leverage is risk. If you don't have money borrowed, you can't be responsible for paying it back. I hear this, a lot, and it's not untrue. Leverage does increase risk. However, I would argue that the increase in risk is *minimal* compared with the increase in lost opportunity cost for what you could have done with that money.

Opportunity cost is defined as "the loss of potential gain from other alternatives when one alternative is chosen." In this case, choosing not to use leverage results in a loss of potential gain you could have experienced had you used it. In this case, opportunity cost would be the great deal you couldn't buy because all your money was tied up in the first deal you bought. You may think you're reducing risk by not using leverage, but are you really?

Stop thinking you are playing it safe by not doing something. Sometimes this is the case. Oftentimes, it's not. Choosing not to buy real estate avoids one type of risk (losing money), but it involves a whole different form of risk (not making money). You can't only look at one side of the coin. You're not being fair, nor honest, with yourself if you think that avoiding leverage is synonymous with avoiding risk.

Leverage forces your money to work for you. It forces you to put it to work. It turns you into an active manager of your wealth, and as a by-product, an active manager of your life. With interest rates this low, you're really not reducing your risk by a whole lot anyway. Sometimes playing it safe is the riskiest thing you can do.

Exit Strategies: How the Refinance in BRRRR Compares with the Sale of a Flip

Bring any deal to an experienced investor, no matter the type of deal, and they will always ask the same question. What's your exit strategy? Every deal has an exit strategy, or at least it should. If you don't have one, you probably shouldn't enter! While there are many kinds of exit strategies, there are two that are the most common in real estate.

1. Selling
2. Refinancing

Of course, this isn't an all-inclusive list. There are many other options including holding a note, holding until you die, holding a property until its useful life has ended, lease options, tearing down and rebuilding something new, etc. However, when you really break it down, most options are some form of selling or refinancing.

When you flip a house, your intention is to buy it, hold it for a short time, then sell it for a profit. By nature, this usually involves a rehab, but the point is to sell for more than you paid. When you successfully sell the house and transfer the title to someone else, you've exited the property. A successful exit is one where you recover all of your capital, and hopefully some extra for your trouble and risk. Flippers enter a deal by looking at the end result they want (sale price or ARV) and base all their analysis and efforts (purchase price, holding costs, rehab budget) off of this end result. They are planning for the exit from the very first move.

In the BRRRR method, we don't sell the property. We refinance it. This is our "exit." We aren't selling the property, but it functions the same as an exit because we are recovering our capital. Capital recovery is the real reason someone exits an investment. This being the case, BRRRR investors function very similarly to flip investors, just with a different exit strategy in mind. The goal is to increase the ARV as much as possible then refinance, as opposed to selling.

Many people refer to this process as "flipping to yourself." In essence, you are buying a piece of junk, making it nicer, then "selling" it to yourself to hold as a buy-and-hold property. This is the same process turnkey providers accomplish, but in most cases (if you do it right) you get the property for a much better price. If you BRRRR correctly, you can "sell to yourself" at deep discounts. This builds your wealth instead of someone else's.

The Argument Against Flipping

So why do we keep a property and refinance it instead of selling? Well, in some cases, you wouldn't. For instance, if you've rehabbed a property that is now worth so much it makes more sense to flip, you should. If you've rehabbed a property and it turns out it won't cash-flow after the refinance, maybe it's a better idea to sell. But, if you've rehabbed a property and you could keep it as a rental instead of flipping, which is better?

The answer depends on your exit strategy. If your goal was to build a large portfolio of cash-flowing homes, it would make sense to keep it. If your goal was to make a quick buck, it would make sense to flip it. We are in a unique position here, however. We can go either direction. Let's say we are trying to choose our exit strategy *now*. Which is the better option?

Let me propose to you that buy and hold is a better, more viable wealth-building option for the long term. Let me also propose that it is better for several reasons, with one of the biggest being its efficiency. The reason? Taxes and commissions.

Selling a Property Is a Costly Endeavor

Here's one of the things nobody talks about in real estate—capital gains taxes. We hear all these great stories of investors who made tens of thousands of dollars flipping houses. You know what you don't hear about? That capital gains taxes are substantial: 25 percent of your profits, or more!

If you own an investment and sell it within a year, that gain gets taxed at the *same rate you pay on your normal income*. If you're doing well, this can be 25, 30, 40, or almost 50 percent. Keep in mind, this isn't like your normal job where you have zero risk. This is on an investment where you could lose it all. If the property is held for more than a year, the long-term capital gains rate kicks in. This is a minimum of 20 percent, and often more. I want you to think about this. If you do *totally crush* a deal, your reward is for the government to then take 20–50 percent of your profits away. Still feeling as excited as you were before?

Well, it gets better (technically, worse). Not only do they tax you at that insanely high rate, but it's a one-way street. If you lose money on a deal, the government doesn't come cut you a check for 25–50 percent of your loss. Nope. If you lose, that's on you. If you win, they show up with their hands out. Capital gains are not talked about enough. They are a huge downside to real estate flipping as opposed to buy and hold.

Now consider this: Capital gains are only assessed upon the *sale* of a property. If you don't sell it, you don't pay capital gains. Sweet deal, right? That's one reason I'm a buy and hold investor as opposed to a flashy flipper. Want to know the other reason? I don't like paying closing costs and commissions.

Now, full disclosure, I'm a real estate agent—and an excellent one. I do a great job for my clients and oftentimes make them tons of money. I expect to get paid for that, and that's normal. I'm not like many shortsighted investors who begrudge their agent's commissions. On the contrary, I often pay agents bonuses for a job well done. My problem with paying commissions isn't the fact I think they are not deserved, it's simply that *they cut so deep into the bottom line.*

Most people understand Realtors typically get paid 6 percent of the price of the home, and that amount is split between both sides (sometimes unevenly). While 6 percent is a fair number and exists for a reason, I'd like you to consider something you may have never considered. You're paying 6 percent of the *sale price*, not 6 percent of your profits.

Let's say you buy a house for $50,000. You put $20,000 into it and sell it for $100,000. This gives you a gross profit of $30,000. Not bad, right? Of the $70,000 you invested, $30,000 is about 42 percent of the total amount you invested. That's a healthy return!

Now consider that you need to pay Realtors 6 percent of the $100,000 ($6,000) and another $2,000 in closing costs. That's a total of $8,000 (or 8 percent). If you apply that $8,000 to the $30,000 profit, it's actually 26.6 percent of the profit. You just lost *26.6 percent of your entire profit,* just to costs associated with the sale of a home. If you weren't selling, you wouldn't have to pay these. And no whining, because these are costs you need to be paying to people who did necessary work.

But that's not all! Now, on top of that 26.6 percent you just lost, you are getting capital gains added to the remainder. After paying your 8 percent in closing costs, you're left with a profit of $22,000. Now, if you're paying your normal income tax at a rate of 30 percent, you can remove another whopping $6,600. This brings your new profit down to $15,400. When you add the closing costs and capital gains together in this example, you are looking at a 48.6 percent loss in initial profit.

Did you see that? You went from a profit in your mind of $30,000 to nearly *half* of that, *solely from capital gains and closings costs.* What makes this even worse is there is no way to avoid these, not legally at least. And keep in mind, this was on an incredible flip where your gross profit was 42 percent of the total you invested.

Here's the rub. Any time a sale of real estate takes place, a whole bunch of stuff needs to get done. It's not a small task. Hundreds of thousands of dollars' worth of property are changing hands between two parties, and there are so many moving pieces. Trying to avoid paying the price for these services is rarely ever prudent. Trying to hire bad agents for discounted commissions almost always loses you money. Trying to avoid paying for title insurance is a big mistake. "For Sale by Owner" escrows rarely ever go smoothly, and when they do, almost always sell for a big discount.

There are so many people involved in the successful and safe sale and transfer of title to real estate that it's just expensive and there is no way around that! The key I want you to take away from this is that *these costs are only associated with the sale of a property*. If a property isn't being sold, both capital gains and closings costs don't apply, meaning you spend less.

Refinancing Is Tax-Free Money

You may hear a lot about "loopholes" in real estate. *Loopholes* is a word that has come to take on a sinister meaning, but it doesn't have to.

A "loophole" is really just a term for "tax break legally found in the IRS code." If you start looking at it from that perspective, it doesn't sound so bad. My recommendation to you would be, start looking at it from this perspective. As I just mentioned in the above segment, there are *lots* of ways the government is going to get from you what it can of your profits, and it surely won't be reimbursing you for your losses. Want to avoid this? Look for ways to save your profits/equity instead of losing them.

Another secret that isn't talked about enough in real estate circles and that many newbies don't know: Refinancing can be a much better option than selling. Refinancing is powerful when it comes to wealth building and very important to consider right now, while you're considering your exit strategy. Refinances aren't taxed like sales are! In fact, they aren't taxed at all! If you're not selling your property, you're not taxed on it. Let that sink in for a second. By *not* selling your property, you can keep *more* of your money. This is one of the most compelling reasons I'm aware of why you should keep property for the long term, not sell it. It makes the BRRRR method that much more appealing when you understand the consequences of paying taxes and commissions.

Additionally, consider that the refinance of a property is much, much simpler than the sale of a property.

During a refinance there is:
- One person (the lender) working on the deal.

During a sale there is:
- A lender
- Listing agent
- Buyer's agent
- Title company
- Escrow company

- Photographer
- Stager
- Home inspector
- Brokers
- and more!

All these people are putting in time and effort. This equals money, and someone's gotta pay it. Guess who that someone is? While refinancing isn't free (there are still closing costs associated with it), it's cheaper than selling a property *and* you don't have to worry about paying capital gains taxes, because you haven't gained capital yet, just equity. Want to access that equity without paying taxes on it? Then refinance instead of selling.

In all of real estate investing, pulling money out of properties via a refinance is one of the only ways you can avoid paying taxes or money associated with cost of sale expenses. I'm not aware of many other investment vehicles that allow you to do this, and I'm certainly not aware of any other options that are as easy to do this as real estate is. This is why so many investors claim long-term buy and hold is the best way to make money in real estate investing. You make money in so many ways!

- You make money from the cash flow your property produces. This is taxed but it's not taxed at the same level of your normal income (like a flip would be) as there are natural tax shelters in real estate investing (depreciation, for one).
- You make money from the rent increasing every year and your cash flow increasing as well.
- You make money from the loan being paid down every month. This is essentially your tenants paying your house off for you.
- You make money from your property increasing in value over time (inflation will do most of the heavy lifting for you).
- You make money from increasing your property's value through a rehab (forced appreciation).
- You make money from buying right (paying less for a property than what it's worth through targeting distressed sellers).

With all of these ways you can make money in real estate, and the only time you get taxed is on the cash flow it produces (at a reduced rate) and when you sell. When you look at the big picture, it becomes pretty obvious that if you never sell, you can avoid paying some pretty serious taxes. If you spread this out over a long period, it becomes money you're saving and then reinvesting, which will be compounding over time to grow even more.

Now, of course there is one caveat. The 1031 like-kind exchange. Section 1031 of the IRS code states an exception to paying taxes on capital gains. It's really less of an exception and more of a deferment. This section allows you to sell a property and reinvest the money into a different property without paying taxes on it until later.

While many investors think this is a way to avoid capital gains taxes, it is not. You will still have to pay them later. In addition to having to pay the taxes down the road, there are strict rules to follow as well. You only get a short period of time to identify a list of potential properties you would like to close on, and then 180 days to actually close on them. There is also a litany of other regulations that must be followed that make executing a 1031 much more difficult in practicality than it sounds in theory.

Consider that when you follow the BRRRR model, you are doing almost the exact same job of a house flipper, but keeping much more of your profits for yourself. At the end of the project you will "exit." You are keeping water in your bucket while the house flipper is spilling a major amount (48.6 percent of the profit in the example I provided above). When you compare the BRRRR model with flipping, it's almost identical except for the "rent" and "refinance" portions. A flipper would follow a model of BRSR (Buy, Rehab, Sell, Repeat). *It's the same amount of work we do as buy-and-hold investors but much less efficient.*

This is the point I'm trying to drive home. If you plan on making a quick buck, flipping a house can work just fine. If you need to build some quick capital, this is a way to do it. But, if you're looking to build long-term, sustainable wealth, owning a portfolio of cash-flowing homes for a long time is the way to do it. Remember how we talked about inflation being like the rising tide of an ocean? How many buoys do you want in that ocean?

Below is a table that compares flipping a property to holding it BRRRR style.

FLIP	BRRRR
Pay commissions	No commissions
Pay closing costs	No closing costs

Pay taxes	No taxes
Build equity then lose a big chunk of it at the sale	Build equity then keep it
Get one payoff then back to looking for a new property to buy	Find deal, rehab it, and benefit from it every month
Access your equity through the sale	Access your equity through the refinance
Don't benefit from appreciation	Benefit from appreciation
Don't benefit from loan pay down	Benefit from loan pay down
Don't benefit from tax shelters	Benefit from tax shelters
No passive income	Passive income

These are the reasons why I rarely flip properties and instead prefer to buy, hold, and refinance. It is a more efficient, cost-effective, and beneficial strategy over the long term. Now you may be saying, but what good is all this equity I'm gaining in a property if I can't use it? I want to invest more. That's the right attitude to have! The key to accessing your equity in the BRRRR strategy is simple—you just refinance again. By paying down your mortgages and monitoring your properties' values as they increase, you can gauge how much equity you have and then refinance later when it makes sense to.

Remember how we talked about rents rising every year? Well the more rents rise, the more you can borrow against a property and still cash-flow positively. Some of the first properties I ever bought in California have increased in value tremendously. This has brought about an increase in rent as well. What was once renting for $1,500 is now renting for $2,150. This is a big difference! With my now-higher rents, I can refinance these homes and pull more equity out to invest with—all while still cash-flowing positive.

The reason is because even though my mortgage increases whenever I pull more money out (the higher loan balance after the refinance results in a higher mortgage payment), the higher rents I'm collecting make up for that higher mortgage. I still cash-flow even after pulling money out. Now, I can go buy more cash-flowing property with that same money and increase my monthly cash flow even more.

Do you see what's happening here? I bought a property. The property went up in value and the rent increased as well. I pulled money out of that property and the increased cash flow paid for it. I used that money to go buy more properties, which will also eventually increase in value and in rent. In essence, I bought a house, that house paid for me to go buy another house, and so on and so forth.

This is like planting a tree that grows to produce fruit. I took the seeds from that fruit and planted more trees. Those trees eventually grew to produce fruit seeds as well, and the cycle continues. Now of course there are tons of variables to this equation, but the principle remains the same. Investing in real estate wisely creates opportunities for you to grow your wealth and invest even more. *Selling a property prevents these opportunities from occurring. You can't expect fruit from a tree that you've chopped down and sold for firewood.*

When a BRRRR Goes Great

So far I've talked about how the one major benefit to flipping vs. holding as a rental is that flipping can make you a quick buck. Selling a property for a profit does put more cash in your pocket, and there is definitely an argument to be made for the value of cash. However, let me propose a wild thought. What about if you can put cash in your pocket using the BRRRR model as well?

I know this is possible because I've done it. Several times. Speaking from experience, there aren't many better feelings in real estate than when you buy a property that cash-flows every month, has been completely renovated so it won't need any major work for a long time, and you get *paid* to own it. Sometimes things like this can sound too good to be true, so let me explain just how this happens.

When you find a lender that will let you borrow against the appraised value (LTV), the price you paid for a property or the time you put into it doesn't matter. The lender is going to look solely at the end result (the

ARV) when determining how much to let you borrow. Now, the key is getting a higher LTV amount. For this reason, I always shoot for 75 percent of the ARV when possible.

Imagine a scenario where you get a great deal on a property. You find a seller headed toward divorce who just wants a quick sell on their investment property so they can pay legal fees. You buy the property, then rehab it very effectively. In this case you paid $45,000 for the property, and spent $20,000 on the rehab, making your all-in cost $65,000. You find a lender that is willing to let you borrow for 75 percent of the appraised value. The property appraises for $100,000.

The lender is going to let you borrow 75 percent of the appraised price, which in this case is $75,000. The property cash-flows at $300 a month after all your expenses. You sign the loan paperwork, complete the loan process, and receive your wire transfer in your checking account for $75,000. Congrats!

Once the money is wired, you realize something. You only spent $65,000 on this project! At the end of the day, you got a full rehab on a great property that cash-flows, and you walked away with $10,000 more than you had when you started. This is not a scam. This is not illegal. There is nothing about this that is wrong or immoral. This is your *reward* for doing a great job as a real estate investor. You got a great deal, rehabbed it well, and got a terrific loan. As a result, you got paid $10,000 to own a cash-flowing rental property.

How many turnkey providers do you know that can provide a return like that? This isn't possible with turnkey because when you buy turnkey you are building someone else's wealth. When you follow the BRRRR model, you are building your own. Now what are you going to do with this extra $10,000 you just made?

- You could buy a car
- You could go on a vacation
- You could buy sports memorabilia
- OR, you could go buy more real estate!

The reason I love putting more cash in my pocket is because it means I can go invest that money into a new deal and turn it into even more. Can you imagine if you got so good that every property you used the BRRRR method for you also received an extra $10,000? More money in your pocket means more deals you can BRRRR—that equals even more money in your pocket.

This is how real estate pays off. When you learn it, when you become a black belt investor, you start getting paid to buy property. That property also pays you every month. The property goes up in value every year, and pays you more every year, and your tenants pay your loans down for you. You can then refinance these properties and buy even more cash-flowing properties. And on and on.

When you pull more out of a property than you put in, it creates a "negative ROI." Now this doesn't mean you are losing money. It means you cannot calculate a return on your investment, because there is no money "invested." You've already pulled out more than 100 percent of the money you invested; therefore, the money can't make you a return.

Think of ROI like the check your money is sending to you every month after you sent it away to work. You send your capital across the country to work for you, and every month your capital sends you the money it's earned for you in a check as proof it's working. This check is the ROI. Now, when you pull more capital out of a deal than you put in, it's like the money went across the country, did its work, and came right back to you right away. There is no ROI, no check to receive, because the capital is already back. But it came back bigger, stronger, and with more friends. Now you can send that money away to your next deal and let it work for you there instead. This is a huge win!

My advice to you if you are somewhat capital restrained is to target properties that are likely to bring you more back than you put in. Of course, this isn't easy, but if this is your goal, even if you miss the mark you'll still likely be in a good situation. If you know your LTV is 75 percent, you need to target properties where you can be all-in for less than that amount. Seventy-five percent is the limit where you will start to lose water (leave money in a property). If you can keep your acquisition and rehab costs below that amount, you'll get to pocket the difference when you're finished.

For instance, let's say you are looking at buying a property and you know the ARV is conservatively $200,000. If you take 75 percent of $200,000, you get $150,000. This becomes your target. Being able to buy and rehab a property for less than $150,000 will leave you with extra money in the bank when it's finished. In order to get a deal this good, you're going to need to find something that is pretty distressed. Usually, this means your rehab budget will be pretty sizeable. Let's call it $50,000.

If I know I want to be all-in for less than $150,000, and I'm planning on a rehab of $50,000, I need to be finding properties with an ARV of $200,000 and buying them for less than $100,000. This sounds difficult, and it is, but isn't that the point of learning how to find great deals? Pulling more money out of a project than you put in is the home run of the BRRRR model. If you want to hit home runs, you have to wait for just the right pitch. Not just any deal will do!

Now, if I find a property for $110,000, that means my rehab needs to be less than $40,000 in order to hit the mark. There is some flexibility here. Understanding these numbers and how to make them work for you is important if you want to be a black belt investor. The good news is, it's an awesome feeling when you can consistently hit pitches like this. You may not be able to right away, but always be building up in this direction.

Once you've got a system of agents, wholesalers, or employees bringing you deals that work like this, you have essentially built a business in which you are getting paid to own cash-flowing property. Can you imagine a better job than that?

Key Points
- Know the difference between LTV and LTC.
- There are several types of loans. The main types are conventional, FHA, VA, jumbo, portfolio, hard money, private financing, owner financing, HELOCs, and 80/10/10s.
- BRRRR maximizes your ability to leverage.
- Real estate investing requires three things: money, knowledge, and hustle.
- Real estate is a hedge against inflation.
- Opportunity cost is the price you pay for missing out on an opportunity because you chose something else.
- Selling a property is expensive.
- Refinancing a property is tax-free.
- A successful BRRRR can pay you to own it!

PART SIX

Repeat: Building Systems to Run Your Business Like a Business

CHAPTER TEN

Building Systems to Increase Your Success

"I fear not the man who has practiced 10,000 kicks once, but I fear the man who has practiced one kick 10,000 times."

—BRUCE LEE

Up to this point, we have learned how to Buy, Rehab, Rent, and Refinance like a pro. Mastery of these core elements to real estate investing *will* lead to not only growing your wealth, but growing it substantially faster and with less stress than simply having a basic understanding of how to find success with real estate. Much like mastering a martial art, it takes time, sweat, pain, and frustration to achieve a level of mastery. While this is sure to grow your wealth and your cash flow, the knowledge alone won't make you a black belt investor. What *will* is the repeated application of the knowledge you have learned so far. Growing your wealth through real estate is a worthy goal, but make no bones about it, it's also a strong opponent.

If you want to achieve financial freedom, you'll need to develop systems to repeat these processes over, and over, and over. With each repetition, you'll grow more efficient, more effective, and more expeditious. The sheer number of reps someone has experienced while practicing *anything* 10,000 times is guaranteed to make them an expert at it.

And that is the goal here, right? We want to be really, really good investors. Black belt investors. Capable of creating and maintaining life-changing wealth through real estate. Learning this stuff is hard, but stick with it. Do you want to go through all that time and stress and stop at a few houses to go chase the next shiny object? Wouldn't it make much more sense to repeat these steps until you've mastered them, then develop a system that runs on autopilot so the work is done over and over without you having to do it?

That's what I did in my business, and that's what I'm going to show you how to do in yours. With everything I've talked about so far, and all four previous parts to this book (Buy, Rehab, Rent, and Refinance), *this* chapter is the most valuable. If you haven't experienced the power of leverage and systems to make a business, process, or cause grow, you are in for a huge treat.

The "Four E's"

From this point forward in the book, I want you to examine everything I talk about through the lens of improving your business according to the "Four E's." Every single time I'm faced with a problem I know I will see again and want to develop a system to ensure the next time around I do it better, I implement the Four E's. The Four E's are:

- Efficiency
- Effectiveness
- Expeditiousness
- Employability

The E's defined:

1. **Efficiency:** The ability to complete a task or accomplish an objective with less effort and money.

   Questions to ask: Where are my actions not efficient? How can I reduce the number of steps to allow fewer opportunities for something to go wrong? How can I make this task simpler to complete? What opportunities do I have to "trim the fat"?

2. **Effectiveness:** The ability to improve my odds of success at accomplishing a goal, achieving a desired result, or completing a task.

   Questions to ask: What can I do to raise my odds? How can I improve my "batting average"? What did I do well in the past that I can isolate and amplify today to give myself more opportunity to succeed?

3. **Expeditiousness:** The speed at which I accomplish a task or objective.

    Questions to ask: Where am I slowing myself down with activities that don't have an impact on achieving my desired goal? Where do I need to increase my sense of urgency? Where am I losing out on opportunity because I am—or my system is—too slow?

4. **Employability:** The ability to put someone else in charge of a task, whether or not you pay them with money or some other form of currency (leads, friendship, support, etc.).

    Questions to ask: What am I doing that someone else could be doing better than I do? What am I doing that isn't crucial to achieving my goal? What am I doing that is slowing me down from achieving my goal?

The Pareto Principle

The Pareto Principle, named after Italian economist Vilfredo Pareto (and also called the 80/20 rule)[15], states that, for many events, roughly 80 percent of the effects come from 20 percent of the causes. Pareto noticed this phenomenon occurring in many instances and became fascinated by its consistent appearance wherever he looked. Pareto found that 80 percent of a farmer's profits came from 20 percent of their crops. That 80 percent of a nation's taxes came from 20 percent of its population. Also, not surprisingly, that 80 percent of a nation's land was owned by 20 percent of its population. Pareto, being an economist, was fascinated by this principle in regard to wealth distribution.

My guess is, if you look at your own life, the same holds true. You wear 20 percent of the clothes in your closet 80 percent of the time. You use 20 percent of the apps on your phone 80 percent of the time. In real estate sales, 80 percent of the business is done through the top 20 percent of the agents, and guess what? In real estate investing, 20 percent of your actions will produce 80 percent of your results. I can't begin to try to understand why this principle works, I just know that I've seen it

---

15 "Understanding the Pareto Principle (The 80/20 Rule)," Better Explained. https://betterexplained.com/articles/understanding-the-pareto-principle-the-8020-rule/

enough to believe it. I also know that once I started to put my faith in it, my success really took off.

Here's how this applies to you. All of us are different. We have different skill sets, strengths, and weaknesses. Because of this, we will all excel in different things. To use a basketball analogy, some people are great three-point shooters, others are great playmakers, and others rebound well. None of us are the same, and trying to run our business like we have to do every single task is a surefire way to sabotage our own success.

I can almost guarantee you may think you understand this, but you're not doing anything about it. If we were all to take an honest look at what we do throughout a day, odds are we are *not* spending 80 percent of our time doing the 20 percent of the tasks that will get us the result we want. A lot of rebounders are spending their time around the three-point line when they should be closer to the hoop. Will they still get rebounds? Of course, about 20 percent of them will make their way all the way out to the three-point line. But wouldn't it make more sense for them to be spending their time closer to the hoop where 80 percent of the rebounds are going to end up?

My point is this—if we don't consciously make efforts to put ourselves in our "20 percent," we won't end up there. Want an effective, quick way to know if you are in your 20 percent? Ask yourself if the task you are working on feels "light" or if it feels "heavy." If it feels heavy (difficult, burdensome, annoying, draining), odds are it's in the 80 percent of tasks you shouldn't be doing.

If you shouldn't be doing it, then who should? That's exactly what we are going to talk about in this section of the book. By developing systems to accomplish the specific tasks you have determined are necessary to succeed in real estate investing, you can isolate those tasks that fall into your own 20 percent, and leverage out the rest. The beauty about creating systems isn't just that you know what to leverage out, it's that once something is systemized, you can leverage it out much easier. All the person you're leveraging needs to do is follow the instructions they've been given. This is much easier for most than having to learn it for themselves.

Creating systems takes time, but once they are in place they allow your business to run much smoother from every level of the Four E's. Think of creating systems as an investment itself. If you want to grow your money, you take it, combine it with your time, and buy a property.

You fix that property up, make it worth more, and your money has grown. Systems work the same way. You take your time, invest it into a process that is not being conducted or managed sufficiently, make it better, and in the end it gives you more of your time back. This is what top businesses do, and there is no reason you shouldn't be doing the same.

Benefits to Building Systems

If we are committed to building systems, let's start off by defining what that means. For the purposes of this book, a "system" will be defined as "a pre-established method or order for conducting the tasks relevant to and necessary for being successful in real estate." A system can be anything that documents a method for conducting a task. This can include checklists, written instructions, spreadsheets, criteria, or even a conversation with someone they remember from that point forward. Now that we've established what a "system" is, let's get started talking about some of the benefits of them!

Benefits to Leverage (or "Employable" Tasks)

As I've already mentioned, there are two major benefits to leverage in your business. The first is it allows you to stay in your "20 percent," only conducting the tasks you are best at. By staying in your zone of expertise, you can work longer (you like what you're doing) and better (it's something you're good at). This leads to better results. In addition to this, leverage helps you accomplish *more*. Having more people working on your behalf to accomplish your goals is obviously going to make you more likely to succeed.

But what if you're not at the point where you have enough money to start hiring people to do tasks? Fear not; there are *many* ways you can take advantage of the power of leverage before you spend a dollar. The trick is to find people who are interested in more of what you have to offer than just your money, and yes, there are plenty of these people out there. For starters, let's begin by talking about those most essential to your success—your team, the Core Four.

Your Core Four consists of your agent, lender, property manager, and rehabber. Without them, you're probably not doing much business. The good news for you is, without you, they aren't either. Your Core Four needs you just like you need them. If the members of your Core Four want to make any money, they need you to be buying properties or sending them leads of others who do. Without you, and people like you, they don't succeed either. This symbiotic relationship is a unique characteristic found in real estate investing that allows you to leverage off parts of your business to others without having to pay them directly.

Here's what that looks like. You need someone to make sure the comps you are getting from your agent are accurate. Of course you could pay an expert to look them over, but if you're not looking at hundreds of deals, that's probably not necessary. If it's just a few deals, why not ask your property manager to do it? If they are a rockstar and an investor them-selves, they should know their stuff. They will be motivated to do this because if you buy the property, they get another property in their port-folio to manage.

You need someone to make sure your contractor is doing the work they agreed to do. Sure, you could pay someone to go check it out, but what if it's just one or two jobs? It makes no sense to hire for that low volume. Instead, ask your agent to double-check. Leverage them to save you some money.

The list goes on and on. There are many tasks we all spend our time doing that we don't have to that others would be willing to do. Start with your Core Four. These are people who genuinely *want* you to be successful, because their success depends in part on yours. Of all the pieces that are involved in a real estate transaction, the buyer is the most important one. Buyers drive markets, and all these other roles are just support roles for buyers. You are that buyer. Understand the power you wield and look for ways to leverage others who make money from being affiliated with you.

When you have the same members of your Core Four doing the same work all the time, it does more than just take the burden off of you, it also creates consistency in the process. Consistency can help limit mistakes. The fewer times someone has done something, the less efficient they are at it, and the more mistakes they are likely to make. Ideally, you'd have the same person doing the same task, every single time. While it may take a long time to build your business up to the point where that's occurring, you can still use the same people for as many of the tasks as they are good at as possible.

When I buy a new property, my agent knows she needs to open up the doors for the home inspector and coordinate with the contractor to get them both in the house on the same day. This allows the two of them to communicate and determine what needs to be done so they can give me a more accurate rehab bid. If I use the same rehabber and the same inspector, the two of them develop a rapport and a system of their own. This allows them to be more accurate, more efficient, and more expeditious. It also guarantees a smoother process with each time we all work together.

By using all the same pieces (agent, rehabber, inspector), I am more likely to get a consistent result and less likely to need to spend extra time explaining to each person what I want each time I do it. This time really adds up over the purchase of several properties, and so do the little mistakes that are bound to happen the first time anybody does anything. By leveraging tasks to the same people every time, you can expect a more consistent result.

If you have a new person trying to complete the tasks you've given them, even if those tasks are systemized, they are still going to go through the "beginner's learning curve" every time. This is not an efficient way to run a business. If you're going to go through the expensive beginner's learning curve (expensive because more mistakes will be made), why would you want to quit and start with someone new every time? Using the same people for the same tasks over and over is a good way to cut down on mistakes as well.

When we really get right down to it, every property we buy is its own little business. It has its own set of books, its own responsibilities, and it makes or loses money on its own. The best businesses do not have any one person doing every single task for the business. They have specialized roles for each employee. If you consider that with the BRRRR method our goal is to buy many of these small businesses, it stands to reason that developing systems for who will do what job, in each transaction, is a much more effective, efficient, and expeditious way to run your business!

How Repetition Increases the Performance of the Four E's

The more you improve the E's, the better and more successful your business will become. On the first day of tryouts to make a team and learn a new sport, none of the athletes will be very good. They haven't learned the movements, let alone practiced them, and they haven't built up the endurance they'll need to be successful. Every coach knows this.

With each new practice, the athletes become better and better. As their minds start to develop new pathways for neurons to travel, their hand/ eye coordination improves. So do their muscle reflexes. The result is more fluid movements, better stamina, and less concentration to perform the basics. Once these movements become "systemized" (meaning, they no longer require active concentration to perform), the athletes can start to focus more on the actions that will actually result in scoring points or being successful.

As a basketball coach, I would see this every year. The players show up and don't understand any of the fundamentals. We start off teaching them a defensive stance, the right way to dribble a ball while keeping their head up to see what's going on, how to rebound, the correct way to shoot, etc. It's only after they have learned these techniques that I can start teaching them the intricacies of the game. Teaching the players how to draw fouls, how to move the ball, and how to get open and recognize when they have an opportunity to score.

It's only when I'm teaching them the more intricate skills that I'm actually teaching them anything that will score points, but we can't get into that until they can perform the basics without thinking about them. Business works the same way. You have to systemize the small stuff, the fundamentals, before you can go on to succeed with the stuff that will actually make you money. The quicker you learn the basics, the sooner you can start making money. It's a one-in-a-billion type person who can show up on their first day, grasp the basics that same day, and start working on the high-level activities before putting their time in to learn.

As a general rule, the first time I do anything new, I expect it's going to go poorly. Not only will the experience likely suck, but more importantly, I will suck at it. I've created this rule as a means of protecting my own self-confidence by establishing a reasonable expectation for myself. This became necessary when I found I was beating myself up for not being that one-in-a-billion person who could show up, excel on day one, and move on to mastery by day two.

I personally suffered through this for a long time. With every new thing I tried and wasn't able to master on the first day, my confidence wavered and I withdrew more. At a certain point, I stopped trying new things to protect myself. Later on, I actively looked into the future to find situations where I might be exposed to something new so I could avoid being put in that vulnerable situation. I developed a lot of anxiety over failure in general and spent a big chunk of my life doing the same things, every day, and never being challenged.

How much growing do you think I did at that point? If I wasn't happy with myself then, do you think I was likely to become happier by avoiding anything that would have helped me develop new skills, new abilities, and new confidence? My fear of failure drove me to avoid new things, and that kept me from ever growing my confidence. A vicious circle. Luckily, I didn't stay there forever.

Once I realized we aren't meant to be great when we first start something, I quit interpreting my failure as an indication something was wrong with me, and I started seeing it as a positive sign I had an opportunity to grow. Now, I see things more clearly. Waiting to be good at something before you start is like waiting to be strong before you begin lifting weights. It's never going to happen. The process of lifting weights *is* what makes you stronger.

The first time you do anything, you're not going to do it well. It's unreasonable to think any different. On every episode of the *BiggerPockets Podcast*, the co-hosts ask each guest: "What sets apart successful investors from those who give up, fail, or never get started?" The overwhelming majority of guests all say the same thing—some form of "persistence." Why do you think that is? Because successful people understand things are always going to be tough in the beginning, and it takes persistence to get through that initial learning phase before you get to the good stuff.

Acknowledging and coming to peace with this is one of the very first things you need to do if you ever want to be good at anything—including real estate investing. My own experience is a testament to this. In 2009, I bought my very first rental property, a bank-owned foreclosure (real estate owned). The property sold at the peak of 2006 for $565,000. By the time I bought it in 2009, I paid $195,000. The property needed nothing but the carpet vacuumed. This was one of those deals that is about as easy as they come.

In spite of that, I still found just about every way to mess it up. My original Craigslist ads didn't include the rent I wanted for it, because I didn't know how to determine what it should be. When I did finally start getting phone calls, I had no plan in place for how to schedule the showings. I ended up dropping what I was doing and driving 20 minutes, each way, for every single potential tenant who called wanting to see it. Oh yeah, I also had no screening process at all. So I showed it to everyone, regardless of whether they had a dime to their name.

Once I finally bought my standard "How to be a Landlord" book, I had a slightly less miserable experience. Spending half a day trying to figure out how to make copies of the potential landlord forms from the book wasn't a great use of my time, and neither was mowing the grass myself, or stopping by every day to put the "for rent" sign back into the grass after it had been blown out. As ineffective as all this was, it's still not taking into consideration all the overtime I did not work because I wanted to save a couple hundred bucks on property management.

Then, things got really bad. I actually found a tenant and rented it out to him and his family. Using the age-old "I'll be good to you and you'll be good to me and we'll all just pretend that's how the world works" mindset, I did not run a credit check, did not collect a big deposit, and did not verify the tenant's employment or rental history. It should not come as a big surprise that he paid the first month's rent, then paid the second and third with money that he stole from me, then started lying that "the check's in the mail" every time we talked after that.

(Curious how he stole my money? When I bought the property, I paid the pro-rated property taxes based on the amount the house was curiously worth in the tax roll: $565,000. Since I was only paying $195,000, I was due a huge refund once escrow closed. Since the title company didn't bother to check and see the house was an investment property, they sent the check to the property itself, as opposed to the house where I lived. My tenant saw the check for nearly $4,000, forged my signature, and got a bank to let him cash it out, hence paying me the next two month's rent with my own money).

Turned out my tenant got into a big fight with his girlfriend and moved out without telling me. He didn't tell her he wasn't paying the rent. Once I realized an eviction was imminent, I tried to save some money and do it all myself. Still not having learned my lesson, I had a friend try to serve the girlfriend with paperwork. The girlfriend, having no doubt been in this position before, knew her legal right and knew not to answer the door when we knocked.

The whole process took four months and ended up costing me over $7,000. All because I wanted to save a couple hundred bucks by not hiring a property manager. Thankfully the property had not appreciated yet, because I would have sold it in a heartbeat and missed out on future appreciation! Today, I use a property manager and the rent has increased from the initial $1,500 to $2,150 a month, and the value has grown from

$195,000 to over $400,000. Good thing I kept it, right?

Here's the thing—the whole experience was horrible because I walked into it thinking, "How hard can it be?" Had I understood we are rarely ever good at anything the first time we do it, I would have hired someone else to manage it and learned from them before I ever considered doing it on my own. Had I understood it was supposed to suck at first, I wouldn't have beat myself up over everything going wrong.

This is just how it goes when you're new at something. You don't know what to expect and your expectations are typically way off. Without the experience you need to help you solve the problems that come up, mole-hills are going to feel like mountains. Here's what I want you to understand: The value isn't found in the first time we do something, it's in the tenth. The first few times we do anything, the goal shouldn't be to excel or even succeed at it. It should be to *learn* from it. The more you learn, the more progress you make, regardless of what results you're seeing.

Just know you won't be an expert when you first start out. But focus on improving your Four E's and you will become more efficient, more effective, more expeditious, and you will employ more and better people to assist you. These E's are what improve your business and eventually your success. Success is a result of continued improvement that comes through repetition.

Persistence Is the Key to Success

The Core Four is *the* best place to start finding help on your investing tasks that won't cost you any money. While it is likely the cheapest way for you to get started, that doesn't mean it's completely free. Even when someone isn't asking for money, they will still likely require your time, energy, and effort. Just like money, these are also finite resources. Protecting them is just as important as protecting your cash.

We want to make this as "cheap" as possible when it comes to more than just your money. In order to do that, I'm going to share some information that should help get everybody on the same page and perform more efficiently. Finding good people is tough, and getting them to understand what you need takes a lot of clear communication. While it's an investment up front, it's well worth it once you're operating like a well-oiled machine!

The most important thing you need to understand when starting a business relationship with someone new is that it's *your* job to set clear expectations of what you want and need from the beginning. It is not their job to know what you want. Many people fall into the trap of "Well, they should know what to do. That's their job." Unfortunately, this is just not true. Not everyone does everything the same way, and it's not reasonable to expect the person you're leveraging to do some of your tasks to know how you want them done.

The fact is most misunderstandings are a result of poor communication. It's my belief that anytime there was a fallout from poor communication, I am the one to blame. I am the only one who has complete control over the choices I make when it comes to communication. By taking responsibility for that, I empower myself to create an environment where those who I'm leveraging are put in a position to be successful according to my standards. This means I have to communicate those standards clearly.

Nobody starts off as a black belt. Every martial artist, regardless of where they end up, starts off as a white belt. This is vital to understand. When you first start working with someone, even if they are really great at what they are doing, they are still a white belt when it comes to working with you. They had their own systems, their own standards, and their own priorities, all operating completely independent of you, so they'll need time to adjust to your standards.

In this example, you are the teacher. The better you are at communicating how to excel to your requirements, the faster they will learn. The process of finding the right person to put on your team isn't an easy one. Realistically, you will go through many different candidates before you find the right one for you. This is okay. In fact, it's pretty much how all the rest of life works. So why would we expect real estate investing to be any different?

Using Funnels to Find Talent

Funnels are everywhere. With just about everything you've had success at, it happened through some sort of a funnel. In summary, a funnel is simply the process of taking a large number of opportunities and weeding them down until you have a much smaller number of only the best opportunities for you. Successful funnels are those that filter out the wrong people, deals, leads, or things. The best funnels are those that do this with efficiency, effectiveness, and expeditiousness, and that can be leveraged to someone or something else.

Whenever you hear the phrase, "It's a numbers game," the person is usually referring to some sort of funnel. Whenever you hear the word "filter," same thing. If you think about it, real estate investing is really just the use of one big funnel. We start with a large number of leads (possible deals), and we filter out all those that don't meet our criteria. Once we are left with a much smaller number, we apply an even smaller filter to find out which of these would work for our needs at a much more detailed level. Once we know that, we write offers on these properties and see which ones are accepted. Of those, we start a whole new process of due diligence to see which ones we want to buy.

If we are successful, at the end of this process we buy a property. This "process" was really nothing more than a funnel with specific principles and criteria involved. The method of creating this funnel to lead to success in real estate investing was the use of a system. This specific system acts as a funnel to filter out bad leads and leave you with only those you want to buy. When we look for someone's help in the process (an agent, a wholesaler, etc.) what we are really doing is trying to jump ahead to a point in the funnel that someone else has gotten to on their own.

Wholesalers use funnels, too. They send out mailers, and a small percentage of people reply. They call back those who reply, and a small percentage of them are serious sellers. They negotiate with these serious sellers, and a small percentage of them are successfully put into contract. *These* are the properties they bring to us investors to buy. As you can see, a wholesaler is just someone who has conducted the first part of a funnel, and they collect an assignment fee to compensate them for the part of the work they've already done for you!

You can choose to build your own funnel and see it from start to finish. You can choose to utilize a wholesaler's funnel and pay them for it. You can choose to use a real estate agent's filtering skills and pay them for their work. Or, you can choose to utilize all three methods and have more opportunities. It's all up to you. What's important is you recognize the way funnels work and you see them in action in ways that lead to your success. A wholesaler is someone who starts at the top of a funnel and completes most of the heavy lifting, then exits from the funnel before the "due diligence" phase. An investor who buys from a wholesaler is just someone who skips the first part of the funnel and jumps in at the very end.

Looking for the right person to help you works the same way! You start off with the entire population, then you whittle that down to only include those with experience accomplishing whatever your objective is. From there, you eliminate anyone who doesn't work in the area in which you need the work done. From there, you start to look for referrals or those highly recommended in that area and eliminate anyone who's not. From there, you get bids from your top contenders and compare prices. From there, you interview those with the most competitive bids to get an idea of what to expect.

This process is roughly the same whether the person you're looking to partner with is a contractor, agent, wholesaler, lender, lawyer, whatever. What you are really doing is creating a system of finding the one rockstar out of the entire group of garage-band wannabes. This process takes time, but it is worth it when you find one! Don't believe me? Consider how much time and resources professional sports teams spend looking for the next big talent.

Professional sports teams have entire divisions devoted entirely to the pursuit of looking for top talent. These individuals start with everyone in the sport (let's say baseball for this instance) and start applying filters to eliminate all the players that don't fit the criteria. In this case, the first filter might be only traveling to see players with a batting average over .300. From there, they may eliminate anyone who has a lower-than-average defensive rating at their position. From there, they may eliminate anyone who is slow on the basepath. From there, they eliminate those with character issues. Eventually, they have a pool of only top-tier talent with which to dig very deep into and find the one they think would be the best fit for their team to draft.

With this in mind, you have to prepare yourself for a journey of looking for talent that will not be an easy one. This is why persistence is so important. You are going to spend a considerable amount of time finding agents, finding lenders, finding rehabbers, etc. This pursuit will not produce money for a significant period of time. You may struggle with thoughts that you are wasting your time, that you'll never get there, that "all the good ones are taken." Keep going. All this effort is an investment that is well worth it. Finding those who can take your business to the next level is a big goal and that means it's going to require a big effort.

One of my all-time favorite stories that illustrates this is that of Stephen Curry. Stephen (or "Steph") was drafted by the Golden State Warriors with the seventh pick of the 2009 draft.[16] Curry's career started off fine, but quickly took a downward dive when his ankles began giving him major problems. Just before his rookie contract expired (when successful players can expect to receive big contracts) Curry went through a series of several ankle and foot sprains that resulted in surgeries. Curry quickly developed a reputation as an injury-prone player that could not be depended on.

This was especially damaging to Curry because coming into the league, the No. 1 criticism against him was he was too small to play in the NBA. His inability to finish a season healthy did not help this stigma. Due to this fact, the Golden State Warriors were able to pay him a contract of "only" $44 million over four years. This was widely considered to be below Curry's market value, but still considered risky for the Warriors because of Curry's injury woes.[17] The Warriors were willing to take the risk because they believed in Curry's talent as an emerging star.

In 2014, Curry went on to make the Warriors look really smart for investing in him, leading the Warriors to their first championship in 40 years. Curry was voted the league MVP and was in the middle of shattering every record for three-point shooting in the books. In addition, the Warriors became so dominant that Steph was able to sit out 17 fourth quarters, not because he was injured, but because his team was winning by so much they didn't need him in the game.

And why were the Warriors so good that Curry didn't need to play? Well, for several reasons. For one, Steph's contract was for so little money for a player of his caliber that the Warriors had more money to spend on other good players. For another, Steph made the other players on his team better, bringing out more of their skills and allowing them to shine in their clearly defined roles. For a third, Steph led the team in becoming so unselfish that role players were valued more than in other franchises—and they played like it!

The following year, Curry went on to become the first ever unanimous MVP of the league (meaning not a single vote went to any other player) as he continued to dominate in his profession. If that wasn't enough, the

---

[16] Cork Gaines, "Where Are They Now? The Players Drafted Before Stephen Curry in the 2009 NBA Draft," Business Insider (June 8, 2016). https://www.businessinsider.com/the-stephen-curry-nba-draft-2016-6#6-jonny-flynn-minnesota-timberwolves-6

[17] Marcus Thompson II, "Five Years Ago, Steph Curry Signed the Contract that Set Up a Dynasty," The Athletic (October 31, 2017). https://theathletic.com/142451/2017/10/31/thompson-five-years-ago-steph-curry-signed-the-contract-that-set-up-a-dynasty/

Warriors had developed a reputation that was so positive and desirable, *other great players in the league wanted to come play there, including a previous league MVP Kevin Durant.* Curry's brilliance had helped create an environment so desirable the Warriors were able to bring one of the best players in the entire league onto a team that was already considered one of the best ever assembled.

Now, why am I talking so much about Stephen Curry? Because he's a wonderful example of the kind of impact that one rockstar can have on your business or organization. Why am I talking about the Golden State Warriors? Because they did everything right in pursuing and developing talent, and as a result they have reaped the benefit of those moves for years. What does this have to do with us? *By replicating what the Warriors did, we can have a similar result in our own business.*

Curry is an example of what can go right when you find talent. He made everyone around him better and did it all at a discount for his team! Wouldn't you like that in your own business? What if you found that one rockstar agent who also brought a rockstar property manager (cough, Kevin Durant, cough) into the fold and you were able to benefit from them, too? What if your agent had advice or support to give your rehabbers so they could get their job done faster and cheaper? What if your rockstar property manager could introduce you to a local portfolio lender to finance your next 100 deals?

I want to highlight the dramatic results that just one rockstar on your team can do for you, so you too can start the process of looking for your next big addition of talent to your business. I also want to point out that once you find a rockstar, you will now find the next one that much faster, because you've already gone through the process of that funnel and will have learned better ways to make the system run smoother the next time around.

Finding deals is great, but isn't it even better to find someone who can bring you deals instead? What if that person could also bring you more than just deals, but referrals to all the other pieces you'll need as well? *Rockstars know rockstars.* Curry didn't just make the Warriors better, he also helped them land Kevin Durant. Finding top talent will attract more talent to you, and that's how you win championships.

Using Your Failures to Improve Your Business

In my opinion, the overwhelming reason most people don't start something new is because they are afraid of failure. As I addressed in the beginning of this chapter, the fear of failure will prevent us from getting started, which also prevents us from learning. When we aren't learning, we aren't improving, and if we aren't improving, we aren't getting any closer to success. I want to make an argument that our failures, when interpreted correctly, allow us to improve our systems and therefore allow us to improve our odds of success in the future. Let me share some examples with you.

My First OOS (Out-of-state) Deal

The story:
The first time I ever bought a property in another state was in Arizona around 2013. I had seen a Realtor on Fox Business News talking about how Arizona still had lots of affordable property as their market had not yet begun the recovery process from the onslaught of foreclosures they had experienced. I, being a California resident, was attracted to this because California had already begun to recover and was recovering so fast I could no longer buy cash-flowing property.

I reached out again and again to get ahold of this Realtor (they were one of the biggest teams in the state) and finally did. After speaking with them, I agreed to fly out, meet, and look at properties together. Two trips to Arizona resulted in zero deals under contract, but I did get a little more comfortable with the thought of buying in a new area.

I ended up buying two deals at the same time that I had never seen. Both deals closed and I was introduced to a property manager to help get them ready to rent. A month into it and my agent stopped returning my calls. It wasn't until another month after that I learned why. My agent had been convicted of money laundering and other criminal charges and was no longer able to practice or speak about real estate.

Not exactly ideal for me. This left me without my security blanket or guide during my first ever foray into out-of-state investing. I was scared, angry, hurt, deceived, and discouraged. I briefly considered selling and taking a loss, then decided it was better to just figure it out. I reached out to the property manager, told him what I needed, and started the process of finding all the pieces to build an OOS investing system.

What I learned that made me better:

During this time, I had to communicate with the OOS PM to let him know what I'd need. Painters, floor installers, handymen, rent estimates, etc. The contractor he found to help me charged way too much, but I learned it was better not to rely on a PM just because he's your PM. For the second house, I went out and found my own contractors and bids from them myself. I then started the process of finding a new PM who would have better contacts and referrals for me. This improved my business and also my system.

I also learned about Rentometer.com and how to use it to find rent estimates myself. When I found my PM was coming in about $100 too low, I asked him to raise it and still got what I wanted in rent. This taught me how to find new resources to verify what I was being told and gave me a powerful tool to help with other investments as well. This became an improvement in my system going forward.

Additionally, I learned never to be too dependent on any one person. When my agent was forbidden from practicing real estate, I felt alone. I decided that wouldn't happen again. From that point forward, I made sure I had a minimum of two contacts for any market I would invest in for each segment of my Core Four: two lenders, two PMs, two deal finders, and two rehabbers. That way I would always have a reserve parachute in case of a worst-case scenario and a second opinion to put me at ease. This became a part of my system going forward.

Finally, I learned that even when it seemed everything went wrong, I still made money. As crazy as that was, it did a ton for my confidence. Had everything gone perfect, I would have expected a perfect experience every time. Thankfully, that didn't happen. My confidence was being built and I began the process of learning how to find what I needed rather than being dependent on someone else. This led to me creating my own system and eventually writing a book to help others do the same, *Long-Distance Real Estate Investing: How to Buy, Rehab, and Manage Out-of-State Rental Properties.*

Not Using a PM on My First Deal

The story:

As I mentioned earlier in the book, on the first rental I ever bought I didn't use a PM. Big mistake! I did about everything wrong I possibly could and lost over $7,000 when it was all said and done. I also added unnecessary stress to my life and wasted massive amounts of time trying to do everything on my own when I could have leveraged a professional's opinion and experience instead.

What I learned that made me better:
The biggest thing I learned was that once I put someone in place who already knew how to do what I needed, everything went so much smoother! I didn't even have a good PM, but just a mediocre one made a huge difference in my business and my peace of mind. By relying on a professional instead of trying to do everything myself, I learned an important lesson: It's one thing to think you've got to do everything yourself, but it's better to feel the support of a team. Learning from those more experienced than me helped me to build my systems better.

I also learned it is very easy to step over dollars to pick up pennies in this business. By trying to avoid $100 a month, I cost myself over $7,000. Sometimes being cheap is the most expensive thing we can do.

The Failure of Trying to Replace My Own Door Locks

The story:
On the second house I ever bought as a rental, I had my first tenants move out and needed to replace the door locks. I am not very handy, and I know this, but still thought I could save myself some money. Wrong. Four trips to the hardware store and half a day later, and I finally installed three new door locks, saving myself the $150 the handyman had said he would do it for.

During this time, I could have worked an overtime shift at my police job and made substantially more money than I saved installing the locks myself. I also could have found a potentially new asset in a handyman that could help whenever the next repair needed to be made.

What I learned that made me better:
If we are considering the 80/20 rule, changing door locks was not in my 20 percent of productivity. I was horrible at it, it became extremely frustrating for me, and I did not have the tools I needed to do the task. Actually, I didn't even know what I needed, and had no business taking

on that job myself. I didn't even consider the opportunity cost (not going to work and making more money).

I learned to stick to my 20 percent and let the handyman stick to his. There are tons of people out there who don't have the drive, skills, or desire to be real estate investors, but they still need work. These people feed their families by providing the skills people like me lack. I should let them do just that. The best use of my time was spent going to work and doing an overtime shift, not being there trying to change door locks and embarrassing myself at Home Depot.

Now, I have a list of vendors for every year that my assistant calls when something breaks or needs to be fixed. I helped her compile the list, and I let her handle the scheduling. I do *nothing* of my own when these things arise, and you can't get much more streamlined than nothing. This experience frustrated me for the day but ultimately improved my system, and for that I am grateful.

Key Points
- The four E's of success are: Efficiency, Effectiveness, Expeditiousness, and Employability.
- The Pareto Principle states that 20 percent of your effort leads to 80 percent of your results.
- Repetition creates mastery.
- Persistence is the key to success.
- Use funnels to locate talent.
- Talent draws more talent to it.
- Stick to your 20 percent!

CHAPTER ELEVEN
Scaling Your System for Increased Success

"There seems to be some perverse human characteristic that likes to make easy things difficult."

—WARREN BUFFETT

As I discussed in the previous chapter, success is based on systems. Systems give us the ability to take something, master it, then repeat that over and over. The more consistent we can get our result, the more predictable we can expect our success to be. Systems are a big part of what helps you reach predictable results. If you don't have predictable results, you can't plan how to scale your business. And scaling your business is the goal, right?

In the beginning of this book, we talked about the vast difference in the results between the traditional method of investing and the BRRRR method. We know the differences are significant, but they only become that way over a significant period of time with a significant amount of action being taken. If you don't have systems, and you don't scale those systems, it will be difficult to reach that level without sacrificing a huge piece of your quality of life.

The goal of every investor is to build wealth and increase passive income. Income that requires constant attention and work isn't passive. If you have to be the one getting involved, making the decisions, and holding it all together, your business isn't going to be that passive—and neither is your income. So what's the key to building systems and running an efficient business? It's taking the time to set things up correctly in the beginning!

Real Estate Is a Get-Rich-Slow Game

By its nature, real estate is a get-rich-slow game. The factors that lead to the most wealth-building in real estate take time. Principle pay down, increased cash flow through rent increases, appreciation—these are all powerful wealth-building tools, but they don't work quickly. Those who attempt to build wealth through real estate too quickly often force strategies that don't work or involve large amounts of risk. It rarely works out well.

Buying real estate is like planting an apple tree. If you plant your seed in the right area, take care of and protect it, and choose the right kind of soil, your apple tree will grow. When the tree matures, it will produce fruit. This fruit can be harvested and eaten (spending your cash flow) or replanted to grow more apple trees (re-invested into new properties). If you play your cards right, you will plant apple trees that turn into orchards. These orchards will continue to produce fruit long into your old age, and can be passed down to future generations as well.

Other forms of investment can work much faster. Bitcoin, stock trading, penny stocks, gold mining, etc. Much like the time spent waiting for a great redwood tree to grow, we can become impatient waiting for big results to be generated from our investments. My advice during the time you are waiting to receive the fruits of your labor is to make use of your opportunity to sharpen your skills. If you know you're going to be waiting for your orchard to grow, you can sit around on your hands, or you can get started learning, improving, and eventually scaling.

Systems Provide Opportunities

When your business is running more efficiently, you can take advantage of opportunities you otherwise couldn't. For example, say the opportunity to flip a home comes your way. You analyze the deal in five minutes and realize you will most likely make a $15,000 profit. This is a low-risk opportunity with the biggest expense being your time.

Do you do it? Well, that depends. If you don't have any systems in place and you have to do everything yourself, maybe not. Planning the rehab, scheduling the contractors, following up on the progress, buying the insurance, doing the market research, choosing the materials, etc. is a lot of work for one person. This process could take well over 100 hours if only one person was doing all of it. Is $15,000, minus capital gains taxes, really enough money to be worth your time? It could be, but maybe not.

Now, what if you had systems in place? People who knew exactly what you wanted and how to accomplish it. People that were anxiously waiting for the next deal to be sent to them so they could jump in and get it done. What if the whole process required a total of five hours of your time. Would that change things?

It should. Systems create efficiency. Efficiency saves time and reduces risk. With an efficient enough system, these smaller deals can work when they wouldn't without a system. The better your system, the more opportunities you can make work for you—and the faster you can build your wealth. Without efficient systems, you can only take on deals that will result in huge profits, and those don't come around too often.

Whenever we see a deal with huge profits and light work associated with it, we call it a "home run." These are the deals every investor brags about to their friends. Who doesn't love a home run? It's the best outcome you can expect. Home runs are not bad because they are freaking awesome. But the problem is they don't come around very often.

Every baseball player understands if you *try* to hit a home run, you usually won't. The act of trying to hit every ball out of the park usually leads to strikeouts and easy putouts. Why? Because not every pitch is conducive to hitting a home run. Trying to force it never works. Real estate is the same way. Trying to take a mediocre deal and turn it into a home run usually results in regret, mistakes, and lost money.

If you want to hit a home run, you have to wait for the right pitch. This usually means a pitcher screwed up and left something hanging for you to crush. You can't *force* a home run, you can only be *ready to take advantage of the bad pitch*. Wise batters understand home run pitches don't just come. You wait patiently, put yourself in the position to capitalize, and then jump on the opportunity.

So what about all the rest of the pitches that *aren't* home run pitches? Do we just stand there with the bat on our shoulder waiting for the perfect pitch or deal? Maybe we have to if the only deals we can make are home runs. But what if you have the right systems in place so you can get hits out of non-home run pitches? What if you learn how to take those deals and make singles, doubles, or triples out of them? Would that make you a more productive player?

The best baseball players know how to make the most of the pitch they are thrown. Every once in a while a home run pitch comes along and they want to be prepared to hit it out of the park. For the rest of the pitches that come their way, they may use different swings for a different approach. For players with a larger skill set that includes a variety of swings, they can hit more and different kinds of pitches, and ultimately end up with better batting averages that make them more successful.

The moral of the story is you want to be able to hit more pitches than other investors. You want to be able to take advantage of deals others can't. We never want to swing at bad pitches because not every deal is a good deal. And we should definitely be picky about what we buy. If we have the right systems in place, we can buy properties other investors can't because we are more efficient, effective, and purposeful. Systems give us the ability to do deals we couldn't otherwise do.

I love this strategy because it allows me to invest at any time, not just when the market cycle is at an ideal point. Real estate, just like everything else in the economy, operates in cycles. Sometimes the market is flooded with cheap housing and sometimes good deals are almost impossible to find. If you don't have systems in place, you're more likely to find yourself in a situation where you are "waiting" for the "market to turn around." People in this frame of mind are always looking for an excuse not to buy. They are a batter who is constantly saying, "I'm just waiting for the right pitch to swing at."

Imagine a world in which you had systems already built. You have a rehab crew who knows how you like your projects to turn out. You have a number of agents and wholesalers actively looking for deals for you. When they find a deal, they call your rehab manager and run it by them first. If that passes, they send it to your property manager, who knows exactly what kind of properties you want to own and what numbers you're looking for. Before the property even makes its way to you, all three members of your team have looked at it and determined it matches your criteria.

With a system like this, very little of your own time is needed to evaluate deals. This is very time efficient. If your rehab crew knows how you like your properties renovated and you've already worked out a lot of the kinks in your renovations, they can do the projects for less money. This is very cash efficient. By creating efficient systems, you increase your ability to buy more properties.

How Systems Help You Master the Five Elements of BRRRR

As I've mentioned so far, mastering the five elements of BRRRR is what will make you a black belt investor. Systems will help you do that. So what systems will you need to help you scale up your business? My recommendation is to start with people. Getting others to help you is what will ultimately allow you to ramp up your business and achieve a level of mastery that will build wealth.

The key to implementing other people into your systems is to effectively communicate your expectations to them. The key to that is to start with checklists. Checklists help you convey exactly what you want and what results you expect. They eliminate the guesswork of someone else trying to understand what you want, and they cut down on mistakes or things falling between the cracks. Most importantly, they force *you* to be clear on what exactly it is that you're doing and just what you're hoping to accomplish.

There is a popular maxim that states, "You learn 90 percent of what you teach." Of all the ways you can learn (seeing, hearing, doing, etc.), teaching by far is the most effective way to learn something yourself. When you create systems for someone else to follow, it is a form of teaching them. This is how you will learn what you're really doing, and it is guaranteed to help you see things that made you successful.

The use of a checklist like this eliminates the possibility I could forget something. While running a project, it's common to get scatterbrained because I'm often thinking about so many things at once. It's easy to let details slip. By putting things onto a checklist, I remove the possibility for human error in the sense of forgetfulness. It also makes it easier for whoever I'm communicating with. By having a checklist they can follow, they don't have to worry about forgetting something themselves.

I like to create a spreadsheet in Google Drive for each of the components of the BRRRR process I want to leverage to someone else.

1. One with the criteria for the agents bringing me deals.
2. One with the criteria for what due diligence is to be done after a deal is put into contract.

3. One with the criteria for how to run the rehab once a property closes.
4. One with the criteria for how someone can make sure the rehab work was completed.
5. One with my lending criteria to share with banks and lenders when reaching out to a new one.
6. One with a list of all the people I do business with and in what areas they serve.

In a perfect world, anytime you do something more than once, you need a system created for someone to follow. If you don't have systems in place, leverage becomes very difficult and you'll find yourself doing it all on your own. By creating different files with the information new people will be asking for, all I have to do is allow them access to see the files with that information, or copy, paste, and send it to them. This allows me to grow the network of people helping me much faster and with very little time once I'm up and moving.

Building Your Network Through Repeat Business

Remember, the purpose of building systems isn't to build systems. It's to allow more people into your world to help you accomplish your objectives. As one person, you can only do so much. As a system of criteria, checklists, and support, you can accomplish much, much more. Think of every person you bring into your world as an extension of you. The more "yous" you have doing work for you, the more you can get done.

These checklists and criteria you create are the "programs" that will run the new "yous." They will need to understand what you're looking for, how they can find it, and how you want it to be presented to them. You don't want to have to explain this over and over again to different people every time you find a new one. This will cause burnout and you'll shrink back from expanding.

I understand this concept can be difficult to accept. For most of us who have had a measure of success in the world, we did it on our own. It can be scary and anxiety-inducing to think about sharing responsibility with others when it comes to your own financial well-being. The old phrase "if you want something done right, do it yourself" comes into play. Many of us have been burned by someone who didn't do a great job or didn't care when their actions caused us loss or pain. Trusting others can sometimes be the most difficult part of scaling a business.

The trick is to learn to create systems to help you determine who to trust. The method of blindly choosing someone from Craigslist and hoping things go well isn't a recipe for success. Once you get good at finding talented people to help you run your business, you may just find you fall in love with the process of leveraging others to help you find your goals. Let me share a story with you to highlight just how powerful the concept of leverage can be.

The Story of a Fisherman's Journey

Jerry was a family man who lived by a large lake in the 1800s. Like many during that time, Jerry married early and started a family young. Now, with five children and a wife, Jerry felt constant pressure to provide food, clothing, and shelter for his family. Every day when he woke up, Jerry felt a firm resolve to provide for them. They were everything to Jerry.

As a young boy, Jerry would watch the men of his village wake up early and launch their boats into the lake to go fishing. Late in the evening, they would return, and Jerry would see who was successful and who failed. As he grew up, Jerry always wondered why all men didn't catch an equal number of fish. They all bought their bait from the same stores, purchased their gear at the same places, and fished on the same lake. It was always a mystery to Jerry why some did well while others did not.

As he grew up, Jerry tried his hand at many things. Growing up poor without extra money to spend on lavish things, Jerry felt a strong desire to be a wealthy man. While he was able to find moderate to high success at everything he did, Jerry always felt like it was the fishermen who had the best jobs.

There was something exciting about catching fish. Unlike other professions, fishermen got to go hunt for their prize. It was up to them to use their wits, experience, and skills to find the fish that would earn them money. Jerry longed for that kind of control in his own life: He fantasized about a life where he would pull the boat in, unload his haul of fish, and feel the gold coins weighing heavily in his pockets as he sold his catch to the highest bidder.

Eventually, Jerry grew up and tried his hand at fishing. Now, Jerry was no fool. He knew someday he'd be trying his hand at fishing and therefore took the appropriate steps to prepare. Jerry spent many nights and weekends learning from the best fishermen in the village. He would take them to bars and buy their beers, getting them loose-tongued enough to share their secrets. Compared with most newcomers, Jerry had a big advantage.

Once he got started, Jerry's research proved to be fruitful and he learned things faster than his fellow fishermen. In his first year, Jerry became one of the most successful fishermen on the lake. By his second year, Jerry was known as a top young talent and respected by others. His hard work had paid off.

Jerry loved his newfound success. He loved the feeling of pulling into the dock and seeing the looks on people's faces as he showcased his catch. When Jerry would stop by restaurants, the staff all knew his name and sometimes other patrons paid for his meals. In a way, Jerry had become a village celebrity. What meant the most to Jerry was the fact he did it in the profession he had always respected the most—fishing.

For several years life went on like this. Jerry would wake up early in the morning so he could get a head start on fishing. Even through the heat of the day, Jerry kept constant focus, ready to reel in fish at a moment's notice. Jerry's success was predicated on how efficiently he could perform, and he took that responsibility seriously.

Late in the evening, Jerry would head back in, after the other fishermen had long since returned. He would bring his catch to the merchants who purchased fish, sell them, and take the remaining fish back to his family. When he got home, his wife would cook dinner based on his catch, and preserve the rest of the fish for future meals. Jerry would tuck his children into bed, ignore their wrinkled noses at the stink of his hands, and kiss them good night. Then, Jerry would pull out his fishing supplies for the next day and start his preparation. Jerry would repair any holes in his nets, stock up his bait, and review his maps for the next day.

While Jerry would prepare for the next day, his wife would talk to him about the children's days. She would fill him in on who got in trouble at school, who had been in a fight, and who was speaking disrespectfully. As the years drudged on, Jerry noticed more and more of the stories revealed problematic behavior from his children. Very rarely was he told good things they had accomplished. More and more he found his wife complaining and becoming frustrated with the way things were turning out. It bothered Jerry, but he was so preoccupied with staying one of the village's top fishermen that he ignored it. The weight of the importance of keeping his family fed and well-kept was too important to be disrupted by the problems his lack of presence was causing.

Month after month, Jerry would continue this process. In time, the pressure of remaining a top fisherman took a toll on Jerry. If he saw another fisherman receiving credit, or heard someone else's name being mentioned in connection with great fishing, he felt pangs of jealousy. Jerry became obsessed with production. He needed to be known as the best, and the ambition he had felt as a young man grew into something much darker. At a certain point, Jerry had provided for his family. Once he reached that, it became more. Jerry needed to be known as the best, and was willing to pay any price to do it.

One day on the lake, Jerry cut his hand while trying to help a fellow fisherman whose boat was leaking water. While rowing to the cove he thought harbored the biggest fish, Jerry was flagged down by a fisherman who was frantically trying to shovel water out of his boat with a bucket. Jerry briefly considered ignoring the man, but eventually gave in and helped. While the boat's owner bailed water, Jerry worked on putting the adhesive in the hole that would stop the flooding. While trying to apply the adhesive, Jerry cut his hand on the jagged edge of the hole.

The cut was so severe he was forced to stay home for many weeks to let the cut heal. Jerry noticed many of the other fishing boats had several fishermen per boat. The fishermen would work as a team and split up the catch at the end of the day. Jerry never liked that approach, because he was afraid others would steal his methods and the ways he found where fish were biting. Jerry always fished alone, so not being able to produce fish meant he made zero income during that time. Jerry couldn't help but feel that helping that other fisherman was a huge mistake.

While staying home and letting his hand heal, Jerry noticed his children's attitudes had become much worse than he assumed. When he would give them commands or direction, they appeared resentful, as they were unused to him doing much other than giving them money and putting them to bed. When he tried to give them advice, they were more likely to listen to strangers in the village than they were to listen to their father. This bothered Jerry as he felt like others were raising his children more than he was.

Additionally, Jerry realized how his relationship with his wife had changed. Unlike the early years when she looked up to him as her hero who could do anything, Jerry's wife had come to see him as a business partner who provided the business capital, while she ran business operations. The closeness they once had vanished, and Jerry missed that. During his time of healing, he had started to realize there was more to being successful than just being a top producer.

One morning Jerry woke before his family and went for a walk. As he walked through the village, he saw things from a new perspective. By mid-morning, Jerry had usually been on the lake for hours, well into catching fish. As he walked through the village streets during the late morning hours, Jerry noticed the merchants with shops set up along the streets. As he walked the streets, Jerry would stop and listen to their conversations, finding himself intrigued by their personalities and lifestyles.

The first merchant Jerry observed was Tim. Tim was slightly overweight and very friendly. Jerry always liked selling to Tim because of his pleasant demeanor, but hated having to wait in line to do so. The line to Tim's shop was always out the door. People would go out of their way to trade with Tim, mostly because he was such a fun and engaging person. Tim did not have the best products, nor did he have the most variety, yet day after day he conducted the most business in the village.

As Jerry observed Tim, he noticed certain things Tim did well. For instance, Tim always remembered people's names and called them by it. Jerry noticed how people's faces would light up with smiles as Tim called them by their first name and asked them how they were. Additionally, Jerry noticed the way Tim would engage with people. Tim didn't just ask surface-level questions. He asked about people's children, their marriages, and their vacation plans. At first, this seemed foolish to Jerry, as it was not likely to lead to Tim making any more sales. In time, Jerry realized Tim sold the most in the village precisely for this reason. People *liked* being around Tim and would go out of their way to do business with him.

As much as Tim's personality was a source of intrigue for Jerry, it wasn't just that. Jerry also noticed how Tim's shop was busy all day long, but Tim wasn't doing all the work. Tim had employees who would arrange the merchandise, bargain with the customers, and set the prices. Sometimes the customers would get in price disputes with the employees (as was customary), but Jerry noted how these disputes were never with Tim himself. Tim remained uninvolved with the haggling and hot temper side of the business and maintained his relationship with his customers as a friendly, caring personality.

All these things got Jerry thinking: Why was Jerry trying to do so much himself? Jerry would wake up early, work all day, and then collapse at home in an exhausted heap, only to wake up the next day and do it all over again.

Eventually, Jerry couldn't take it anymore. His hand wasn't healing as fast as he'd like and his bitterness toward the fisherman he'd tried to help that day was growing. Things were going so good, finally! Why did his good fortune have to be ruined? Jerry had begun to wallow in self-pity, and somewhere deep inside realized he needed to find a way to turn things around before it was too late.

Jerry's desperation led him to ask Tim out to lunch. Tim, being the happy and pleasant man that he was, was happy to oblige. During lunch, Jerry opened up about the worries of his heart. Tim listened intently as Jerry shared where he had come from, what he had accomplished, and how he was feeling. As Jerry began talking, it all poured out. Jerry himself realized how unhappy he was with life and how painful the whole thing had become.

Jerry asked Tim how he was able to entrust the workings of his business to his employees. How did he know they weren't stealing? How did he know they wouldn't learn all his methods and leave to build their own shop? There were so many things that could go wrong, Jerry just didn't see how this was all possible.

Tim said he remembered how he too had once thought this way, but chose to see the good in people. Tim explained to Jerry that he wasn't the only one running a business this way, that in fact the streets were *completely lined with various merchants who all followed the same model while selling different merchandise*. While Jerry was amazed that Tim could make this process work, Tim was honest with Jerry about the fact that he wasn't even the most successful merchant on the street.

In fact, Tim worked fewer hours, and did less to make his business grow than other merchants, and was *still* very profitable. For Tim, being the top business wasn't most important. He just wanted to enjoy life. Jerry was inspired and couldn't help but ask Tim just how much he made. Tim's answer was the final piece of the puzzle Jerry had been waiting for: Tim made an annual profit that was roughly four times what Jerry made on his best year, all while working about one third as hard and in half the time.

Jerry's head spun as he asked Tim to explain how on earth he kept things running smoothly and prevented his employees from stealing from him. Tim explained he used a system that relied on multiple levels of checks and balances. As one employee was responsible for collecting the money from customers, another would enter that purchase into the ledger, and a third would ensure the business's stock was matching up. In order for someone to steal from his business, all three employees would have to be in cahoots with one another. To further increase his security, Tim put a fourth employee in charge of making sure all of the other three were doing their jobs and producing the results that were expected. Tim made sure he never had to be the bad guy as there was always someone else in place to play that role if need be.

Jerry realized he had been so focused on producing and the notoriety that brought that he had missed out on better opportunities. His lack of trust in other people and his desire to be the best had cost him a lot. Jerry didn't know exactly what he was going to do, but he knew something needed to change.

When Jerry's hand healed, he returned to fishing, but found it wasn't the same. Jerry wasn't able to maintain the same amount of focus he had before. As he went through the motions, Jerry still caught enough fish to support his family, but he noticed his heart wasn't in it anymore. Jerry had begun the initial stages of breaking his cycle of production. Jerry knew the ins and outs of fishing, and he knew he was great at it, but his perspective had changed. Being the best wasn't as important anymore.

Weeks later, Jerry had his epiphany. After returning home from a successful day at the lake, Jerry saw a sign advertising that one of the merchants was paying nearly double per pound of fish. Not being a fool, Jerry approached his merchant and asked why his price was so high.

The merchant blushed and apologized as he explained the sign was old and reflected afternoon prices. In the haste of the day, the merchant had forgotten to change it out with the evening prices. Jerry was confused and asked what the merchant meant—why were there two different prices? The merchant, equally as confused, explained to Jerry that obviously villagers were willing to pay more for fish in the afternoon before dinner was to be cooked than they would in the late evening. Those buying fish at the end of the day were clearly buying it to preserve it and eat later. The freshness of the day's catch was not important to those who planned to salt and preserve the fish.

Again, Jerry felt foolish and naïve. All this time he had been selling his fish for almost half of what he could have fetched in the afternoon because he was so obsessed with catching the most fish! Jerry had no idea he was selling at a discount, and this new realization only served to confirm he was too wrapped up doing things on his own to see all the opportunities that were available to him.

Jerry explained what he had learned to Tim and Tim explained to Jerry one of the reasons he took an afternoon nap was to be awake when the evening catch came in, as he could pay nearly half as much for the same amount of fish! Tim explained to Jerry he could go learn to fish as well (if he'd wanted), but instead chose to pay half price for fish from fishermen who had no one else to sell to. Most of the village shops closed by late afternoon, and the few who were still open could find "distressed" fishermen with no one else to sell to.

Finally, the light bulb went off in Jerry's head. He had two choices: He could continue on in his pursuit of becoming the top fisherman in the village, or he could target other fishermen he knew and buy their fish from them at a discount. Jerry realized his respect within the fishing community was good for more than just his ego—it could be converted into the ability to buy fish from them first, before anyone else had the chance.

Jerry ran home and told his wife of his plan. Rather than going fishing every day of the week, he would take one day off to spend with his family, repairing the relationships that had soured. Of the remaining six days, he would fish for three of them himself to catch enough food for his family, and the other three he would spend building relationships with other fishermen. In the beginning, Jerry would teach them how to improve their techniques. Then, once they began to catch more fish, he would buy the remains of their catch they were unable to sell—at discounted prices. Jerry would then take these fish and have them preserved, where he would sell them to other shops himself.

Jerry's plan worked brilliantly. In a few short months, Jerry wasn't fishing for himself at all, and was working six days a week forming relationships with other fishermen and buying the remains of their catch they were unable to sell. Eventually, Jerry rented out his own fishing boat to another fisherman and split the proceeds with him 50/50. As Jerry taught this talented young man more about fishing, he found his 50 percent growing monthly.

One day, Tim approached Jerry to congratulate him on his new business success. Jerry thanked Tim for his mentorship, and explained his biggest problem was the amount of time it took him to preserve the fish himself and sell them to the merchants. Tim provided a solution. Tim and Jerry would partner up and Tim's employees would salt and preserve the fish. Then, they would sell the catch out of Tim's store, splitting the profits between them. Jerry agreed, and soon saw the time he was working reduced dramatically, while the income he was bringing in steadily increased.

Jerry began to spend more time with his family, rest more, and grew as a businessman. His mind became sharp as he formed new business ventures and relationships, and his reputation as a wise businessman grew instead of his former reputation as the top fisherman. He became a mentor to young fisherman, teaching them to improve their catch, and was often the first person they would sell their excess fish to after a successful day's work. Jerry's wealth grew and grew, and not just financially. His family, health, and overall well-being all grew together, and Jerry finally found the life he had always been looking for.

Using Systems to Find Deals Through Others

While Jerry's story is clearly fictional, the principles are absolutely true. It is one thing to find great deals. Like a great fisherman, you can be taught to do so. It is another thing, however, to find great fishermen and buy their deals *from* them. Letting others do the work of finding the deal and swooping in to buy it at a discount is my preferred method of investing. I don't want to just be the best fisherman, I want to find those with too many fish to eat themselves, and buy those fish at a discount.

How does this work in practical application? The answer is wholesalers. Wholesalers are like the fishermen in the story. It is their job to search the lake to find the fish, catch them, and then look for somebody to buy them. Some of these wholesalers will keep some of their deals to flip or hold themselves, but for many of them, they simply don't have the capital to keep everything. In these instances, I want to be the first person they turn to when they need to move the deal.

If you look at the job of a wholesaler, they are basically doing all the heavy lifting of finding and landing a deal, but don't have the capital to "capitalize" on that deal. These are the fishermen who are catching fish but don't have the means to sell them themselves, and instead must rely on a merchant to do that for them. Because of this, they have to sell at a discount to keep their end buyers happy. If you wanted to cut out any part of the "fishing" process, wouldn't it be the hard work of waking up early, launching the boat, and laboring away on the water? I sure would. For this reason, I look to people like wholesalers to bring me deals.

While this works well for wholesalers, it isn't exclusive to wholesalers. "Bird dogs" can work the same way. A bird dog is someone who goes out and pounds the pavement looking for deals. When they find them, they notify you about them or put them under contract for you. Some bird dogs do this for a monetary reward, others for more of a mentorship and knowledge-based reward. Regardless of how you set this up, a bird dog is a great resource to put to work on your behalf to find you deals, or get you fish!

This principle of changing your approach from catching fish to looking for those with too many fish can work anywhere. Think of the possibilities. I send them emails and make an effort to stay in touch with them because I want to stay top of mind. The following are samples of emails I send to those who I think are likely to come across deals or those who hunt for deals.

Lenders

Hello! My name is _____, and I am a real estate investor who buys properties in the _____ area. I'm writing to you because your name came up through several people I know as an elite level lender with experience working with real estate investors.

I wanted you to know I'm actively looking for property to buy, and willing to be pre-approved through your business for you to provide me lending on deals that pass my way. I'm hoping you can send me your loan application and we can set up a quick phone call to discuss my file, what I'm looking for, and how we can help each other's businesses.

Additionally, I know as a lender you often put in massive time on a file that for various reasons beyond your control does not close. I wanted to let you know I would be extremely grateful for you to let me know when anything resembling a great deal falls out of escrow or otherwise crosses your path. If at all possible, I'll buy it and let you represent me on the sale, refinance, or both.

I would love to learn more about how I can help you as well, what programs you offer, and what kind of clients I can refer you to. Please let me know when a good time for a follow-up phone call will be. I'll be happy to leave you a positive review on the platform of your choice after we do.

Looking forward to working together!

Thanks!

(Name)

Property Managers

Hello! My name is _____, and I am a real estate investor who buys properties in the _____ area. I'm writing to you because your name came up through several people I know as an elite level property manager with experience working with real estate investors.

I wanted you to know I'm actively looking for property to buy, and willing to have you manage the property once I do. I'm hoping you can send me your application and we can set up a quick phone call to discuss my file, what I'm looking for, and how we can help each other's businesses.

Additionally, I know as a property manager you often manage properties, stabilize them, then have the owners sell them. I wanted you to know if you find one of your clients selling a property you manage, I would be extremely grateful if you would let me know first. If I can buy it, I'll keep the property in your portfolio to manage, as well as any additional properties I buy. Furthermore, if any of your clients comes across a deal they cannot buy, I would be grateful for the opportunity to buy the property and have you manage it.

I would love to learn more about how I can help you as well, what programs you offer, and what kind of clients I can refer you to. Please let me know when a good time for a follow-up phone call will be. I'll be happy to leave you a positive review on the platform of your choice after we do.

Looking forward to working together!

Thanks!

(Name)

Wholesalers

Hello! My name is _____, and I am a real estate investor who buys properties in the _____ area. I'm writing to you because your name came up through several people I know as an elite level wholesaler with experience working with real estate investors.

I wanted you to know I'm actively looking for property to buy, and willing to be pre-approved through your business. I'm hoping we can set up a quick phone call to discuss my file, what I'm looking for, and how we can help each other's businesses.

Additionally, I know as a wholesaler you often put in a lot of time on a property that for various reasons beyond your control does not close. Whether it's your buyer backing out or your seller being unwilling to make concessions, I would love to know about deals you come across that need a strong buyer to close. I would be extremely grateful if you could let me know if anything resembling a great deal falls out of escrow or otherwise crosses your path. If at all possible, I'll buy it, refinance it, then buy from you again.

I understand the need you have for strong buyers to follow through on their word. I am an experienced investor who can get due diligence done very quickly, close quickly, and keep my word.

I would love to learn more about how I can help you as well, what programs you offer, and what kind of clients I can refer you to. Please let me know when a good time for a follow-up phone call will be. I'll be happy to leave you a positive review on the platform of your choice after we do.

Looking forward to working together!

Thanks!

(Name)

Agents

Hello! My name is _____, and I am a real estate investor who buys properties in the _____ area. I'm writing to you because your name came up through several people I know as a highly skilled and effective real estate agent with experience working with real estate investors.

I wanted you to know I'm actively looking for property to buy, and willing to be represented by you during this process. I'm hoping you can send me your criteria of what is needed to be able to work successfully together, and we can set up a quick phone call to discuss my goals, what types of properties I'm looking for, and how we can help each other's businesses.

Additionally, I know as an agent you often put in a lot of time on a file that for various reasons beyond your control does not close. I wanted to let you know I would be extremely grateful if you could let me know if anything resembling a great deal falls out of escrow or otherwise crosses your path. If at all possible, I'll buy it and let you represent me on the sale, then list it if it's a flip property.

I would love to learn more about how I can help you as well, what programs you offer, and what kind of clients I can refer you to. Please let me know when a good time for a follow-up phone call will be. I'll be happy to leave you a positive review on the platform of your choice after we do.

Looking forward to working together!

Thanks!

(Name)

Attorneys

Hello! My name is _____, and I am a real estate investor who buys properties in the _____ area. I'm writing to you because your name came up through several people I know as an elite-level attorney who often comes across situations with clients needing to find a solid, fast buyer for their property.

I'm hoping you can keep me in mind, and we can set up a quick phone call to discuss my situation, what I can do to help you out, and how we can help each other's businesses.

Additionally, I know as an attorney your goal is to represent your clients' interests, and I wanted to let you know I would be extremely grateful if you could let me know of anything resembling a great deal crosses your path. If at all possible, I'll buy it and prove to you I am reliable, honest, and trustworthy. My goal is to become a resource and an asset to your business to help you serve your clients better.

I would love to learn more about how I can help you as well, what programs you offer, and what kind of clients I can refer you to. Please let me know when a good time for a follow-up phone call will be. I'll be happy to leave you a positive review on the platform of your choice after we do.

Looking forward to working together!

Thanks!

(Name)

Family/Friends

Hello! I'm writing to you as a friendly reminder that YOU can help me with a very big part of my life—finding financial freedom through real estate.

As you may already know, I'm looking for real estate deals to buy and rent out or sometimes flip. Not every deal will meet my criteria, so I spend a considerable amount of time looking for the right one! I would love it if you kept me in mind whenever you hear about someone who needs to sell their house quickly. The condition of the house does not matter, as sometimes the crappier ones are better!

I've found that unfortunate circumstances can lead to crises. Some of these situations are unexpected/expected deaths, divorces, sudden relocations, or "hoarder houses." If you hear of anyone experiencing any of these problems, please keep me in mind and contact me. I want to be the person who can make one aspect of their lives easier in these situations. I always take measures to be kind, compassionate, and professional, and often buy homes people don't want real estate agents to show for various reasons.

Thank you so much for your cooperation with this, and please let me know what goals you have so I can reciprocate! I would love to hear more about what you'd like to achieve and how I can assist with that. Thanks again for keeping me top of mind!

Sincerely,

(Name)

Staying Top of Mind

There is a game I often play with investors or new real estate agents to prove the power of staying top of mind. I tell them I'm going to say the name of an item, and when I do, I want them to spit out as fast as they can the first two brands that come to mind. As an example, I tell them if I say "shoes" they might respond "Nike and Reebok." I then take a piece of paper and write something down on it they can't see. Right after that, I say "toothpaste."

So far, every time I've done this practice the only two answers I've ever heard are "Crest" and "Colgate." I show them that's exactly what I wrote down on the paper after they give those two names. The point of the exercise is to show that if you want to be thought of right away, you need to be the first or second name someone thinks of when a good deal comes their way. We all know there are probably 20 brands of toothpaste. Had I given the person 10 minutes to think of more brands, they might have thought of 20. However, how much time and effort are people going to put into thinking of who to talk to when someone casually mentions a great real estate deal? The overwhelming majority who hear it will, if nobody immediately comes to mind, let it pass right out of their brain as they go about their day.

Why is it that everyone thinks "Crest" and "Colgate"? Brand recognition. They own the real estate in our brains when it comes to toothpaste. If you want to be the person someone thinks of when a good deal crosses their path, you need to own that prime real estate in their brain. How do you do that? Constant, systematic contact.

This is one of the most powerful systems you can develop—your "lead generation" system. Remember, a lead is anything a business can convert into a profit, and you are running a business. Staying in touch with property managers, lenders, agents, family, etc. is one of the ways you are running your business to help you find deals. So, what's the best way to do this? Well, you can buy a system, or you can build one.

For those wanting to build their own system (and maybe save the most money), many people create a spreadsheet. You can use any program like Excel, Numbers, or Google Sheets—they all work similarly. To use a spreadsheet, you'll enter all the names of those you want to stay in touch with in one column, with additional columns to keep track of their profession, address, phone number, email address, etc. You'll then continue to add rows for every time you speak with them including notes to track what was said and what date the conversation occurred. Setting aside time every day to update this spreadsheet is something that will ultimately make you a lot of money once you become the "Crest" or "Colgate" in their mind!

If this seems like too much work for you, I recommend using some form of CRM (customer relationship manager) to organize your contacts and conversations. In my experience, many of these systems can be used for $15 to $50 dollars a month; quite affordable. Some CRMs, like Podio, are free and can be built to serve the purposes you want them to. While you might initially think you don't want to spend money on anything, I would strongly urge you to reconsider.

The purpose of a CRM is to keep you in contact with leads, period. Many CRMs will also provide a feature where you can track leads as progress from first hearing about them to close. CRMs are powerful business tools. Just keeping in touch with people you already know and staying top of mind with them alone will lead to you finding deals. If you can find a way to use a CRM to help you accomplish this goal, you just may find a system that makes real estate investing and deal finding much easier than you expected.

If you *do* take the CRM route, you can build it to remind you who you should be reaching out to, what you last spoke about, and which deals need what once they are in your pipeline. You may already see where I'm going with this. If you create a computer system to remind you what to do and how to do it, you can now leverage this task to someone else. Once you have a CRM built with reminders to stay in touch with your database, you can hire someone else to do that. Paying someone (or finding an intern to work for free) to stay in touch with agents, PMs, attorneys, etc. is a great way to make progress through leveraging others to be an extension of yourself!

The Impact of Compound Interest

When you understand how powerful compound interest is, it will change the way you look at money. Many people have gone to huge lengths to save money once they realized the impact it could have on their future financial lives. Just like my analogy of planting the seeds from your fruit rather than eating them, if you keep reinvesting your profits, eventually you grow entire orchards from your trees.

On my website, GreeneIncome.com, I have a spreadsheet listed under the "info" tab. On it, you can see just how powerful compound interest is when allowed to run its course over time. The spreadsheet shows how an initial investment of $125,000 can be optimized to produce significant results (you can plug in your own numbers once you download it). In my initial sample, I show how if you purchased a property for $125,000 cash, then pull out 80 percent of the money, you're left with $100,000. If you were to reinvest this money at 12 percent (buying notes, for example) and use that income to pay down your $100,000 mortgage, you'd pay it off in only 5.8 years.

If you then refinanced, pulled out another $100,000, then reinvested that money at 12 percent again, you'd pay the new mortgage off in only 3.4 years if you applied your profits directly toward the mortgage principle. This cycle could continue on and on, letting the power of compound interest work its magic as you paid each mortgage off progressively faster each time.

If you check out the second tab in the spreadsheet, you can see over a matter of years just how fast the money grows. After 33 years, your initial investment of $125,000 will be producing over $50,000 *a month*. And this is assuming zero growth in the value of the home or rental income over a 33-year period. Not a very likely scenario! By all reasonable measures, your wealth would have grown much, much more than this over that period. This is what compound interest does.

Why do I bring this up in a book about fixer-upper properties and the BRRRR strategy? Because just like compound interest can grow your money quickly, so can leveraging people and systems in your business. The compound effect of other fishermen bringing you fish, cleaning those fish, and selling them for you works the same way compound interest does to grow your wealth. Getting more people involved in the process and supervising their work is immensely more effective than trying to do it all yourself.

Many people have grasped the concept of compound interest. Books have been written on it, speeches given, theories created, etc. It's a simple but powerful concept. I want to encourage you to take that same principle of compound interest and apply it to people. By getting others involved in your business, finding other fishermen to go fish for you and empowering and teaching them how to do it, you can go from being the hardworking fisherman to the happy business owner. The secret is understanding leverage and applying it wisely.

What makes compound interest work is consistency over time. By making a return, reinvesting it, then making a return on that, you can turn small numbers into large ones over a long period of time. If you look at this philosophically, what you're really doing is making good, small decisions, over and over and over. Wealth is built this way, whether it's through real estate or the stock market.

The principle of compound interest is easy to understand. What you may not understand is there are two ways it can be put to practice. If we consider the effect that compound interest has on your wealth as "progression," we see there are two types of progression—linear progression and geometric progression.

Linear progression is steady, predictable, and even. It is getting the same return, over and over, year after year. It is "non-compound interest." Linear progression is getting a 10 percent return on a $100,000 investment, every year. On a graph, linear progression is a straight line that never changes its angle. It is earning $10,000 on that $100,000 investment every year. After ten years, you'd have $100,000.

Geometric progression is much more exciting. It behaves more like "compound interest." Geometric progression is the concept of doubling your returns every year as opposed to earning the same 10 percent every year. Geometric progression isn't a straight line. It's more of a "hockey stick" curve on a graph. Geometric progression starts off slowly, gains momentum, then takes off. When it takes off, it really takes off! Geometric progression doesn't happen by repeating the same act over and over. It happens by capitalizing on new opportunities, creating opportunities out of those opportunities, then creating opportunities out of all those.

In the beginning of the book, we compared the traditional method of buying real estate with the BRRRR method of buying real estate by looking at two investors who started off in the same position but built their portfolios in the different ways: Traditional Tom and Mastery Mike.

Traditional Tom used a method consistent with linear progression. He bought the same number of homes, every month, over the whole time period. Tom worked the same hours, bought the same type of homes, and got the same results. At the end of his career he achieved a very predictable result.

Mastery Mike, who used the BRRRR method, had a result more consistent with geometric progression. He continued to work and earn the same money, but he deployed that capital in a much more efficient way. Mike was able to geometrically increase his results and ended up far better off than Tom.

When you focus on geometric progression, you look for ways to take everything you've learned and put those skills to work for you looking for new opportunities. Geometric progression is the act of learning how to find properties that meet your criteria, then teaching those criteria to five agents who all start looking for you. As you start receiving more deals than you can afford to buy, you start wholesaling them and earning money off that, or raising private money to buy then refinance them.

Once you've got a large number of deals coming in, you use what you've learned to train contractors on your rehab process, then hire a project manager to manage all the projects that are coming in. As you learn more about the industry, you start leveraging your contacts to find lenders that will work with investors, then leveraging the volume you do to get better deals from those lenders. By combining all these new skills and abilities, you help the success of your business.

I want you to start thinking in a geometrically progressive way. Look for ways to grow and find new opportunities with *every single new thing you learn*. This is how you maximize the "repeat" element of BRRRR. Learning to Buy, Rehab, Rent, and Refinance will make you money. Learning to Repeat will change your life. Don't waste all the effort you put into learning real estate investing by buying a few properties and stopping. Once you've put in all the hard work and sacrifice, you deserve to reap the rewards.

Value Through Volume: How Investing at Scale Gives You a Competitive Advantage

So far in this chapter we've been looking into why scaling the systems you have built is advantageous to you. Most of what I've shared so far has been related to how systems make your life easier and your business run smoother. While these are important reasons to build systems and stick to them, they aren't the most important reason. The most important reason to rely on systems is the ability they give you to increase your volume. Volume makes everything easier, and real estate investing is no exception.

I want to share with you some of the ways increasing your volume will not only grow your wealth, it will also increase your profitability. When I talk about buying turnkey properties, I use an analogy that buying turnkey is like buying a soda from a convenience store, while learning to invest is like buying from a bulk warehouse. Costco is known for having very low prices, and often tempts people to buy way more than they ever planned on buying while they're there. What's Costco's secret? Volume.

Costco sells items to its consumers in bulk. The more items someone buys at one time, the more Costco makes, so the cheaper they can price each individual item. Costco also drives large amounts of customers to its stores, largely due to its low prices. As more and more people buy from Costco, the sales go up. As sales increase, the store can ask for discounts from its suppliers on the items they sell (buying in bulk themselves). Wherever you have this increased volume, you're likely to find a lower price point and higher profitability.

When investing in real estate, this same principle is at play. Using the same team member over and over will allow you to develop a rapport with them and a familiarity in how they work. This will not only save you time, it will also likely save you money. You are much more likely to get discounts from every vendor or team member you use when you use them more than once. This repeat business, or volume, will save you money on your costs of sale.

I'm going to share with you ways you can save money with several of the people associated with buying and fixing up rental property. These are some of the ways I've structured my relationships to work with each of my team members, and creative concepts I've used to help keep our relationship "win-win." While I can't list every single strategy you can use, if you can understand the point of the concept, you'll likely come up with some original ideas that will work in your own business with the people you partner with.

Contractors

Doing repeat deals with the same contractor who values your business is one of the single best ways you can save yourself money investing in real estate, primarily because rehab costs are often the biggest expense in the entire process. Going after ways to eliminate costs on your big-ticket items is always a much better idea than trying to nickel and dime providers of much smaller cost items. Always start from the top and work your way down from there.

When you use the same contractor, you can develop a system with that person. The contractor knows how you want to receive bids, how soon you'll pay them, what they need to do to keep you happy, etc. Once this familiarity is established, the contractor will save time communicating with you. Saving this time also saves them money. Once your contractor knows what you want the jobs to look like when they are finished, they are less likely to need to send crew members back to finish the job. This saves them money, also.

Once you are saving your contractor money, it's okay to expect them to save *you* some money. Asking to reduce their profit margin on the jobs they are bidding for you is an accepted business practice if you are providing them with a significant number of properties to work on. The volume you provide them allows them to justify a smaller profit margin (just as Costco does). When you have systems in place to raise money, to buy property, and to rehab efficiently, you can ramp up your volume and consequently pay your contractors less. Going bigger in your investing will save you money on your construction costs.

Property Managers

Property managers are the people who look after your properties when you can't. If you are going to scale your business through leverage, and truly "repeat" this whole BRRRR process, there will eventually come a time when property management is not an option, it's a necessity. One of the benefits to increasing the volume at which your portfolio grows is you have more negotiating power with property managers to get them to lower their fees.

Part of this process is establishing a rapport with the property manager and creating a system both of you are comfortable with that saves each of you time. Coming up with a plan for which types of problems the PM can solve without your approval, lists of phone numbers of the handymen you want the PMs calling when things break, and details of how lease renewals will be handled helps the PM to know how much time and effort they'll be spending on your portfolio. Your goal is to make it as efficient for them as possible so they spend the least amount of time they can on your properties.

If you can accomplish this, you can ask for a reduction in the amount of money you pay them every month. The PMs' entire argument for why they won't reduce their fees is that it takes them too much time to do the work. If you have already eliminated that argument, it's tough for them to stick to it. Once I have three to four properties with one PM, I ask for a 1 percent decrease in the fee they charge me to manage the property.

Once I get six to seven properties, I ask for a 2 percent decrease. Once I hit ten or more, I ask for a 3 percent decrease. This is how I routinely pay 7 percent to property managers when the going rate is 10 percent. It's not that I'm a cheapskate, it's that I'm providing them value through volume, so they can afford to give me a better price. This is something I couldn't accomplish if it wasn't for systems, volume, and maximizing the "repeat" part of BRRRR!

Lenders

Working with the same lender, over and over, helps you in many ways. The first and obvious way is you don't have to fill out a new application and jump through all the initial hoops each time. This saves you a lot of time. For this reason alone, many investors stay loyal to the same lender even if they could get better terms elsewhere. While I don't always agree with that, I want to share with you a way you can keep the efficiency of using the same lender while also saving yourself money.

When a lender originates a loan, they typically sell it off to someone else who packages it with other loans and sells them to a mortgage backed securities (MBS) fund. The originator of that loan gets paid for selling it, and the salesperson (loan officer) gets a chunk of that money. If this is the case with your lender, you can ask for a "lender credit," or something similar. This is the lender crediting you back money that comes out of their bottom line. While it's not good business practice to ask for this right off the bat, it can be okay to do so if you're doing several loans with the same lender. If you're going to do this, make sure you're providing volume, and make sure your files are quick and easy to close. If you are a high-maintenance client, you shouldn't be asking for a credit back.

If you're doing your loans through a company that's *not* selling them to a fund (a portfolio lender, for example), I recommend only asking for a lender credit if you are already providing this lender plenty of referrals. The concept of value through volume applies here as well if you're providing volume through referrals instead of just through your own business. Thinking creatively like this can save you money, and it's another example of how you can get better returns by scaling your business.

Agents

If you're using an agent to find you deals, this is a quick and easy way to save money on the process. The key is to being an "easy" client. How do you do that? Let your agent do their thing, give them clear direction and standards for what you want, and then get out of their way. If you can establish a consistent and simple system with the real estate agent you're using, you can save them time. Once you've done that, you can expect a discount if you're bringing them volume.

The key to making this work is finding an agent who also has a system. If your agent has a system for managing sales, they won't be spending as much of their own time, and they are more likely to give you a discount. How does this discount work? The best way is to negotiate a lower commission when it comes to selling houses. The second-best way is to negotiate yourself higher into their chain of supply when it comes to who gets the first phone call when a great deal crosses their desk.

If you're a house flipper, you can pay less to your listing agent if you're consistently bringing them business. The same standard applies if you're sending them constant referrals. Combining this with being easy to work with is the best way to get an agent to lower their commission. Additionally, if you have an agent who doesn't do much for you other than write offers and make sure the deal closes, you can ask for a piece of their commission as well. Now, understand this is treading on thin ice. You're already getting their services for free, and it can be especially greedy to ask for even more. My recommendation is you *only do this* if you are making their job incredibly easy.

In my opinion, a much better way to capitalize on the value through the volume you are bringing someone is to let them know you expect to see the best deals first. This will make you way more money in the long run than saving a couple hundred or thousand by shaving it off the agent's commission. Asking for an agent's commission can actually backfire, because it makes them more likely to bring their best deals to someone else. They make more doing it that way. If you were in their position, you'd do the exact same thing. Remember, by being the person who buys the most properties, you can expect the best service, the best prices, and have the opportunity to build the best system.

Materials

This concept can work on a smaller scale in hardware stores where you'll buy the materials for your properties. If you buy enough from these stores, you can get set up for a "contractor's discount," or something similar. Stores want people shopping from them over and over, so if you're buying in volume, they want your business. Ask a representative the next time you're at one what it is you'll need to do to receive these discounts, and what kinds of discounts they are.

Types of Properties

This same concept of volume works when it comes to the types of properties you buy as well. Multifamily investors are often found quoting the favorable economies of scale found in large apartment buildings with many doors under one roof compared to those of single-family investors with their portfolios scattered around a large geographic area. This close-knit conglomeration of properties works to keep costs lower in several ways.

The first and most obvious way is you can have one group of people managing many units when there is a system in place for how this will be managed. One large apartment complex of 100 units can operate very efficiently from a management perspective when they have one form of marketing, one policy and procedure manual, one way to collect rents, one person to call for maintenance issues, etc. Having one central hub of management, on-site, allows for a few employees to manage a large number of tenants.

As you can see, anytime you are doing something at a great volume there are several inherent advantages for you. Whether it's the fact that repetition (another way of expressing the concept of volume) makes you better, or the fact that profit margins increase through volume (so you can ask for a piece of that increase), volume is your friend. This is why systems are so important. They serve to help you create a process that is easily replicated and makes volume more achievable, and that means you can make a lot more money!

Key Points

- Real estate is a "get-rich-slow game."
- Sharpen your skills before you begin for better results.
- Systems provide opportunities.
- Build your network through repeat business.
- Systems help you master the five elements of BRRRR.
- Stay top of mind to get deals first. You must be either Crest or Colgate.
- Compound interest is key!
- Investing at scale gives you a competitive advantage.

PART SEVEN

Digging Deeper

CHAPTER TWELVE
Arguments Against BRRRR

"Everyone hears only what he understands."

—JOHANN WOLFGANG VON GOETHE

So far, you've absorbed a lot of material relating to how to build wealth in real estate—much of which may have seemed new, confusing, or too good to be true. If you're a human and not a robot, you no doubt have some objections, or at the very least questions about why BRRRR actually works or if it's superior to the traditional model when it comes to buying real estate. I want to help you out with that.

There's a few commonly asked questions when it comes to using the BRRRR method to buy fixer-upper properties and, while I'm sure I didn't catch them all, I do believe I have a solid list of the most common objections, misunderstandings, and myths about both the BRRRR method and real estate investing in general. If you've had that annoying little voice in your head the whole time you've been reading that is causing you to doubt, here's where we can finally silence it.

1. BRRRR is bad because having more equity in the property is safer.
One common objection is putting a large down payment on a property is safer because more equity in the property gives you a "cushion" in case the market drops. Those with this mind-set are looking at how to protect

themselves against price drops and believe equity is the best way to do that.

Why I disagree:
First off, equity does not protect against losing an asset. Cash flow does. As I've mentioned before, cash flow does not make you rich. At least not for a long, long time. Cash flow by design is meant to keep you from losing a property. Your cash flow covers your expenses. If you have analyzed a property correctly (which you will if you read *Part Four: The Rental Process* in this book), your cash flow will protect you. The amount of equity you have in a property is largely inconsequential when it comes to affecting your cash flow.

After cash flow, it is your reserves that will protect you, not your equity. Keeping a significant amount of capital in reserves in case something goes wrong will prevent you from experiencing a foreclosure. You can only lose a property if you can't make the payment, and reserves will keep you afloat should you encounter a situation where you can't make the payment. Reserves are a hedge against vacancy, unexpected repairs, or big-ticket items needing to be replaced (roof, HVAC, etc.).

Equity only has a purpose if you're considering selling a property or perhaps refinancing it. Remember, if we use the BRRRR method correctly, we are still left with equity in the property. The difference is, that is equity we *created*, not capital we *put down*. Even if a property does lose equity, it only matters if you are selling a property. You can avoid needing to sell if you make sure the property cash-flows positively. Cash flow plus reserves allow you to weather any storm in the market and sell at a date that makes financial sense for you to do so.

Lastly, leaving equity in a property can actually be *more* risky than taking it out. If you are considering the worst-case scenario like losing a property to foreclosure, the equity you leave in a property is the only money you can lose. If you don't have any of your own capital left in a property during a foreclosure, you can't lose any of it. There is an old poker adage: "You can only lose what you put in the pot." That fits here as well. Leaving equity in a property increases your exposure and therefore your risk to losing capital.

To be blunt, seeing equity as a way to protect against loss is the lazy person's way of protecting themselves and it shows that person doesn't have a firm grasp of real estate principles. Don't be sucked into that kind of thinking. It may make sense on the surface, but it doesn't really pass muster once we look closer at it. Cash flow and reserves protect your investment, not equity.

2. The BRRRR method takes too long. I want to get started now!
This argument has its root in the fact that you need to save up more cash to buy than if you just save up a 25 percent down payment plus reserves. In the Chapter One story of Traditional Tom vs. Mastery Mike, Tom was able to get started faster than Mike did. For those who are impatient, this can feel like time being wasted when all you want to do is get started.

Why I disagree:
Even though you get started later, as we saw from the story of Tom vs. Mike, Mike made way more in the long run. Taking more time to start is a wise investment if it allows you to BRRRR over a significant period of time.

The second reason I don't like this argument is it assumes the only way to buy a BRRRR/fixer-upper property is with your own cash. That's simply not true! There are tons of ways to short-term finance a BRRRR property if you're in a hurry to get started. Some of the easiest are:
- Partner with someone who has money.
- Borrow private money.
- Use a hard money loan to buy/rehab, then refinance into a better, long-term loan.
- Take out a HELOC on a different rental property.
- Take out a business loan.
- Take a note against your car.
- Find someone with a self-directed IRA and borrow from them.
- Borrow against your own retirement plan (when applicable).
- Use seller financing for the short term.

With this many options, it's a little shortsighted to assume the only way to buy a BRRRR property is to save up your own cash. The more you know about real estate investing, and the more contacts you make, the more opportunities you have to find a way to finance a fixer-upper that won't qualify for traditional financing.

3. BRRRR is riskier because you have to invest more money when you buy.

This argument is to me the easiest to debunk, but it's also the objection I hear more than anything else! The argument states that BRRRR investing is riskier because you are putting more money up front initially and that means you have more to lose.

Why I disagree:
If I'm paying $100,000 to buy and rehab a property, that is a bigger number than a $25,000 down payment with a small $5,000 rehab budget. Because $100,000 is more than $30,000, BRRRR is therefore scarier and riskier. Here's why this doesn't add up. It takes too narrow of a focus on the initial part of the process. If you zoom out a bit and take a broader view of the whole process, it very quickly becomes apparent the BRRRR model is actually far less risky than the traditional model.

Those afraid to put money into the deal in the beginning stages are usually those newer to real estate investing who don't understand that they aren't dumping money into a fund, buying stocks, buying Bitcoin, or making a business loan. In all these examples, you are giving money to someone else and "hoping" you get your money back—preferably with a return. If someone is looking at real estate investing this way, it makes sense they would be hesitant to put more money into the deal.

The problem with this argument is real estate investing isn't the same as the examples I just gave. You aren't investing into a business, idea, or person, you are purchasing an asset with a hard value that's easy to appraise and improve its value. You are investing in a chunk of land with a property attached to it. It's not an apples-to-apples comparison.

The BRRRR method is actually less risky than the traditional model for several reasons.
- You are buying undervalued property.
- You are taking control of the ability to improve a property's value.
- You are buying a property with a plan that allows you to improve its value.
- You will be able to get more of your money out of the deal when you're done, leaving less capital in the investment and reducing your risk.
- The equity you are creating gives you creative measures to raise money from others. Using OPM (other people's money) is a less risky form of investing.

If your concern is you may put all this money in a home and then not be able to get it out, you can solve that problem by getting approved ahead of time. In the case that something goes wrong before you can complete your refinance (e.g., you lose your job before the loan funds), you now have an asset with an improved value in which you have created equity that you can sell, recover your capital on, and still make a profit.

At the end of the day, you *are* putting more money in a deal initially, but that is only for a short time. You end up putting much less money in the deal at the end, improving your ROI, and reducing your risk, all at the same time.

4. BRRRR only works if you're willing to do a massive rehab.

While it's true more BRRRR purchases tend to be bigger remodels, this doesn't necessarily have to be true. What *does* have to be true is you are paying significantly under market value for a property that will appraise for more than you paid for it when you go to refinance. Does this mean you have to buy a fixer-upper? Nope. Does this mean you need to get a great deal? Yup. Are most fixer-uppers great deals? Usually, but it doesn't have to be so.

Why I disagree:

The BRRRR model works because it's so much more efficient, not because it requires you to buy a fixer-upper. I have used the BRRRR model successfully several times buying deals from wholesalers that needed very little rehab work. I'm talking a thorough cleaning and some paint—that's it. While these aren't as common as the fixer-uppers, they do still occur. You do not have to buy a fixer-upper to BRRRR successfully.

5. BRRRR is for cash buyers and I'm sorry, but that's just not me.

Many different kinds of investors use the BRRRR formula and BRRRR-related strategies to increase their returns, the velocity of their money, and the number of deals they can take down. So why do people think it's only for cash buyers? Probably because that's who uses it most. While it's true that cash buyers likely make up the lion's share, many different buyers use the BRRRR method to structure their deals.

Why I disagree:

Let's start with apartment syndicators as an example. I have been a partner on several different big projects where a group of investors all put our money together and bought a large, multiunit apartment complex together. The properties were purchased with about 75 percent "agency debt" (a bank loan), then we investors kicked in the remaining 25 percent of the down payment plus the rehab costs. The rehab money was used to clean up the apartment complexes, and in the process, increased their value. Once the apartments had a higher value, we had an asset we could borrow against again.

Approximately two years into the project we refinanced them and paid the investors back a chunk of their original investment. Three years after that, the property was either sold or refinanced again to give everyone their profit. Apartments are not the same as small single-family houses, yet this principle works the same. Buy a property however you want (your money, someone else's, both, etc.), improve its value, then refinance it. In this example, we are *not* buying $7 million properties with cash. We still use debt, then refinance that debt later. These BRRRR strategies work even if you're not an all-cash buyer.

6. What happens if the appraisal comes in low and I can't get all my money back?

A low appraisal can be a wet blanket on many a real estate deal. We can't control what an appraiser is going to determine, and anytime there is uncertainty like this, anxiety is sure to follow. For many investors, or would-be investors, they just can't bring themselves to live or work in an environment that provides this much uncertainty. The inability to know the future and know what a property will appraise for throws a lot of people off.

In the case of a low appraisal, there are three main options you can consider. The first is to challenge the appraisal, present your comps, and try to get a better result the second time around. The second is to pay for a new appraisal (if your lender will let you) and hope for a better result. The third is to consider selling the property and hope for a higher sales price than your appraisal, and banking on the fact your buyers will order their own appraisal that will be higher than yours.

If none of these ideas are appealing to you, there is still hope. You can still accept your disappointment, refinance the property, start making money, and look to get 'em next time!

In the case of a low appraisal, it's true you may not recover 100 percent of your capital. This doesn't have to be discouraging, however, because it's not a sign you failed. To me, recovering 100 percent of my money is considered a home run. I may aim for this on every deal, but I don't expect it. In reality, even if you don't get the appraisal you hoped for, you're still likely to get a much better result than if you'd used the traditional model. It's a healthier perspective in my opinion to compare your BRRRR results to traditional results rather than comparing getting 100 percent of your money back vs. "only" 90 percent of it.

As we've discussed several times in the book, if you leave $5,000–$10,000 in a deal because of a low appraisal, you'll still end up with a super high ROI, and just as important, much more of your capital back to reinvest. That's not a bad consolation prize! By keeping the perspective that the point of BRRRR investing is to receive *more* of your capital back, not necessarily all of it, you can overcome the "what about a low appraisal" objection and get on your way to creating wealth through real estate.

7. BRRRR remodels are always big remodels and that intimidates me.

This isn't necessarily an argument against BRRRR, but more against rehabbing in general. While I can relate to those who are intimidated by a remodel, I really can't agree it's healthy or wise to stay in that place. Real estate investing is all about adding value—especially BRRRR investing. If you never learn how to manage a rehab, or find someone else who can, you are severely limiting your ability to add value to a property. This will have an impact on your ability to grow wealth through real estate.

A rehab is one of the easiest and simplest ways to add value to a property *precisely because nobody wants to do them*. If everybody was willing to do rehabs, there would be no opportunity there for investors. People looking to buy a home to live in would be snatching up all the properties because they were cheap. Opportunity exists because a rehab can be intimidating and therefore creates a barrier to entry.

Here's the thing with rehabs—you don't have to be the one doing them. There are lots of people who don't want to invest in real estate, they just want to fix up somebody else's house. It's your job to find these people, or find the people who will find them. It can be more work up front, but will pay huge dividends once you find the right handyman or contractor.

When it comes to adding value, every asset you can invest in has a way you can add value. Each asset class is valued differently and therefore needs different strategies to accomplish adding value. Apartment complexes have their value increased by improving NOI. Small businesses have their value increased by improving profitability and reducing the amount of time an owner needs to spend working. A stock's value is increased through the company announcing increased profits. For a SFR property, value is increased through improving the appearance, size, and functionality of a property. This is all accomplished through a rehab.

What does this mean? Whatever you have to do to get over your fear of rehabs, you have to do it. Buy books, listen to podcasts, talk to friends, hire a coach. Whatever you have to do, do it. If you can't do it, put your efforts toward finding someone else to do it for you. Pay another investor who is good at it to manage yours, then just make sure there is enough meat on the bone in your deal to justify this extra expense. Don't let something as formulaic as a rehab intimidate you into not taking action. Too much is at stake!

Key Points

- Equity will not keep you safe in the case of a market correction. Cash flow and reserves will.
- BRRRR is not riskier than the traditional model.
- BRRRR is not only for fixer-uppers.
- BRRRR can work even if you buy with financing.
- Even if the appraisal comes in lower than you expected, the BRRRR model is still more efficient than the traditional model.

CHAPTER THIRTEEN

How You Should Expect BRRRR to Improve Your Results

"The successful warrior is the average man, with laser-like focus."

—BRUCE LEE

Quite frankly, learning and mastering the BRRRR method changed my life. I went from a committed but casual real estate investor having a moderate level of success, to a respected authority on the topic being asked to speak, teach, and write about how to pull it off successfully. How did I accomplish this in a manner of a few short years? I achieved mastery through repetition, just like a black belt martial artist.

These results aren't unique to me. Anyone can achieve them; that's why I'm teaching you how. If you commit to following this path, you too will eventually achieve mastery. I want to share with you some of the results you can expect if you commit to this process, based on mine and other investors' experiences. Once you see how impactful it is, it's hard not to be excited to get started!

1. BRRRR forced me to analyze deals more thoroughly

Before BRRRR, I analyzed every property I considered buying through one metric—ROI. If I was looking into buying one property vs. another, I asked myself which had the higher ROI. If I was considering buying vs. not buying, I asked myself if the ROI was better than I could expect on a different investment. If I still wasn't sure, I asked myself if the ROI was worth the time I would have to put in. Basically, ROI was the scope through which I viewed all of real estate investing.

When I started BRRRR investing, I was forced to look at many more aspects of each property I was considering buying. Rather than solely looking at ROI, I started analyzing other factors as well. Equity, for example, became much more important to me. Before BRRRR, I was paying pretty close to fair market value and then just waiting to see if my properties would appreciate while I collected cash flow. After BRRRR, I was looking at how much I could make a property worth, how little I could spend to do that, and how little I could pay for the property in the first place. This new perspective taught me to focus on finding *deals*, not just finding a return.

This was big! Your wealth grows quickly once you start finding great deals. BRRRR forced me to do that. Once I realized I only wanted to buy great deals, I started looking for where I could find these deals. Rather than speaking with "my Realtor," I started reaching out and looking for many Realtors. Do you think this helped my ability to determine quickly if an agent could find me properties I would want to buy? Yup. Here are some of the other ways that helped me.

- I got better at developing a system to find talented agents.
- I developed my "army of agents" looking for deals for me.
- I looked into more than just one market.
- I increased the roster of other members of my "Core Four" as each agent was able to provide me with more referrals.
- I increased my own knowledge of real estate as I developed relationships with many more "teachers," helping improve my own knowledge and experience.

It wasn't just agents, either! As I began my journey of finding where the best deals were, I started finding new wholesalers, bird dogs, and sources to find off-market deals. My knowledge and the value I could bring others increased exponentially, and this opened up even more doors for myself. Book deals, opportunities to write for powerful business publications, news appearances, and an opportunity to host the

BiggerPockets Podcast. All of this happened simply because I learned to BRRRR and that led to real estate mastery.

2. BRRRR forced me to add value through rehabs

As previously mentioned, if you want to build wealth through real estate, you need to learn how to run a rehab. Kind of like if you want to become a black belt martial artist, at some point you're going to need to learn how to punch. It's a fundamental skill required for combat, just like rehabbing is for real estate investing.

When I started to BRRRR, I had to get much better at this. I had to learn to create systems to get bids from contractors. I had to find agents who understood rehab costs themselves. By sheer immersion in this environment, I learned about electrical panels and roofing procedures and the permitting process. Becoming a BRRRR investor helped me to learn how to manage a rehab, and enabled me to write the entire part of this book about rehabs!

Through BRRRR, I learned how to:
- Find referrals for contractors from others
- Interview contractors
- Develop systems for receiving bids from contractors
- Develop a system for running rehabs
- Develop a system for determining likely ARVs
- Add square footage, bedrooms, and bathrooms to add value
- Develop relationships with commercial lenders to continue funding my deals
- Apply due diligence when buying properties at online auctions

This is honestly just a small portion of the things I've learned. It would have taken me years to learn this, if I learned anything at all, using the traditional model and barely moving the needle of my own success. If you commit to achieving mastery through BRRRR, you can expect similar results.

3. BRRRR taught me to work only with the best and form a dream team

When you're buying lots of properties, you end up doing a lot more work. In order to prevent yourself from burning out, you start relying on other people more. Once you're forced to rely on other people, you quickly start to demand excellence where once mediocrity was fine. It is truly the power of your team that determines whether you will succeed or not.

The unexpected result of surrounding myself with top talent is how they helped me do my job better. Having top-level contractors helped me do my job by putting me in touch with other investors and wholesalers with resources I needed. My opportunities to succeed began to increase exponentially with each all-star I added to my team.

Working with talent like this forced me to step up my own game as well. As I demanded more from others, I had to do more myself. This caused me to get more out of myself and increase my own success. The BRRRR method, and the volume you can do with it, will open up these doors for you as well.

4. BRRRR helped remove my "FOMO" (fear of missing out)

Before BRRRR, I only had so much capital to go around. This led to a horrible case of FOMO. "If I buy here, I cannot buy there—which is best?" This created a nasty cycle of anxiety as I tried to pick the best markets to invest in. The problem was, I would take so long to get back to agents or wholesalers about deals that they stopped bringing them to me. It was not good for my business, or my mental health.

With BRRRR, I know I'll be getting capital back after the purchase, so I don't have to worry about "missing out" on the next deal. I can buy here, *and* I can buy there, because I have enough capital to do both. I cannot stress enough how powerful this mind-set is for your own ability to make progress and take action. This more efficient model of investing opened doors for me that seemed sealed shut before.

What Kind of an Investor Do You Want to Be?

In Chapter One we compared the two strategies of Traditional Tom vs. Mastery Mike. Their results were vastly different and incredibly impactful when compared side by side. You can retire with massive wealth, or you can retire with pretty good wealth. Both are better than nothing, but why wouldn't you want the vastly superior results?

Getting better at something is how you improve your own position in life. It works whether you are trying to get a promotion at work, establish better relationships, or build more wealth. Considering that mastery is *built* on repetition, why would you avoid it? Mastering BRRRR is, by definition, mastering real estate investing. It covers each step of the process from buying a property to refinancing it and moving on to the next one. Getting good at BRRRR is getting good at real estate investing, and *that* will build your wealth.

To put it candidly, all the best investors I know are using some form of the BRRRR method or its principles in their investing business. It is simply the most efficient, most effective, and overall best way to purchase real estate. If you bought this book, you are clearly interested in growing wealth through real estate. I can tell you, speaking from experience, substantial wealth is possible through real estate investing. It is the single best way I know of to build wealth, and the BRRRR method is the single best way I know how to do it. Don't sacrifice your future by not taking action today!

Acknowledgments

To Brian Burke, who first turned me on to the idea of return on equity vs. return on investment, thank you for planting the seed that grew into this book.

To Brandon Turner, who coined the phrase "BRRRR," thanks for being so busy you let me write this book instead of you.

To Katie Miller, who had the vision to see what this could be and the determination to see it through, thank you for your diligence and confidence in me.

To Scott Trench, for manning the ship like a true captain should and for setting a great example of what it takes to succeed.

To the listeners of the *BiggerPockets Podcast*, you're the best audience in the world, and together we are building life-changing content!

Special thanks to Katie Golownia, Mark Amundsen, Kaylee Pratt, Wendy Dunning, Katelin Hill, and Jarrod Jemison.

More from
BiggerPockets Publishing

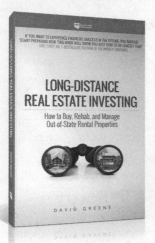

Long-Distance Real Estate Investing

Don't let your location dictate your financial freedom: Live where you want, and invest anywhere it makes sense! The rules, technology, and markets have changed: No longer are you forced to invest only in your backyard. In *Long-Distance Real Estate Investing*, learn an in-depth strategy to build profitable rental portfolios through buying, managing, and flipping out-of-state properties from real estate investor and agent David Greene.

The Book on Tax Strategies for the Savvy Real Estate Investor

Taxes! Boring and irritating, right? Perhaps. But if you want to succeed in real estate, your tax strategy will play a huge role in how fast you grow. A great tax strategy can save you thousands of dollars a year. A bad strategy could land you in legal trouble. That's why Big-gerPockets is excited to offer *The Book on Tax Strategies for the Savvy Real Estate Investor!* You'll find ways to deduct more, invest smarter, and pay far less to the IRS!

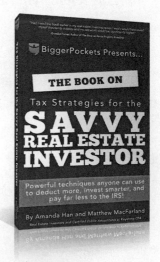

If you enjoyed this book, we hope you'll take a moment to check out some of the other great material BiggerPockets offers. BiggerPockets is the real estate investing social network, marketplace, and information hub, designed to help make you a smarter real estate investor through podcasts, books, blog posts, videos, forums, and more. Sign up today—it's free! **Visit www.BiggerPockets.com.**

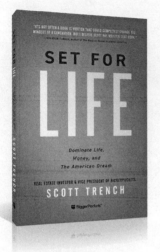

Set for Life: Dominate Life, Money, and the American Dream

Looking for a plan to achieve financial freedom in just five to ten years? *Set for Life* is a detailed fiscal plan targeted at the median-income earner starting with few or no assets. It will walk you through three stages of finance, guiding you to your first $25,000 in tangible net worth, then to your first $100,000, and then to financial freedom. *Set for Life* will teach you how to build a lifestyle, career, and investment portfolio capable of supporting financial freedom to let you live the life of your dreams.

Raising Private Capital

Are you ready to help other investors build their wealth while you build your real estate empire? The road map outlined in *Raising Private Capital* helps investors looking to inject more private capital into their business—the most effective strategy for growth! Author and investor Matt Faircloth helps you learn how to develop long-term wealth from his valuable lessons and experiences in real estate. Get the truth behind the wins and losses from someone who has experienced it all.

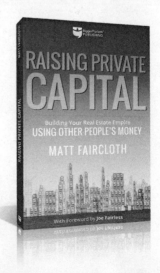

Connect with BiggerPockets

and Become Successful in Your Real Estate Business Today!

Facebook
/BiggerPockets

Instagram
@BiggerPockets

Twitter
@BiggerPockets

LinkedIn
/company/Bigger
Pockets

Website
BiggerPockets.com